Reading Rancière

Also available from Continuum:

Chronicles, Jacques Rancière
Dissensus, Jacques Rancière
The Politics of Aesthetics, Jacques Rancière
Jacques Rancière: An Introduction, Joseph J. Tanke
Jacques Rancière: Education, Truth, Emancipation, edited by Gert Biesta and Charles Bingham

Forthcoming:

Althusser's Lesson, Jacques Rancière
Mallarmé, Jacques Rancière
Jacques Rancière and the Contemporary Scene, edited by Jean-Philippe Deranty and Alison Ross

Reading Rancière

Edited by
Paul Bowman
and
Richard Stamp

continuum

Continuum International Publishing Group
The Tower Building   80 Maiden Lane
11 York Road   Suite 704
London SE1 7NX   New York, NY 10038

www.continuumbooks.com

© Paul Bowman, Richard Stamp and Contributors, 2011

All rights reserved. No part of this publication may be reproduced or transmitted in any form or by any means, electronic or mechanical, including photocopying, recording, or any information storage or retrieval system, without prior permission in writing from the publishers.

British Library Cataloguing-in-Publication Data
A catalogue record for this book is available from the British Library.

ISBN: HB: 978-1-4411-9037-6
      PB: 978-1-4411-3781-4

Library of Congress Cataloging-in-Publication Data
Reading Rancière / edited by Paul Bowman and Richard Stamp.
   p. cm.
Includes bibliographical references.
ISBN: 978-1-4411-9037-6 – ISBN: 978-1-4411-3781-4
1. Rancière, Jacques. I. Bowman, Paul, 1971- II. Stamp, Richard, 1968- III. Title.

B2430.R274R43 2011
194–dc22   2010043094

Typeset by Newgen Imaging Systems Pvt Ltd, Chennai, India

Contents

Notes on Contributors	vii
Introduction: A Critical Dissensus Paul Bowman and Richard Stamp	xi
The Thinking of Dissensus: Politics and Aesthetics Jacques Rancière	1
The Politics of the Police: From Neoliberalism to Anarchism, and Back to Democracy Samuel A. Chambers	18
On Captivation: A Remainder from the 'Indistinction of Art and Nonart' Rey Chow and Julian Rohrhuber	44
Politics without Politics Jodi Dean	73
Out of Place: Unprofessional Painting, Jacques Rancière and the Distribution of the Sensible Ben Highmore	95
The Wrong of Contemporary Art: Aesthetics and Political Indeterminacy Suhail Malik and Andrea Phillips	111

The Second Return of the Political: Democracy and the Syllogism
   of Equality   129
Oliver Marchart

Police Reinforcement: The Anti-Politics of Organizational Life   148
Linsey McGoey

Paul de Man and Art History I: Modernity, Aesthetics and
   Community in Jacques Rancière   163
Martin McQuillan

Film, Fall, Fable: Rancière, Rossellini, Flaubert, Haneke   185
Mark Robson

On the Shores of History   200
Alex Thomson

Anti-Sociology and Its Limits   217
Alberto Toscano

Against an Ebbing Tide: An Interview with Jacques Rancière   238
Jacques Rancière

Select Bibliography   252
Index   259

Notes on Contributors

Paul Bowman (Cardiff University) is author of *Post-Marxism versus Cultural Studies* (2007), *Deconstructing Popular Culture* (2008) and *Theorizing Bruce Lee* (2010). He is editor of numerous journal issues and several other books, including *The Truth of Žižek* (2006), also co-edited with Richard Stamp and published by Continuum.

Samuel A. Chambers teaches political theory at Johns Hopkins University. He has recently published *The Queer Politics of Television* (IB Tauris 2009). His previous publications include the monographs *Untimely Politics* (NYU 2003) and *Judith Butler and Political Theory* (with Terrell Carver, Routledge 2008), edited volumes on William Connolly and Judith Butler, respectively, and numerous journal articles. His current teaching and research revolves around intersections between queer theory and contemporary political thought and is oriented to the task of rethinking democracy outside the terms of contemporary liberalism. He is currently writing a book on the politics of social orders in which he tries to link Althusser's understanding of ideology and Rancière's conception of police with the American political thought of Madison and Bentley.

Rey Chow is Anne Firor Scott Professor of Literature at Duke University. She has published extensively on literature, film and cultural theory, with a focus on the discursive encounters among modernity, sexuality, postcoloniality and ethnicity. Before Duke, Chow was Andrew W. Mellon Professor of the Humanities at Brown University. The books she has authored include *Woman and Chinese Modernity, Writing Diaspora, Ethics after Idealism, The Protestant Ethnic and the Spirit of Capitalism* and *Sentimental Fabulations, Contemporary Chinese Films*. Her current work includes a co-edited special issue, 'The Sense of Sound', for the journal *differences*, and an essay collection in progress, *Entanglements: Trans-medial Thinking about Capture*. *The Rey Chow Reader*, ed. Paul Bowman, is available from Columbia University Press.

Jodi Dean is Professor of Political Science at Hobart and William Smith Colleges in Geneva, New York, and Erasmus Chair in the Humanities in the Faculty of Philosophy at Erasmus University, Rotterdam, Netherlands. She is co-editor of the journal *Theory and Event*. Her ninth book, *Democracy and Other Neoliberal Fantasies*, was published in 2009 from Duke University Press.

Ben Highmore is Reader in Media and Cultural Studies at the University of Sussex. His most recent books are: *A Passion for Cultural Studies* (Palgrave 2008); *Ordinary Lives: Studies in the Everyday* (Routledge 2010); and the edited collection *The Design Culture Reader* (Routledge 2009). Currently he is working on a book called *The Great Indoors: An Intimate History of the British House* (due to be published in 2012).

Suhail Malik is Reader in Critical Studies in the Department of Art, Goldsmiths, London. Malik is currently working on a philosophy of American power and (with Andrea Phillips) a book on transnational aesthetics.

Oliver Marchart is Professor at the Department of Sociology, University of Lucerne. His books include *Post-foundational Political Thought: Political Difference in Nancy, Lefort, Badiou and Laclau* (Edinburgh University Press 2007), and *Laclau: A Critical Reader*, ed. with Simon Critchley (Routledge 2004).

Linsey McGoey is Lecturer in Sociology at the University of Essex. She completed a PhD in Sociology at the London School of Economics, followed by postdoctoral work at the University of Oxford. Her research examines the uses of ignorance as a productive tool for exonerating blame and asserting expertise in modern liberal democracies.

Notes on Contributors   ix

Martin McQuillan is Professor of Literary Theory and Cultural Analysis and Dean of Arts and Social Sciences at Kingston University, London. His books include *Deconstruction after 9/11* (2009), *The Origins of Deconstruction* (Ed., 2009), *Deconstruction Reading Politics* (Ed., 2009), *The Politics of Deconstruction* (2007) and *Paul de Man* (2001). Forthcoming books include *Roland Barthes (Or The Profession of Cultural Studies)*.

Andrea Phillips is Reader in Fine Art at the Department of Art, Goldsmiths, University of London, and Director of the Doctoral Research Programme. She works on art, architecture, politics, institution-making and urban regeneration, and her current research projects include the aesthetic formatting of transnational space and its relation to contemporary art, the future and implications of practice-based research, and 'Building Democracy', a set of publications and discussions that forefront critiques of participation in contemporary art and architecture.

Jacques Rancière is Emeritus Professor of Philosophy at the University of Paris-VIII (Saint-Denis). Born in Algiers in 1940, he is the author of numerous books dealing with aesthetics, politics and their relationships. His oeuvre includes such diverse landmarks as *The Nights of Labour*, *The Ignorant Schoolmaster* and *The Flesh of Words*, as well as *Disagreement* and *Film Fables*. His most recent book in English is *The Emancipated Spectator*.

Mark Robson teaches at the University of Nottingham. His publications include *Stephen Greenblatt* (2008), *The Sense of Early Modern Writing* (2006) and *Language in Theory* (with Peter Stockwell, 2005). He edited the collection *Jacques Rancière: Aesthetics, Politics, Philosophy* (2005).

Julian Rohrhuber is Professor of Music Informatics and Media Theory at the Institute for Music and Media, Robert Schumann Hochschule, Düsseldorf. He works in the areas of philosophy of science, art and media theory. Actively involved in computer language programming development, he designed the synthetic sound tracks for the experimental documentary films *Alles was wir haben* (2004) and *Oral History* (2009). His recent publications include the chapters 'Network Music' in *The Cambridge Companion to Electronic Music* (2007), 'Mengenlehre' in *Unmenge – Wie verteilt sich Handlungsmacht?* (2008), 'Implications of Unfolding' in *Paradoxes of*

Interactivity (2008), 'Artificial, Natural, Historical: Acoustic Ambiguities in Documentary Film' in *Transdisciplinary Digital Art* (2008) and 'New Mathematics and the Subject of the Variable' (in *Variantology* 4, 2010).

Richard Stamp teaches cultural studies at Bath Spa University. He is an editor of the open access journal *Film-Philosophy* and has co-edited (with Paul Bowman) *The Truth of Žižek* (Continuum, 2007) and an issue of *Parallax* on the work of Rancière (no. 52, 2009). He has also written on Rancière and the queer politics of friendship for *borderlands* e-journal (2009).

Alex Thomson is a Senior Lecturer in the Department of English Literature at the University of Edinburgh. He is the author of *Deconstruction and Democracy: Derrida's Politics of Friendship* (Continuum, 2005) and of *Adorno: A Guide for the Perplexed* (Continuum, 2006).

Alberto Toscano is Senior Lecturer in Sociology at Goldsmiths, University of London. He is the author of *Fanaticism: On the Uses of an Idea* (2010) and *The Theatre of Production: Philosophy and Individuation between Kant and Deleuze* (2006). He is an editor of the journal *Historical Materialism*.

Introduction: A Critical Dissensus

Paul Bowman and Richard Stamp

> [T]hose who are venturing into this labyrinth should be honestly forewarned that no answers will be provided them.
> (Rancière 1989: xii)

It seems to be a peculiarly consistent characteristic of the importation of French philosophy and theory into English-speaking academic and intellectual cultures that successive Francophone thinkers are lauded as the next 'master thinker' – or, to capture the proper linguistic register of discipleship, '*maître à penser*'. To limit this claim simply to the post-war period, one need only think of the ways in which Sartre, Althusser, Lacan, Foucault, Deleuze, Lyotard, Bourdieu or Derrida have each in their time been posed or counter-posed – according to the non-chronological production of translation and commentary, and thus never fully synchronized with contemporary French intellectual (let alone academic) contexts[1] – as the most 'important/radical/contemporary' figure of intellectual modernity. Indeed, this tendency was brought into stark light in the wake of the death of Jacques Derrida in 2004, which all-too swiftly generated 'debates' over which proper name would become the 'next Derrida', the next *maître* (regardless of how much he would have shuddered at such an appellation): would it be Jean-Luc Nancy, echt deconstructive philosopher? Or perhaps Alain Badiou, already proclaimed by Peter Hallward as 'perhaps the only serious rival of Deleuze and Derrida for that meaningless but unavoidable title of "most important contemporary French philosopher"'? (2003: xxi)

Both 'meaningless' and 'unavoidable' are dead right here. There is something rather blackly comical in such claims and counter-claims, always made *on behalf of* the thinker who would never claim such a title himself (and it is always *him*-self, it seems) – for this is a rivalry between *disciples*, not (at least, in this context, not directly) their chosen 'masters'. So perhaps we should nominate Jacques Rancière, who like Badiou is a former student of Louis Althusser and of whom it can also be claimed (according to the editors of the first English-language collection of essays on his work) that he 'has written some of the most significant philosophic work to be published in French in the last forty years' (Rockhill and Watts 2009: 1). We will not. For the simple reason that over this 40-year period, Rancière's work has never ceased to call into question the status, rhetoric and authority of mastery. From his refusal of Althusser's 'philosophy of order' (1974: 9) and the founding of *Les Révoltes Logiques*, via his nineteenth-century archival work on workers' history and the forgotten pedagogue, Joseph Jacotot, through to his more recent thinking of politics and aesthetics in terms of the 'distribution of the sensible', Rancière's work has been characterized by polemical interventions into an increasingly diverse range of fields; but they do not add up to a 'system' or a 'theory'. Rather he has described his 'method' as consisting in making interventions into always particular situations, specific instances in which ideas are 'at work': 'What Rancière tries to point out in any situation is the polemical nature that makes it an object of thinking, that situates it in a field of tensions' (Rancière 2009a: 116). Ultimately, these always-specific interventions aim to present his readers with scenes of struggle over what politics is, of a disagreement or dissensus that interrupts and redistributes that system of places – the distribution of the sensible – that allots to each his or her proper role and function. In Rancière's work, the very place of (theoretical) mastery and therefore struggle over the object or territory to be analysed – whether it be a political ontology, the figure of the worker or the aesthetics of the sublime – always gives rise to the fundamental question: 'who is qualified for thinking at all?' (Rancière 2009a: 116)

This is the question at the heart of what remains Rancière's most explosive book, *The Ignorant Schoolmaster* (1991 [1987]), which recounts the forgotten nineteenth-century pedagogical experiments of Joseph Jacotot.[2] Half-adopting the polemical tone of Jacotot's own writings, Rancière aligns himself with the basic presupposition of his 'method': 'The same intelligence is at work in all the acts of the human mind' (1991: 16).

The near-universal assumption of all pedagogical method – that those who have mastered knowledge transmit it to those who have not through explication – thereby vanishes. From this perspective, even (or rather, especially) the most enlightened method of explication remains embedded in a 'principle of *enforced stultification* [*l'abrutissement*]' that preserves the distinction and the distance between intelligences (Rancière 1991: 7). This is why, for Jacotot, the only authority to be exercised is to teach what one does not know – 'I must teach you that I have nothing to teach you' (cited in Rancière 1991: 15) – in order to oblige the student to exercise his or her own (equal) intelligence. The only pedagogical act for such an 'ignorant master' is emancipatory:

Whoever teaches without emancipating stultifies. And whoever emancipates doesn't have to worry about what the emancipated person learns. He will learn what he wants, nothing maybe. He will know he can learn because the same intelligence is at work in all the productions of the human mind, and a man can always understand another man's words. (1991: 18)

In this way, Jacotot's 'non-method' of 'universal teaching' proclaimed that anyone could learn without a master, which meant that 'a poor and ignorant father could, if he was emancipated, conduct the education of his children, without the aid of any master explicator' (Rancière 1991: 18). The explosive power of Rancière's book (first published in France in 1987) is not only to make this (ultimately failed) experiment from the past resonate with contemporary French debates over educational reform, but also to refuse once again the mastery and authority of methodological and disciplinary territory. This 'transgressive imperative' is succinctly phrased by Rancière in an interview that Alex Thomson re-contextualizes in his contribution to the present volume: 'it is imperative to revoke the authoritative principle derived from the succession of historical events. [...] To conceptualize the "contemporaneity" of thought requires the reliance on a certain anachronism or untimeliness.' (2000: 121) Thomson's chapter traces the 'trouble' that Rancière's work poses for those wishing to classify it. He emphasizes the twin strategic importance of anachronism and poetry in Rancière's work, generating 'something like an interference pattern' between history and philosophy – the disciplines with which Rancière is most closely identified. It is by contesting the disciplinary boundaries for producing knowledge about politics, Thomson argues, that Rancière's work each time seeks to reassert the equality of the democratic subject of history with the authoritative voice of the historian or philosopher.

This 'untimely contemporaneity' might be borne in mind in the way that the present collection of critical responses to the work of Jacques Rancière is 'book-ended' by two 'responses' written by Rancière himself: it begins with a revised version of the paper that he gave in response to papers presented at a conference on his work, *Fidelity to the Disagreement: Jacques Rancière and the Political*, held at Goldsmith's College, University of London, in September 2003; and it closes with a new interview in which he responds to a series of questions posed by the editors during preparation of this book in the summer of 2010. We chose to include his 2003 paper, 'The thinking of dissensus: Politics and aesthetics', for two reasons: first, it presents a number of important responses to several of his most 'critical readers' (Badiou and Žižek, for example) as well as setting out a succinct account of his own critical distance from several contemporaries (such as Agamben, Derrida, Lyotard, Negri) to whom he has been compared; and second, it has been cited as an unpublished manuscript in a number of secondary texts on his work (including a number in the present volume), but has not hitherto been available more widely.[3]

The 'thinking of dissensus' by which Rancière identifies his 'method' is taken up by a number of the contributors here in chapters that, in turn, seek to re-stage, critique or simply contest his formulations of 'politics' and 'police', the distribution of the sensible, democracy and the 'rarity' of politics. Indeed, just as dissensus is critical to politics for Rancière, we can track the forces as well as fault lines that arise in response to reading Rancière – a critical dissensus that is staged in and between the different readings of his work in this volume. For instance, a recurrent point of critical dissensus appears in the considerations of Rancière's alignment of equality and democracy with contingency. Jodi Dean, Oliver Marchart and Alberto Toscano each take issue with what they describe – albeit according to slightly different modulations – as the identification of democracy with contingency in Rancière's account of politics in *Disagreement* (1999) and subsequent texts. In a contentious essay that we originally published elsewhere (Bowman and Stamp 2009), but decided to republish here because of the polemical reactions it has already elicited (as evidenced again by several of the chapters included here), Dean charges that although Rancière recognizes that there can be no pure politics, he disavows its 'obscene supplement'. That is, to read the equal absence of qualification for rule (which distinguishes democracy from all other political systems) in terms of contingency results in 'a kind of hysterical pure politics of resistance' that remains intentionally blind to the necessary dirtiness of politics. Following a Žižekian characterization of Rancière as a 'post-political' thinker, Dean's diagnosis is that Rancière chooses fantasy over actuality.[4] Both Marchart and Toscano make comparable charges of utopianism, but from the position of defending two of Rancière's principal targets: political ontology (Marchart) and sociology (Toscano). In each case it is forcefully argued that it is Rancière's apparent suspicion of institutionalization and organization that is the weak point of his insistence on the emancipatory presupposition of equality. Thus, they argue, Rancière's account of emancipatory politics remains in need of supplementation by the very disciplinary objects he so vehemently rejects.

As if in response to these charges, Samuel Chambers patiently undertakes an excavation of the key conceptual relation of politics and police in Rancière's work. Detailing the misrepresentations of that relation in Todd May's *The Political Thought of Jacques Rancière* (2008), Chambers argues that the very occasionality of politics means that it cannot be thought outside of its relation to a specific police distribution of what can be said, thought and felt: the task for Rancière, *pace* his critics as much as those who recruit him to a given political (or theoretical) position, is not to reject any order or organization, but to demonstrate the effects of the actualization of politics as a dissensual intervention into always particular situations. In this spirit, Linsey McGoey focuses on just such a particular situation within the organizational governance of pharmaceutical trails. Contra Dean, McGoey defends a certain understanding of the 'rarity' of politics by insisting on the fragility and ephemerality of dissensus in the struggle over what counts as a political act.

There are other dimensions to and other species of critical dissensus in the readings of Rancière presented here, which accentuate the ongoing interrogation of the relation between politics and aesthetics in his work. The very concept of 'dissensus', he reminds us in this 2003 paper, 'means a difference between sense and sense'. In this way, his paper's subtitle ('Politics and aesthetics') in turn gives the heading for a series of responses focussed on different modalities of this relationship, ranging across the fields of art, literature, cinema and the status of 'professionalism'. In their co-authored essay on aesthetics as 'capture', Rey Chow and Julian Rohrhuber pick up Rancière's axiom that art is that which blurs the distinction between art and non-art, but undertake to restage his affirmation of 'indistinction' from what they diagnose as the contemporary 'postmodern globalist' rhetoric of 'flows'. In a rereading of such boundary indistinctions in terms of 'medial reflexivity' – from *Madame Bovary* to *The Lives of Others* – they have produced a subtly critical shift in Rancière's aesthetics of dissensual 'tension' by exposing it to Ernest Gell's cultural anthropology of art, whose emphasis on aesthetic experience as 'abduction' or 'capture' allows them to supplement Rancière's emancipated spectator with a 'captivated' one. Mark Robson undertakes an intriguingly parallel account of the relation between Rancière's reading of Emma Bovary's fate and contemporary film, which shares Chow and Rohrhuber's interest in the artwork as 'trap'. In this case, the blurring of literature and film is mediated through Rancière's readings of Rossellini's *Germany Year Zero* and *Europa '51* to produce a critical rebuttal of political critiques of Michael Haneke's *Hidden*. Robson's guiding thread is the different acts of suicide whose resistance to explanation is played out in each of these 'novelistic' works, thereby arming 'a trap to those viewers and critics who would seek to go beneath its surface'.

Suhail Malik and Andrea Phillips's contribution shifts critical attention to the potential effects of Rancière's reconfiguration of aesthetics and politics upon the political claims of contemporary art. Mapping Rancière's recent critical readings of the political aspirations of 'critical art' (2009b) back onto his earlier accounts of political subjectification of 'wrong' (1999), Malik and Phillips argue – in a fashion that bears some comparison with Toscano's chapter – that while the constitutive undecidability of what they rename 'aesthetics-art' always occasions the 'political inventiveness' (2009b: 60) of the principle of equality, it does so only ever at the risk of leaving untouched the very political orders in which it takes place. The question of whether the 'aesthetic regime of art' redistributes the established order of the institutions of art also forms the focus of Ben Highmore's contribution, which takes as its example the apposite case of the 1938 exhibition of 'Unprofessional Painting' by the so-called Pitmen Painters of the Ashington Art Group. Highmore takes this example not simply because of obvious parallels with the proletarian poets of Rancière's *Nights of Labor*, but for the way in which the exhibition was structured by a dissensus over what it means (and who can claim) to be 'professional' or 'unprofessional'. The value of Rancière's contribution to debates in the history of art, Highmore argues, lies in a similar 'refusal to "know your place"' that can reanimate not just our thinking about art, but about 'the aesthetic dimension of our social worlds'.

In contrast, Martin McQuillan's polite but polemical 'disappointment' with Rancière's work on aesthetics addresses (by way of a reading of de Man) what he sees as its resistance to reading and commentary. Diagnosing Rancière's growing 'popularity' in the Anglophone academy as part of a retreat from a deconstructive interrogation of philosophy, McQuillan's complaint is not that Rancière forsakes philosophy but that his conceptual vocabulary of 'regimes of art', 'aesthetics', the 'sensible' remains too resolutely dialectical-philosophical. He therefore reads Rancière's own pedagogical position as 'master' in *The Emancipated Spectator* (2010b) against the grain of the 'emancipated community' that the book envisions, thereby issuing a challenge to its readers: *what can we do with Rancière's texts?*

It is also for this reason that we chose to close the book with an interview with Rancière: not out of a wish to give him the final word or right of reply (since he did not read the contributions in advance), but because his responses to the questions we had posed to him inevitably reflected on the 'untimely contemporaneity' of his research and interventions – the accidents, chance events, contingencies, yet also the remarkably consistent element of this 'refusal to "know [his] place"'. Such a refusal might in turn be read as Rancière's own profession of faith, what he refers to in his answers as 'the refusal to follow an ebbing tide, a refusal to decree that all these ideas of emancipation and revolution were an error or a crime'. This refusal of all conceptions of the end ('of illusions, of utopias, of politics, of history') is sustained by the accompanying conviction that such proclamations with regard to 'the crimes of Marxism' simply worked to preserve the same orders of mastery and authority, thereby disguising the continuity of a more disastrous abandonment of 'an entire revolutionary tradition' of emancipation and equality. This is why Rancière chooses to identify the 'common thread' of his work as an 'attention to the ways in which arguments circulate between reasons of order and the reasons of those who claim to attack it'. Rancière's 'method' of dissensus amounts to a refusal of mastery since he forewarns us it will provide no answers, that it will only teach us that it has nothing to teach us, professing only to expose the disagreement at the heart of every cosy consensus – including that of opposition. As he states, slightly differently albeit with the same modesty, in 'Thinking the dissensus':

By reconstructing the logic of my thinking of dissensus, I was not willing to say how we must think and act. I was just trying to explain why I went that way. I realise that my practice of philosophy makes the reading of my work difficult. This is why I am very grateful to those who accepted to discuss it. Let me stress in conclusion that the main point is not *understanding* what I wrote. It is moving forward together in the discussion of the issues we are facing today. For those who want to thread a new way between consensual thinking and the ethical absoluticisation of the wrong, there is still much room for discussion.

It is therefore in the spirit of this critical dissensus that the contributions to the present book have sought to move these discussions forward.

* * *

We would like to thank all of the present contributors for responding to the task of reading Rancière with such critical diligence and persuasive passion. Thanks also to our editors at Continuum: Sarah Douglas for encouraging its inception, and Tom Crick for patience in our steering the book to delivery. Our final thanks must go to Jacques – for supporting this and other projects in which we've been involved, for being generous with his time and feedback, and for so graciously and patiently responding to yet another set of interview questions.

Notes

1. For example, Derrida draws attention to 'complex, contradictory [. . .] and overdetermined' situation for his own work, strongly identified with a French, and 'more narrowly', he adds, 'Parisian university and cultural scene', while noting the growing 'antipathy' to it in the French press and universities (1995: 416).
2. Rancière's argument in this book has been widely recounted, but perhaps the best discussion of its theoretical ethical, pedagogical, institutional and political implications remains Kristin Ross's Translator's Preface to the English translation (Rancière 1991) as well as her article 'Rancière and the practice of equality' (1991).
3. It is important to point out that the 2003 Goldsmith's conference – in the wake of *Disagreement* (Rancière 1999) and 'Ten Theses on Politics' (Rancière 2001; reprinted in Rancière 2010a) – marked for many (the editors included) the first contact with Rancière's work, and as such contributed a decisively to its wider dissemination or 'polemicization' (Arditi and Valentine 1999). Accordingly, we would like to thank one of the *Fidelity to the Disagreement* conference organisers, Benjamin Arditi, for suggesting and for making available this text for inclusion in the present volume. Also, of course, we thank Jacques Rancière for consenting to its inclusion here.

4. Rancière's own response to an earlier version of Dean's argument forms part of a rather playful text called 'A few remarks on the method of Jacques Rancière' (2009a).

Works Cited

Arditi, Benjamin, and Valentine, Jeremy (1999), *Polemicization: The Contingency of the Commonplace*, Edinburgh: Edinburgh University Press.

Bowman, Paul and Stamp, Richard (2009), eds, *Jacques Rancière: In Disagreement*, *Parallax* 52, 15 (3), (July–September).

Derrida, Jacques (1995), 'Honoris causa: "This is *also* extremely funny"', in *Points . . . Interviews, 1974–1994*, ed. Elisabeth Weber and trans. Peggy Kamuf & others, Stanford, CA: Stanford University Press: 399–421.

Hallward, Peter (2003), *Badiou: A Subject to Truth*, Minneapolis: University of Minnesota Press.

May, Todd (2008), *The Political Thought of Jacques Rancière: Creating Equality*, Edinburgh: Edinburgh University Press.

Rancière, Jacques (1974), *La Leçon d'Althusser*, Paris: Gallimard.

— (1989), *The Nights of Labor: The Workers' Dream in Nineteenth-Century France*, trans. Donald Reid, Philadelphia: Temple University Press.

— (1991) [1987], *The Ignorant Schoolmaster: Five Lessons in Intellectual Emancipation*, trans. Kristin Ross, Stanford: Stanford University Press.

— (1999), *Disagreement. Politics and Philosophy*, trans. Julie Rose, Minneapolis: University of Minnesota Press.

— (2000), 'Dissenting Words: A Conversation with Jacques Rancière', interview with Davide Panagia, *Diacritics*, 30 (2): 113–26.

— (2001), 'Ten Theses on Politics', *Theory and Event*, 5: 3.

— (2009a), 'A Few Remarks on the Method of Jacques Rancière', *Parallax* 52, 15 (3), (July–September): 114–23.

— (2009b), *Aesthetics and Its Discontents*, trans. Steven Corcoran, Cambridge & Malden: Polity.

— (2010a), *Dissensus: On Politics and Aesthetics*, ed. & trans. Steven Corcoran, London & New York: Continuum.

— (2010b), *The Emancipated Spectator*, trans. Gregory Elliott, London: Verso.

Rockhill, Gabriel, and Watts, Philip (2009), 'Introduction – Jacques Rancière: Thinker of Dissensus', in *Jacques Rancière: History, Politics, Aesthetics*, Durham: Duke University Press: 1–12.

Ross, Kristin (1991), 'Rancière and the Practice of Equality', *Social Text* 29: 57–71.

The Thinking of Dissensus: Politics and Aesthetics

Jacques Rancière

What does it mean to think politics and aesthetics under the concept of dissensus?[1] Obviously dissensus is not only the concept of what politics and aesthetics are about. This notion also sets up the theoretical stage on which politics and aesthetics themselves are thinkable and the kind of relations that tie their objects together. At the most abstract level, dissensus means a difference between sense and sense: a difference within the same, a sameness of the opposite. If you assume that politics is a form of dissensus, this means that you cannot deduce it from any essence of the community, whether you do it positively in terms of implementation of a common property such as communicative language (Aristotle) or negatively in terms of a response to a destructive instinct that would set man against man (Hobbes). There is politics because the common is divided. Now this division is not a difference of levels. The opposition between sense and sense is not an opposition between the sensible and the intelligible. Political dissensus is not the appearance or the form that would be the manifestation of an underlying social and economic process. In reference to the Marxist conceptualization, class war is the actual reality of politics, not its hidden cause.

Let us start from the first point. In *Disagreement* I re-examined the old Aristotelian definition of the political animal as a speaking animal. Some critics saw it as 'a return to the classics', which also meant to them a return to an old view of language and an old theory of the subject that would ignore Derrida's deconstruction or Lyotard's *différend*. But this view is misleading. Starting from the Aristotelian 'speaking animal' does not mean returning to the definition of an anthropological disposition to political life, to the idea that politics is based on the human capacity of speaking and discussing, as Aristotle opposed it to the merely animal capacity of the voice which expresses pleasure and pain. On the contrary, I show that this 'common' capacity is split up from the very beginning. Aristotle tells us that slaves *understand* language but don't *possess* it. This is what dissensus means. There is politics because speaking is not the same as speaking, because there is not even an agreement on what a sense means. Political dissensus is not a discussion between speaking people who would confront their interests and values. It is a conflict about who speaks and who does not speak, about what has to be heard as the voice of pain and what has to be heard as an argument on justice. And this is also what 'class war' means: not the conflict between groups which have opposite economic interests, but the conflict about what an 'interest' is, the struggle between those who set themselves as able to manage social interests and those who are supposed to be only able to reproduce their life.

I started from philosophers who defined politics as the implementation of a human disposition to the community because I wanted to show that it is impossible to draw such a deduction, that this 'common' sensory quality is already the stage of a dissensus. This leads me to a methodological remark: disagreement is not only an object of my theorization. It is also its method. Addressing an author or a concept first means to me setting the stage for a disagreement, testing an operator of difference. This also means that my theoretical operations are always aimed at reframing the configuration of a problem. The same critics that suspect me of 'returning' to the classics think that the distinction between politics and police in *Disagreement* or in the 'Ten Theses on Politics' amounts to a search for the purity of politics. Marxists see it as a reminder of the old 'populist' opposition of spontaneity to organization, deconstructionists as an uncritical return to an old metaphysics of identity. But both miss the polemical context of my argumentation. My analysis of what 'politics' means was entirely aimed at challenging and overturning a given idea of that purity. It was a response to the so-called return of the political or return to politics which nearly overwhelmed us in the 1980s in France. At that time we could hear everywhere this motto: we have now broken away from the subjection of the political to the social, to social interests, social conflicts and social utopias. We have thus returned to the true sense of politics as the action on the public stage, the manifestation of a 'being-together', the search for the common good, and so on. The philosophical ground for that return was taken mainly from two philosophers, Leo Strauss and Hannah Arendt, who – in some way – had brought the legacy of Greek philosophy to modern governmental practice. Both theorists had emphasized the opposition between the political sphere of public action and speech and the realm of economical and social necessity. Their arguments were strongly revived, even more so as they could be substituted for the old Marxist opposition of 'economism' and 'spontaneism' to true revolutionary practice.

That conjunction was made obvious during the strikes of 1995 in France. The old Marxist denunciation of 'trade-unionism' and the Arendtian denunciation of the confusion between the political and the social could merge into one and the same discourse of support to the 'political courage' of the government in charge of the common good and of the future of the community *against* the archaic privileges advocated by the strikers. Therefore, it appeared that the return to the 'purity' of the political meant in fact the return to the identification of the political with state institutions and governmental practice. Consequently, my attempt at defining the specificity of politics was first an attempt at challenging the mainstream idea of the return to pure politics.

There is no 'pure' politics. I wrote the 'Ten Theses on Politics' primarily as a critique of the Arendtian idea of a specific political sphere and a political way of life. The 'Theses' aimed at demonstrating that her definition of politics was a vicious circle: it identifies politics with a specific way of life. Ultimately, however, this means identifying it with the way of life of those whose way of life already destined them to politics. It is the circle of the *arkhê*, the anticipation of the exercise of power in the 'power of beginning', in the disposition or entitlement to exercise it. The core of the problem lay precisely in the idea of 'disposition' or 'destination'. It lay in the idea of the opposition between a political and a non-political life or a 'bare life'. This distribution is precisely the presupposition of what I call the police: the configuration of the political community as a collective body with its places and functions allotted according to the competences specific to groups and individuals. There is politics when this presupposition is broken by the affirmation that the power belongs to those who have no qualification to rule – which amounts to saying that there is no ground whatever for the exercise of power. There is politics when the boundary separating those who are born for politics from those who are born for the 'bare' life of economic and social necessity is put into question.

This means that there is no political life, but a political stage. Political action consists in showing as political what was viewed as 'social', 'economic' or 'domestic'. It consists in blurring the boundaries. It is what happens whenever 'domestic' agents – workers or women, for instance – reconfigure their quarrel as a quarrel concerning the common, that is, concerning what place belongs or does not belong to it and who is able or unable to make enunciations and demonstrations about the common. It should be clear therefore that there is politics when there is a disagreement about what is politics, when the boundary separating the political from the social or the public from the domestic is put into question. Politics is a way of re-partitioning the political from the non-political. This is why it generally occurs 'out of place', in a place which was not supposed to be political.

Let us draw some consequences from this analysis. First, this does not mean that my view of politics is 'value-neutral'.[2] Sure, it refuses to ground politics on an ethical idea of the common. More precisely, it puts into question the idea that politics, as a set of practices, has to be regulated by ethics conceived as the instance pronouncing values or principles of action in general. According to this view, disasters and horrors would happen when you forget to ground politics in ethics. I would put matters the other way around. In the age of George Bush and Osama bin Laden, it appears that the ethical conflict is much more violent, much more radical than the political one. Politics then can be conceived as a specific practice of antagonism, capable of soothing the violence of ethical conflict.

Yet I do not reduce politics to a mere agonistic schema where the 'content' is irrelevant. I am far away from the Schmittian formalization of antagonism. Politics, I argue, has its own universal, its own measure that is equality. The measure never applies directly. It does so only through the enactment of a wrong. However, not every wrong is necessarily political. It has been argued against my theses that there are also anti-democratic forms of protest among the oppressed, shaped by religious fanaticism or ethnic identitarianism and intolerance. Ernesto Laclau (2005) put this as the blind spot of my conceptualization of dissensus (246–7). But it is clear that in my view a wrong is political when it enacts the basis of political action, which is the mere contingency of equality, which is evidently not the case of 'popular' movements asking for the purity of the blood, the power of religion, and so on. But I also refuse a widespread tendency to stigmatize any form of protest under the name of 'populism'. The concept of 'populism' is a hotchpotch which allows old Marxists and young liberals at once to put in the same basket struggles for maintaining the welfare system and ethnic or religious riots.

The 'people' is a name for two opposite things: demos or ethnos. The ethnos is the people identified with the living body of those who have the same origin, are born on the same soil or worship the same god. It is the people as a given body opposed to other such bodies. The demos is the people conceived as a supplement to the parts of the community – what I call the count of the uncounted. It is the inscription of the mere contingency of being born here or there, as opposed to any 'qualification' for ruling, and it makes its appearance through the process of verification of that equality, the construction of forms of dissensus. Now it is clear that the difference is not given once and for all. The life of the demos is the ongoing process of its differentiation from the ethnos.

Second, this does not mean that I reduce politics to exceptional and vanishing moments of uprising. The mere enactment of the political principle rarely – if ever – appears in its purity, but there is politics in a lot of 'confused' matters and conflicts, and politics makes for a memory, a history. There is a historical dynamic of politics: a history of events that break the 'normal' course of time, a history of events, inscriptions and forms of subjectivization, of promises, memories, repetitions, anticipations and anachronisms.[3] There is no point in opposing exception to process. The debate is about the conception of the process. The history of politics, as I view it, is not a continuous process, going along with economic and social development. It is not the unravelling of any 'destinary' plot either.

Thirdly, the opposition between politics and police goes along with the statement that politics has no 'proper' object, that all its objects are blended with the objects of police. In an earlier text, I proposed to give the name of 'the political' to the field of encounter – and 'confusion' – between the process of politics and the process of police (see Rancière 1995). It is clear for me that the possibilities for a political intervention reframing a situation have to be taken from a given setting of the political, understood in that way. This is why, against the Marxist opposition of real and formal democracy, I emphasized the part played by all the inscriptions of the democratic process in the texts of the constitutions, the institutions of the states, the apparatuses of public opinion, the mainstream forms of enunciation, etc. It is a point that clearly differentiates me from some radical political thinkers who want to tear the radicality of politics apart from any confusion with the play of state institutions. Alain Badiou, who merely sees democracy as the form of state and way of life of our Western societies, suspects me of clinging to that consensual view. Slavoj Žižek opposes the risk of the 'radical political act' to the 'legalistic logic of transcendental guarantee' that is provided by the democratic law of the majority.[4] But I never identified the democratic process with the functioning of our states or with the 'opportunistic insurance' (Žižek) provided by the law of the majority. I identified it with the political supplementation that confronts this functioning with the 'power of anyone' which grounds it at the cost of disrupting it. The unequal order cannot work without its egalitarian presupposition. Conversely the egalitarian struggle itself often uses the weapons of the police description of the common. Let us think for instance to the role played in feminist struggle by the medical, moral and pedagogical standards of sexual complementarity, or by the reference to the 'property' of work in workers' struggles. Equality has no vocabulary or grammar of its own, only a poetics.

Politics does not stem from a place outside of the police. I agree on this point with some of my contradictors (cf. Thomson 2003). There is no place outside of the police. But there are conflicting ways of doing things with the 'places' that it allocates: of relocating, reshaping or redoubling them. As I recall in the 'Ten Theses', the space of democracy was opened in Greece by such a displacement, when demos, which first meant 'district', became the name of the subject of politics. We know that it did so when Cleisthenes reshaped the Athenian tribes by putting together three 'demes' that were geographically separated – a measure that made two things at once: it constituted the autonomy of the political space and deprived the aristocracy of its locally based power.

This gives me the opportunity to say something more about my use of spatial categories or metaphors that has been underlined by several commentators.[5] Speaking of the 'space' of democracy is not a mere metaphor. The delimitation of the demos is at once a material and a symbolical matter. More precisely it is a new form of (dis)connection between the material and the symbolical. The institution of democracy meant the invention of a new topography, the creation of a space made of disconnected places against the aristocratic space that connected the material privilege of the landowners with the symbolical power of the tradition. This disconnection is at the core of the opposition between politics and police. So the issue of space has to be thought of in terms of distribution: distribution of places, boundaries of what is in or out, central or peripheral, visible or invisible. It is related to what I call *the distribution of the sensible* (see Rancière 2004b). By this I mean the way in which the abstract and arbitrary forms of symbolization of hierarchy are embodied as perceptive givens, in which a social destination is anticipated by the evidence of a perceptive universe, of a way of being, saying and seeing. This distribution is a certain framing of time and space. The 'spatial' closure of Plato's *Republic* which wants that anybody be at its *own place* is its temporal partition as well: the artisans are initially figured as they who have no time to be elsewhere than in their place. I called my book on worker's emancipation *The Night of the Proletarians* (translated into English as *The Nights of Labor* (1989)) to stress that the core of emancipation was an attempt to break away from the very partition of time sustaining social subjection: the obvious partition being that workers work during the day and sleep during the night. Therefore, the conquest of the night was the first step in social emancipation, the first material and symbolic basis for a reconfiguration of the given state of things. In order to state themselves as sharing in a common world and as able to name the objects and participants of that common world, they had to reconfigure their 'individual' life, to reconfigure the partition of day and night that, for all individuals, anticipated the partition between those who were or were not destined to care for the common. It was not a matter of 'representations' as historians would claim. It was a matter of sensory experience, a form of partition of the perceptible.

In other words, my concern with 'space' is the same as my concern with 'aesthetics'. I already tried to explain that the shift perceived by some commentators between my work on history and politics and my work on aesthetics is not a shift from one field to another. My work on politics was an attempt to show politics as an 'aesthetic affair'. What I mean by this term has nothing to do with the 'aestheticization of politics' that Benjamin opposed to the 'politicization of art'. What I mean is that politics, rather than the exercise of power or the struggle for power, is the configuration of a specific world, a specific form of experience in which some things appear to be political objects, some questions political issues or argumentations and some agents political subjects. I attempted to redefine this 'aesthetic' nature of politics by setting politics not as a specific single world but as a conflictive world: not a world of competing interests or values but a world of competing worlds.

If that part of my work dealt with the 'aesthetics of politics', I would say that my later work dealt with the politics of aesthetics. I do not understand by this term the question of the relationship between art and politics, but rather, the meaning and import of the configuration of a specific sphere – the sphere of aesthetics – in the political distribution of the perceptible. Already in my 'political' work, I have tried to demonstrate how the existence of the political and the existence of the aesthetic are strongly interconnected: the exclusion of a public scene of the demos and the exclusion of the theatrical form are strictly interconnected in Plato's *Republic*. This does not mean, as it is often said, that Plato excluded art to the benefit of politics. He excluded politics *and* art, both the idea of a capacity of the artisans to be 'elsewhere' than at their 'own' workplace and the possibility for poets or actors to play another identity than their 'own' identity.

I also tried to show how modern democracy and modern revolution are connected with this new distribution of the sensible that delineates a specific place for art, a specific feeling called aesthetic feeling. It is not a mere coincidence that made the art museum emerge at the time of the French Revolution; neither is it a mere factual influence that led from Schiller's idea of a specific 'aesthetic state' to Hölderlin's idea of a new, sensory revolution and to the Marxist revolution of the producers. Modern democracy is contemporaneous with the emergence of the aesthetic. By this, I mean a specific sphere of experience suspending the forms of domination governing the other spheres of experience: the hierarchies of form and matter, of understanding and sensibility, that predicated domination on the opposition of two humanities, differentiated from the very constitution of their sensory experience. This re-partition of the spheres of experience is part of the possibilities of refiguring the question of places and parts in general. As we know, it did so in an ambiguous way: it was not for casual reasons but because of the exceptionality of aesthetics that replicated the paradoxical 'exceptionality' of politics.

The exceptionality of politics has no specific place. Politics 'takes place' in the space of the police, by rephrasing and restaging social issues, police problems, and so on. Aesthetic autonomy, on the contrary, has specific places. But the definition of those specific places is bound up with the equation between a form of art and a form of life. The solitude of the aesthetic experience was bound, from the very beginning, with the promise of a future community where there would be no more art or politics as separate spheres of experience. This means that, from the beginning, aesthetics has its politics – which, in my terms, is a metapolitics, a manner of 'doing politics' otherwise than politics does. Aesthetics opposes to both the practices of political dissensus and the transformations of state-power the metapolitical project of a sensory community, achieving what will always be missed by the 'merely political' revolution: freedom and equality incorporated in living attitudes, in a new relationship between thought and the sensory world, between the bodies and their environment.

This project has taken a variety of shapes and undergone many transformations that eventually led to its reversal: Schiller's aesthetic education, the new mythology dreamed by Hegel, Schelling and Hölderlin, the human revolution of the young Marx, the constructivist project of the Soviet artists and architects, but also the surrealist subversion, Adorno's dialectics of the modern work, Blanchot's idea of May '68 as a 'passive' revolution, Debord's 'derive', or Lyotard's aesthetic of the sublime.

Here I have to spell out what is at stake in my discussion of Lyotard's late work, a point which remains unclear in *Disagreement* and that I have tried to develop in some subsequent essays (see Rancière 2003b, 2004a, 2004d). What is at stake is the understanding of dissensus, which Lyotard turned, through the category of the sublime, into a new form of absolute wrong. That absoluticization was not apparent in *The Differend* but it became more and more obvious in the following books. That turn has been obscured in the Anglo-American reception of Lyotard by the concepts of poststructuralism and postmodernism. Lyotard's thinking of differend and wrong has been too easily aligned with a poststructuralist critique of the subject and a postmodern perception of the end of grand narratives, which would result in a relativist view of the plurality of languages and cultures. That perception conceals what is at stake in Lyotard's theory and in the way of thinking dissensus that his late books epitomized but which characterizes much more widely what I call the 'ethical turn' of aesthetics and politics.[6]

The absoluticization of the wrong began in fact with the so-called postmodern affirmation of a break between a modern epoch where the proletarian would have been the universal victim, subject of a great narrative, and a postmodern time of micro- or local narratives. This break has no historical evidence. All my historical research had been aimed at deconstructing that presupposition, at showing that the history of social emancipation had always been made out of small narratives, particular speech acts, etc. So the argument of a breakaway from the time of the great narrative and the universal victim seemed to me beside the point. More accurately, it was beside the point unless it was in fact embedded in another narrative of an absolute wrong. My assumption is that this was precisely the point. What Lyotard was doing was not breaking away from the grand narrative of the victim. It was reframing it, in a retrospective way, in order to make a new use of it.

From this point of view, *Heidegger and "the jews"* (Lyotard 1990) can be considered as a switching point that gives to the so-called postmodern argumentation a meaning that perhaps was not there and certainly was not obvious at the beginning. This meaning is that of the substitution of a narrative and of a substitution of the victim. In this text, the Jews became the subject of the new narrative of modernity, the new narrative of the Western world. It was no longer a narrative of emancipation, the one-way plot of the fulfilment of a promise. Instead, it was another one-way plot: the narrative of the absolute crime that appears as the truth of the whole dialectic of Western thought, the end-result of the great attempt at forgetting the original debt of thought with respect to the Other, the Untameable or the Unredeemable.

The idea of the unredeemable debt, as we know, is itself the last stage in the transformation of the exceptionality of the aesthetic state. Lyotard interprets the aesthetic exceptionality through the grid of the Kantian sublime: as an experience of impotence. The exceptionality of the aesthetic state would mean the radical dis-agreement of sense and thought. The Kantian inability of Imagination to present the idea of Reason is overturned into a power of the *aistheton* that escapes the power of thinking and bears witness to an original 'disaster': the immemorial dependence of the mind, its 'enslavement' to the law of otherness. The first name of this Otherness is 'the Thing', the Freudo-Lacanian *Das Ding*. Its second name is the Law.

In this way, the Jewish obedience to the Law is the same as the obedience to the original experience of the 'disaster' or 'disempowerment' of the mind. Thus, the Nazi extermination of the European Jews could be interpreted as the disaster resulting from the denial of the original disaster, the last accomplishment of the project of getting rid of *Das Ding* or the Law, of getting rid of the immemorial dependence to otherness. This properly means interpreting the aesthetic experience as an ethical experience, debarring any process of emancipation. In such a plot, any process of emancipation is perceived as the disastrous attempt to deny the disaster that enslaves the mind to otherness. This thinking of a new kind of radical evil currently leads – at least among French intellectuals – to two kinds of attitudes regarding politics: one is abstention and other is support for another kind of absoluticization of the wrong, support for the current campaigns of the forces of Good against the axis of Evil.

Therefore, what is at stake in my research on politics and what ties it up with a research on aesthetics is an attempt to think a specificity of politics as disagreement and a specificity of the aesthetic heterogeneity that break away from the absoluticization of the dissensus as wrong or disaster. It is an attempt to think such exceptionality outside of a plot of purity. What is at stake in Lyotard's last work is clearly a transformation of the Adornian interpretation of the aesthetic separateness. In Adorno, the aesthetic experience had to be separated in order to hold the purity of the aesthetic promise. In Lyotard, the aesthetic purity of the work boils down to the status of sheer testimony of the Untameable.

Similarly, the Arendtian idea of the separation between political life and bare life was reversed in Agamben's theorization of the 'state of exception'. The latter becomes the great narrative of Modernity as the subsumption of political life under 'bare life'. This subsumption accounts for Hobbes' theory as well as for the Rights of Man, the French revolutionary sovereignty of the people, or genocide. The idea of the purity of politics leads to its contrary, to empty the stage of political invention by sweeping aside its ambiguous actors. As a result, politics comes to be identified with the act of a power that appears as an overwhelming historico-ontological destiny: we are all, from the outset, refugees in the homogeneous and pervasive space of the camp, entrapped in the complementarity of bare life and exception (cf. Agamben 1998; Rancière 2004c).

If, at the beginning of the 1990s, I was addressing the standard theories of the return of the political, I found myself more and more concerned with this infiniticization of the logic of exceptionality, with this double reversal of the political and the aesthetic exceptionality whose conjunction constitutes the 'ethical' trend. I try to oppose to it a way of thinking aesthetical and political dissensuality apart from the idea of purity. The exceptionality of politics is the exceptionality of a practice that has no field of its own but has to build its stage in the field of police. And the autonomy of art, in the aesthetic regime, is heteronomy as well: art is posited as a specific sphere falling under a specific experience, but no boundary separates its objects and procedures from the objects and procedures belonging to other spheres of experience.

The global logic of my work aims at showing that pure politics and pure aesthetics are doomed to be overturned together in the radicalization of the infinite wrong or infinite evil. I try to think disagreement as the wrong that cannot be settled but can be processed all the same. This means that I try to keep the conceptualization of exception, wrong or excess apart from any kind of ontology. The current trend has it that you cannot think politics unless you trace back its principles to an ontological principle: Heideggerian difference, Spinozist infinity of Being in Negri's conception, polarity of being and event in Badiou's thought, re-articulation of the relationship between potency and act in Agamben's theory, etc. My assumption is that such a requirement leads to the dissolution of politics on behalf of some historico-ontological destinary process. This may take on different forms. Politics might be dissolved in the law of being, like the form that is torn up by the manifestation of its content. In Hardt and Negri's *Empire*, the Multitudes are the real content of the empire that will explode it. Communism will win because it is the law of being: Being is Communism. Alternatively, all political wrong could appear as the consequence of an original wrong, so that only a God or an ontological revolution can save us.

My first concern from the beginning has been to set aside all analysis of political matters in terms of metaphysical destination. For this, I think it necessary to dismiss any temporal teleology, any original determination of difference, excess or dissensus. This is why I have always tried to define specific, limited forms of excess, difference or dissensus. I do not ground political dissensus in an excess of Being which would make any count impossible. I link it with a *specific* miscount. The demos does not embody the excess of Being. It is primarily an empty name. On the one hand, it is a name for a supplementary count that has no necessity, and on the other, this 'arbitrary' count enacts the 'egalitarian' condition inherent in the legitimization of inequality itself. There is no ontological gap but a twist that ties together the contingency of equality and the contingency of inequality. The power of the demos does not enact any original excess of being. It enacts an excess inherent in any process of nomination: the arbitrariness of the relationship binding names and bodies together, the excess of names which makes them available to those who are not 'destined' to give names and to speak about the common. Difference always means to me a specific relationship, a specific measure of incommensurables.

This is what keeps me at a certain distance from Derrida's spectrality, though, obviously, I have to tackle the same kind of issues as he does. For instance, the Derridean problematic of ghosts and spectrality ties together two issues whose knot is crucial to me too: disidentification and the status of anachronism. It deals with the same problem that I confront: how are we to think the 'existence of the inexistent', how are we to think the 'supersensible-sensible'? However, in my view, Derrida gives too much presence, too much flesh to the inexistent. While deconstructing identity, he is always on the verge of reinstating it by overstating the 'identity of alterity' or the presence of the absent. As he puts it in *Specters of Marx*, we know nothing about the reality of the ghost. Yet we know that he looks at us, that he sees us and speaks to us. We do not know its identity but we have to bear its gaze and obey its injunction.

I am fully aware of the weight of 'otherness' that separates us from ourselves. What I refuse is to give it a gaze and give to its voice a power of ethical injunction. More precisely, I refuse to turn the multiplicity of forms of alterity into a substance through the personification of Otherness, which ultimately reinstates a form of transcendence. The same goes with the issue of temporal dis-junction. I also deal with the issues of anachronisms, repetitions, and so on, but I refuse to unify them in the idea of a 'time out of joint'. I rather think of it in terms of multiplicities of forms and lines of temporality. In the logic of dis-agreement, as I see it, you always consider a dis-junction as a specific form of junction (and a junction as a form of dis-junction) instead of constructing an ontology of dis-junction.

I am aware of the flipside of this argument. If there is no original structure of temporal 'disjunction', it is difficult to think the horizon of an emancipatory fulfilment. To put in other terms, if there is no ghost, there is no Messiah. If I translate the messianic proposition in prosaic terms, the question runs as follows: is it possible to ground politics on its own logic? Do we not need to frame a specific temporality, a temporality of the 'existence of the inexistent' in order to give sense to the process of political subjectivization? I prefer to reverse the argument by saying that the framing of a future happens in the wake of political invention rather than being its condition of possibility. Revolutionaries invented a 'people' before inventing its future. Besides, in the context of the 'ethicization of the political' that is ours, I think that we have to focus first on the specificity of the 'aesthetics of politics', the specificity of political invention.

Therefore when Derrida speaks of ghosts, opposing them to the binarism of 'effectiveness' and 'ideality', I prefer to speak of fictions – a term which, in my view, plays the same role but keeps us from substantializing the part of the 'inexistent'. The inexistent for me is first of all words, texts, fictions, narratives, characters – a 'paper life' instead of a life of ghosts or *Geist*. It is a poetic framing of specific appearances rather than a phenomenology of the unapparent. So when Derrida proposes to frame a 'hauntology' that would be wider and more powerful than an ontology, I prefer to speak in terms of poetics. Ontology or 'hauntology' are as fictitious as a political invention or a poem. Ontology claims to provide a foundation to politics, aesthetics, ethics, and so on, whereas a 'hauntology' purports to de-construct this pretension. In my view, it does so at the cost of substantializing the 'otherness' that undermines the foundationalist project. Now, the substantialization of Otherness is at the core of the 'ethical' enterprise. I am fully aware of the distance separating Derrida from the mainstream ethical trend and its obviously reactive politics, but I think that 'otherness' has to be de-substantialized, de-ontologized if we want to escape this trend.

This leads me to answer some questions regarding the sense of my work or the status of my discourse. Rather than founding or deconstructing, what I always tried to do is to blur the boundaries that separate the genres and levels of discourse. In *The Names of History* (1994), I proposed the notion of a 'poetics of knowledge'. A poetics of knowledge can be viewed as a kind of 'deconstructive practice', to the extent that it tries to trace back an established knowledge – history, political science, sociology, and so on – to the poetic operations – description, narration, metaphorization, symbolization, and so on – that make its objects appear and give sense and relevance to its propositions. What is important to me is that this 'reduction' of scientific discourse to the poetical moment means its reduction to the equality of speaking beings. This is the meaning of the 'equality of intelligence' that I borrowed from Jacotot. It does not mean that every manifestation of intelligence is equal to any other. Above all, it means that the same intelligence makes poetic fictions, political inventions or historical explanations, that the same intelligence makes and understands sentences in general. Political thought, history, sociology, and so on use common powers of linguistic innovation in order to make their objects visible and create connections between them. So does philosophy.

For me this means that philosophy is not the discourse that grounds the other forms of discourse or spheres of rationality. Instead, it is the discourse that undoes the boundaries within which all disciplines predicate their authority on the assumption of a specific methodology fitting the specificity of their field of objectivity. My practice of philosophy goes along with my idea of politics. It is an-archical, in the sense that it traces back the specificity of disciplines and discursive competences to the 'egalitarian' level of linguistic competence and poetic invention. This practice implies that I take philosophy as a specific battlefield, a field where the endeavour to disclose the *arkhê* of the *arkhê* simply leads to the contrary, that is, to disclosing the contingency or the poetic character of any *arkhê*. If much of my work has been elaborated as a rereading of Plato, it is because his work is the most elaborated form of this battlefield. The *Republic* tells us that the inequality of destination is a 'noble lie' and lets us understand that the 'lack of time' that prevents the artisan to be elsewhere is a proscription of the *elsewhere* as such. *Phaedrus* shows us the link between the proscription of writing and the proscription of democracy. It draws a radical line separating the space-time of the cicadas-philosophers and the space-time of the workers, and it promises to tell us the truth about Truth. However, the truth about Truth can only be told as a myth. The equality of fairy tales underpins the whole hierarchy of discourses and positions. If there is a privilege of philosophy, it lies in the frankness with which it tells us that the truth about Truth is a fiction and undoes the hierarchy just as it builds it.

An egalitarian practice of philosophy, as I understand it, is a practice that enacts the aporia of foundation, which is the necessity of a poetical act to constitute an *arkhê* of the *arkhê*, an authority of the authority. I am aware that I am not the only person committed to this task. What is thus the specificity of my position? It is that I refuse to ontologize a principle of the *aporia*. Some thinkers put it as *difference*, at the risk of conjuring up a spectre of transcendence. Others identify it with the *infinity* or *multiplicity of Being*. We have in mind Hardt and Negri's *multitudes* or Badiou's theory of Being as pure multiplicity. Both Negri and Badiou set out to ground the unbinding of authority in a law of Being *as* unbinding. But, from this point on, it seems to me that they can complete the enactment of the unbinding power in specific spheres of practice only at the cost of some sleights of hand which in my view reinstate the principle of authority. I prefer not to set a principle of the aporia, not to put Equality as an *arkhê* but to put it just as a supposition that must be verified continuously – a verification or an enactment that opens specific stages of equality. These stages are built by crossing the boundaries and interconnecting forms and levels of discourse and spheres of experience.

By reconstructing the logic of my thinking of dissensus, I was not willing to say how we must think and act. I was just trying to explain why I went that way. I realize that my practice of philosophy makes the reading of my work difficult. This is why I am very grateful to those who have accepted to discuss it. Let me stress in conclusion that the main point is not *understanding* what I wrote. It is moving forward together in the discussion of the issues we are facing today. For those who want to thread a new way between consensual thinking and the ethical absoluticization of the wrong, there is still much room for discussion.

Notes

1. This text transcribes with some slight modifications the paper presented at the conference *Fidelity to the Disagreement: Jacques Rancière and the Political,* organized by the Post-Structuralism and Radical Politics and Marxism specialist groups of the Political Studies Association of the UK in Goldsmiths College, London, 16–17 September 2003. I express my gratitude to Benjamin Arditi, Alan Finalyson and James Martin who organized that conference.
2. On this point, cf. Thomson (2003).
3. See my response to Mick Dillon in the discussion about the 'Ten Theses' (Rancière 2003a).
4. Alain Badiou makes this point against me in his *Metapolitics* (2005). Žižek's criticism of the 'democratic trap' has been most clearly coined in the essay 'From Politics to Biopolitics... and Back' (2004).
5. Cf. the contributions of Mustafa Dikeç and Michael Shapiro to the 2003 Goldsmith's conference.
6. In his contribution to the 2003 Goldsmith's conference, Sam Chambers has argued that I endorsed, against the Lyotardian differend, an Aristotelian view of language that prevented me not only from understanding Lyotard but also from completing my own project of rethinking politics. But I referred to Aristotle in order to show the gap or the wrong lying in the heart of the classical equation man/speaking animal/political animal. The whole problem is how we conceive of this wrong. Cf. Chambers, 2005.

Works Cited

Agamben, Giorgio (1998), *Homo Sacer: Sovereign Power and Bare Life*, trans. Daniel Heller-Roazen, Stanford: Stanford University Press.
Badiou, Alain (2005), *Metapolitics*, trans. Jason Barker, London: Verso.
Chambers, Samuel (2005), 'The Politics of Literarity', *Theory & Event*, 8 (3). (Original version presented at *Fidelity to the Disagreement: Jacques Rancière and the Political,* Goldsmith's College, University of London, September 16–17.)
Derrida, Jacques (1994), *Spectres of Marx: The State of the Debt, the Work of Mourning, and the New International*, trans. Peggy Kamuf, London & New York: Routledge.

Dikeç, Mustafa (2003), 'The place of space in Rancière's Political Thought', unpublished paper from *Fidelity to the Disagreement: Jacques Rancière and the Political*, Goldsmith's College, University of London, September 16–17.
Hardt, Michael and Toni Negri (1999), *Empire*, London & Cambridge: Harvard University Press.
Laclau, Ernesto (2005), *On Populist Reason*, London: Verso.
Lyotard, Jean-François (1990), *Heidegger and "the jews"*, trans. Andreas Michel and Mark S. Roberts, Minneapolis: University of Minnesota Press.
Rancière, Jacques (1989), *The Nights of Labor: The Workers' Dream in Nineteenth-Century France*, trans. Donald Reid, Philadelphia: Temple University Press.
— (1994), *The Names of History: On the Poetics of Knowledge*, trans. Hassan Melehy, Minneapolis: University of Minnesota Press.
— (1995), 'Politics, Identification, Subjectivization', in *The Identity in Question*, ed. John Rajchman, New York: Routledge: 63–72.
— (1999), *Disagreement: Politics and Philosophy*, trans. Julie Rose, Minneapolis: University of Minnesota Press.
— (2001), 'Ten Theses on Politics', trans. Rachel Bowlby and Davide Panagia. *Theory & Event*, 5 (3).
— (2003a), 'Comment and Responses', *Theory & Event*, 6 (4).
— (2003b), *Le destin des images*, Paris: La Fabrique.
— (2004a), *Malaise dans l'esthétique*, Paris: Galilée.
— (2004b), *The Politics of Aesthetics: The Distribution of the Sensible*, trans. Gabriel Rockhill, London & New York: Continuum.
— (2004c), 'Who is the Subject of the Rights of Man?' *South Atlantic Quarterly*, 103 (2–3) (Spring/Summer): 297–310.
— (2004d), 'The Sublime from Lyotard to Schiller: Two Readings of Kant and their Political Significance', *Radical Philosophy*, 126: 8–15.
— (2007), *The Future of the Image*, trans. Gregory Elliott, London: Verso.
Shapiro, Michael (2003), 'Radicalizing democratic theory: Social space in Connolly, Deleuze and Rancière', unpublished paper from *Fidelity to the Disagreement: Jacques Rancière and the Political*, Goldsmith's College, University of London, September 16–17.
Thomson, Alex (2003), 'Re-placing the opposition: Rancière and Derrida', unpublished paper from *Fidelity to the Disagreement: Jacques Rancière and the Political*, Goldsmith's College, University of London, September 16–17.
Žižek, Slavoj (2004), 'From Politics to Biopolitics . . . and Back', *South Atlantic Quarterly*, 103 (2–3) (Spring/Summer): 501–21.

The Politics of the Police: From Neoliberalism to Anarchism, and Back to Democracy

Samuel A. Chambers

Jacques Rancière does political theory, if he does it at all, by staking out provocative positions and making provocative claims.[1] As Davide Panagia puts it, for Rancière 'politics is the practice of asserting one's position [in a way that] that ruptures the logic of *arkhê*' (Panagia 2001: §2).[2] And one way to rupture a given order or logic is to rename or redefine terms. Rancière does this most famously with politics itself. *Disagreement* (1999), Rancière's best-known work in English translation, made the bold and controversial move of redefining as 'the police' (*la police*) most of what political theorists and everyday political actors all traditionally recognize as politics. This has led to certain dislocations within the field of political thought. Some theorists have scrambled to make sense of Rancière's radical (at best) or non-sensical (at worst) conception of politics as occurring only when the logic of equality interrupts the logic of domination. Others dismiss Rancière for conceiving of politics too narrowly (e.g. Dean 2009). These criticisms, however, miss their mark precisely because Rancière himself admits (or perhaps proclaims) that politics happens 'very little' (1999: 17).

That politics happens so infrequently only raises the question of how we are to understand the workings and functions of the police. It also leads us to ask: what is at stake in the police? On one level, my title, 'The Politics of the Police' gestures first of all to this simple but important query. At another level, however, my title looks like a contradiction in terms; since 'politics' and 'police' are diametrically opposed in Rancière's thought, there can be no politics *of* the police. I will argue here that the degree to which we take 'politics of the police' to be an impossibility depends upon how we translate 'politics' and on how we conceptualize police. Finally, on a third level, 'politics of the police' points to the distinct ways in which particular theorizations of the police lead to different political articulations. My subtitle maps the movements I wish to track here: from Rancière's critique of neoliberal interest-group politics, to Todd May's vigorous defence of anarchism, to my own effort to return to a reworked (both with and against Rancière) democratic politics.

I. Mise en Scène

Rancière produces his concept of 'the police' precisely so as to redefine neoliberal consensus models (interest-group liberalism) as nothing more than 'orders of the police'. This gives him the space to articulate his novel conception of politics, posed in stark and consistent opposition to police. But, despite its apparent centrality to his entire politico-theoretical framework, Rancière seems content to leave 'the police' somewhat undertheorized. He gives us a few pages on it in *Disagreement*, devotes one thesis to it in 'Ten Theses on Politics', and offers barely two short mentions of it in *Hatred of Democracy*. More than this, Rancière appears untroubled by the fact that most of what we typically take for politics has been redefined by this minimally developed concept of police. This makes politics special, and as Rancière says 'rare', but if the world we live in can only ever be a world of police orders, then do we not need to think more carefully and critically about the nature, extent, structure (and structural weaknesses) of those orders? Rancière offers few options, but he seems to imply that politics must be revolutionary, since political moments will prove so infrequent.

Into the space that Rancière opens but does not work within, Todd May inserts his own anarchist politics. In a book putatively devoted to Rancière's political thought – it is titled, simply enough, *The Political Thought of Jacques Rancière* – May develops an account of anarchism as the only *true* democratic politics, the only politics committed fully to the Rancièrean verification of equality in the face of social orders (i.e. police orders) of hierarchy and domination. To make this case, May must give a particular account of police orders precisely because his anarchist politics will remain committed to the complete obliteration of police. Along the way, I suggest – and precisely because police remains such an underdeveloped concept in Rancière's political theory – May makes a significant contribution to a theory of the police.

My own efforts here to think through, augment, refine and perhaps reorient Rancière's notion of 'the police' will be based partly on a critique and rejection of May's anarchist project. May's commitment to anarchism requires him to depart from Rancière precisely by misreading him. May wants to supplant police with politics. Therefore, for him, there can be no politics of the police; politics must destroy police. Put differently, May embraces the element of impropriety that proves central to Rancière's thinking of politics, but he fails to retain any faith in Rancière's concomitant commitment to an *impure politics* – to a rejection of any and all philosophical projects (from Plato to Althusser to Arendt) that would render politics pure (Rancière 2003c: 3). Thus, in this paper I call for a shift from May's anarchism to a rearticulation of Rancière's allegiance to democracy. But Rancière's 'democracy', as he frequently reminds his readers, is not a regime. As he polemically explains, 'we do not live in democracies' (Rancière 2006b: 73). A theory of democracy inspired by Rancière – which may or may not remain a 'Rancièrean' theory of democracy – requires a theory of the politics of the police. It demands further development of Rancière's provocative but elliptical comments concerning the 'neutrality' of *la police* and about the superiority of some police orders to others.

This essay clears the ground for such developmental work by taking on May's reading of Rancière's political thought, in section III. I challenge both May's understanding of 'the police' in Rancière and the theory of anarchist politics that he develops from it. Most importantly, I show the essential connection between the two, thus indicating that there is a 'politics of the police' to just the extent that divergent readings of police will give rise to divergent politics. Prior to that encounter and preparatory to it I lay out, in section II, Rancière's theory of the police such as it is developed in his writings, and I link his theory of the police with his practical intervention into and critique of neoliberalism. At the same time, I stake out the terms for further thinking of this crucial element in Rancière's thought, suggesting a number of possible avenues for thinking the police. Finally, in section IV, I make the case for 'the politics of the police', an argument that offers a particular rendering of Rancière's political theory and that demands further attention to the police.

II. Redefining Neoliberal Consensus Politics: *la police*

Rancière's perhaps path-breaking, or perhaps merely curious, definition of politics is now well known in contemporary English-speaking political theory, and because of this, Rancière's concept of 'the police', or 'police orders', also has some currency within the field. The two go together, of course, because Rancière *redefines* most of what we typically take to be politics, and relocates it under the broad heading of *la police*. This key move appears early on in Rancière's best-known text in English, *Disagreement*. There he writes: 'Politics is generally seen as the set of procedures whereby the aggregation and consent of collectivities is achieved, [it denotes] the organization of powers, the distribution of places and roles, and the systems of legitimizing this distribution'. He then goes on to state quite flatly that he would like to apply a wholly different name to such a system: 'I propose to call it *the police*' (1999: 28). If the reversal enacted here does not come through loudly enough, Rancière had already announced in the preface that he will 'propose . . . the term *policing*' for 'what normally goes by the name of politics' (1999: xiii).

This unique redefinition of almost everything we usually call politics, this renaming of a broad swath of phenomena under the category of 'police' obviously opens up the space for a new way of thinking politics. It comes us no surprise, then, that most accounts of Rancière's political theory immediately move on to his definition of politics: a logic antagonistic to all policing, a logic that disrupts and rearranges that order by countering the police order's logic of domination with the political assumption of equality (1999: 29). But in making this move so quickly, these commentaries on Rancière account for his concept of police as little more than a foil for the more important argument about politics (e.g. Panagia 2006; Dillon 2003). It seems worth noting, then, that in his own presentation in *Disagreement*, Rancière spends a great deal more time sorting through the meaning of police before moving on to his conception of politics.

My wager is as follows: that closer attention to these passages in Rancière's texts will produce a subtle but significant reorientation of our understanding of Rancière's political thought. The formal starkness of Rancière's claims about politics may tempt his readers into playing up the singularity of his thinking, particularly when it comes to a definition of politics that from some angles looks like nothing one has ever heard before. Perhaps this makes Rancière into a 'unique' thinker of the political, but it simultaneously makes his thought less salient for making sense of the political world we inhabit. To put it bluntly, if all we take from Rancière are rare and beautiful political moments, which are easily boiled down to revolutionary moments, then how do we orient thinking or action within the realm of police orders that are our lives? In other words, if we take Rancière's concepts of police and politics seriously, do we not also have to admit that we live in police orders, not in a space of politics? Politics is not really a space in Rancière, as it is for Arendt, but merely a disruptive force. We cannot live in, nor even aspire to live in, Rancière's 'political' in the way we might with Arendt.[3] Our realm is that of police, and it therefore seems prudent for us to take seriously Rancière's understanding of police.

Critical attention to Rancière's 'police orders' has often been avoided by reducing the idea of 'the police' to little more than a creative renaming exercise. In other words, the equation 'Rancière's police = our politics' makes space for the new term, 'Rancière's politics'. But to take police as a simple substitution for 'regular' politics prevents us from seeing the links between Rancière and other thinkers. That is, taken in context, Rancière's approach to the police may not turn out to be so strange or curious as it has appeared to some of his North American readers. We should note then, the tradition of understanding *la police* as something far broader, something more historically and politically significant than officers on the streets. What's more, on this point – and *unlike* so many others – Rancière actually signals his own continuity with this history and with other thinkers. In other words, while in general Rancière appears to studiously avoid citing other thinkers (*especially* contemporary French thinkers), and while he vigorously resists having his thought associated with other (perhaps more famous) French theorists, when it comes to his concept of the police, he notes its connections to one of the most famous French thinkers of all, Michel Foucault. Immediately after introducing the term in *Disagreement*, Rancière himself freely admits that it surely 'poses a few problems'. It is here that Rancière first insists that we dissociate his thinking of 'police orders' from the actions on the ground of either beat cops or feds. But Rancière stresses that the distinction should be drawn not as a matter of definitional fiat, since a 'narrow definition [of police] may be deemed contingent' (1999: 28). And we know this because of the work of Foucault, whose lectures on seventeenth- and eighteenth-century 'reason of state' showed that 'the petty police is a more general order that arranges that tangible reality in which bodies are distributed in community' (Rancière 1999: 28).[4]

The link to Foucault and the argument made here prove crucial: they show already, in the first page, that Rancière introduces the term 'police', that a police order is a partition of the sensible (*partage du sensible*). That is, 'police order' designates not only phenomena much more general than the 'petty police' but also irreducible to simple domination or inequality. A police order is not just an order of powers, it is '*an order of bodies* that defines the allocation of ways of doing, ways of being, and ways of saying, and sees that those bodies are assigned by name to a particular place and task; it is an order of the visible and the sayable' (Rancière 1999: 29, emphasis added). Here we see what it means to say that the police order is one specific partition of the sensible. In his 'Ten Theses on Politics' Rancière introduces the term police in a manner parallel to the presentation in *Disagreement*. But here again, Rancière has a great deal more to say about police than to state the mere fact that it re-describes our everyday, conventional understanding of politics. Indeed, the presentation in 'Ten Theses' indicates something of the broader significance that Rancière places on the concept. First, Rancière claims that there are two ways of (ac)counting (for) the parts of the community. He then says: 'we will call the first *police*[: it] only counts empirical parts – actual groups defined by differences in birth, by different functions, locations, and interests that constitute the social body, *without any supplement*' (Rancière 2001, §19).[5] The explanation for this definition comes not from a theory of politics (Rancière would refuse the idea that he has such a thing) but rather from a linking up of 'police' with *partage du sensible*. The 'police order' names a particular type of partition of the sensible. The 7th thesis states: '*the police is a partition of the sensible whose principle is the absence of a void and of a supplement*' (Rancière 2001). The police order distributes bodies without remainder and without exclusion; there is nothing it does not account for, nothing left over or external to its process of counting.[6]

But this does not, according to Rancière, make the police order totalizing in the sense of determining a repressive State order. Hence the importance of the other intellectual context that Rancière provides, when he subtly suggests that the concept of police order must not be confused with Althusser's concept of State Apparatus (1999: 29).[7] State apparatus, says Rancière, cannot be disconnected from a conception of State standing in opposition to society, a notion that depends, from Rancière's perspective, on *confusing* politics with police. But more than this, to take police as a repressive force is to miss the crucial disclaimers that Rancière offers concerning his concept of 'police order'. In other words, while as readers of Rancière we tend to celebrate politics in its very opposition to police, it would be too easy to simply dismiss or denigrate all police as repression or violence. But Rancière warns his readers to avoid such a faulty interpretation.

I wonder if we have paid proper heed to these alerts. Perhaps they are worth enumerating:

1. Police is a neutral and non-pejorative term (1999: 29).
2. Police can be reduced neither to repression nor even to 'control over the living' (2001: §19).
3. Police is not a leveling mechanism; not all police orders are the same (1999: 30).
4. 'There is a worse and a better police' (1999: 30–1).
5. Police orders may make more or less space for the emergence of democratic politics (2006b: 72).

This list opens up an enormous area of inquiry for explaining and developing Rancière's understanding of police, its role in his political theory and its salience for a broader thinking of contemporary politics. I will come back to these dimensions later, for now I simply want to bring my logic here to some closure by pointing out the limitations to an approach that would take police in Rancière as nothing more than a counterweight to politics. If we refuse to reduce police to a mere first postulate, a *given* necessary to Rancière's thinking of politics, then we are left with a different set of questions. Most important among them: what work does the concept do for us? In the context of Rancière's writings from the mid-1990s, I argue that police serves to specify and *to focus a political critique*. Here I mean 'political critique' in its ordinary language sense: an argument meant to challenge the form of the political regime, the actions of its leaders or the dynamics of its processes. This suggests one possible interpretation of my always potentially oxymoronic title (a danger I return to in greater detail in my final section, below). There is a politics of the police in that Rancière's concept of the police serves particular ends within the specific political circumstances in which he publishes. Put in another way, we might say that Rancière's use of 'the police' has significance in the way that it speaks to a particular political context. This claim can be made to resonate more broadly when we consider that Rancière introduces the term 'police' somewhat late in his career and he drops it relatively quickly.[8] In other words, does it matter that Rancière proposes the term police at a particular historico-political juncture? I contend that the timing proves more than coincidental, as it appears concomitantly with Rancière's critique of what he often calls consensus politics, or 'post-democracy'. As Todd May has helpfully articulated, Rancière's critique of consensus democracy – which Rancière calls a 'conjunction of contradictory terms' (1999: 95) – implies a radical challenge to neoliberalism (May 2008: 146).

As we know, 'interest groups' and the interactions between them are the basic building blocks of neoliberal politics. But for Rancière 'conflicts of interest', the very core of what we call 'interest group politics', are exemplary and exclusively matters of the police. What Rancière calls politics has nothing to do with the coordination of interests: '*the political dispute is distinct* from all conflicts of interest between constituted parties of the population' (1999: 100). Neoliberalism forms and founds a particular police order. However, to say only this would be to miss the force of Rancière's critique, since he is not content to throw names at neoliberalism (by calling it 'police'). Neoliberalism, or consensus democracy, articulates a particular arrangement between any given police order and the potentially disruptive force of democratic politics. In other words, it is not just that neoliberalism is not politics, but that *neoliberalism seeks the end of politics*. As leverage for his critique, Rancière refers to this neoliberal form of consensus democracy as 'postdemocracy'. He defines it as follows:

Postdemocracy is the government practice and conceptual legitimation of democracy *after* the demos, a democracy that has eliminated the appearance, miscount, and dispute of the people and is thereby reducible to the sole interplay of state mechanisms and combinations of social energies and interests. (Rancière 1999: 102)

Rancière's understanding of democracy, as I will discuss in greater detail below, will always depend upon the centrality of struggle. 'Consensus democracy', in contrast is committed to the degradation and possible elimination of struggle. Consensus democracy is thus the end of democracy – 'in a word, the disappearance of politics' (Rancière 1999: 102; see also May 2008: 146).

The concept of 'the police' provides the crucial leverage for the critique of consensus democracy. Rancière's ability to take the neoliberal marketing of 'consensus' and show how it boils down to the curious and feeble form of 'post-democracy' depends upon the critical lens provided by *la police*. Rancière's polemic here amounts to much more than merely decreeing that consensus democracy contains no politics, that it is only police. That is, of course, true. But on Rancière's terms it would also be true of almost all institutionalized political regimes. The key to the critique lies in showing that consensus democracy commits itself to the elimination of politics. It is a police order devoted to its own pure and perpetual preservation, a police order that *strives for its own perfection as a police order*. Thus, consensus democracy is post-democracy in the same way that the Platonic *kallipolis* would be post-democracy; it does not merely exclude politics from policing, it puts an end to politics. Doubtless, it does this self-consciously in calling for just that, 'the end of politics'. This means that post-democracy operates in a similar manner, although on very much distinct terrains, to political philosophy. For Rancière, the latter is a *philosophical* ordering project designed to replace politics with police. The former is a putatively 'political' project aiming for the same goal. Both use the name 'politics' as a banner under which to seek the elimination of politics.[9]

Here then I have suggested one significant sense in which we find a 'politics of the police'. That is, to just the extent that the concept of police works in the service of Rancière's own political interventions. In this context I want also to emphasize the different levels on which Rancière's most explicitly 'political' texts operate (i.e. *On the Shores of Politics*, *Disagreement* and *Hatred of Democracy*). *Disagreement*, for example, can easily be read as an abstract and detached philosophical work. After all, it opens both its preface and its introduction with quotes from Aristotle; it operates on a dense and philosophically obtuse level of logical reasoning; it seems to cite only historical examples, and to do so in the service of very broad and general points. And, indeed, most commentators read *Disagreement* the way they might read Arendt's *The Human Condition* or any other work in political theory: as a project of philosophy or of political ontology. This approach can be encouraged by assigning students only the first 60 pages of the text to read (I plead guilty). Perhaps this is why most explorations of Rancière's political theory centre themselves on the first half of *Disagreement*, supplemented by some of the theses from 'Ten Theses'.

The worry is that such an approach turns Rancière into a political philosopher, when he himself has mounted a damning critique of the project of political philosophy. How do you theorize politics while avoiding the trap of political philosophy? Perhaps you link your political ontology to your assessment of and engagement with the contemporary political situation. Thus, to engage with Rancière's thinking of politics means to work with his political interventions as well. And if we broaden our reading of Rancière, we see those engagements peppered throughout the very texts in which he articulates his concepts of politics and police.

For example, Chapter 5 of *Disagreement* – which contains the critique of post-democracy that I have just been discussing – troubles those readings that would turn Rancière into a thinker of concepts. In that chapter Rancière engages not with Plato or with Marx but with the contemporary discourse of 'consensus democracy'. The essays in *Shores* and *Hatred* also ill fit any attempt to make Rancière into a philosopher, since these are direct political engagements; many of the essays that make up those two books were previously published in popular periodicals. And Rancière has himself argued that we might read *Disagreement* backwards, seeing it *first* as a political intervention (Rancière 2003a: §4; Thomson 2003: 9).

Therefore, to get at the politics of the police, we need not only to take the concept of the police more seriously and to read it much more broadly, but also to draw the connections between Rancière's thinking of the police and his political interventions. In this section, I have connected the dots between Rancière's own use of the police and his critique of neoliberalism. I now turn to a very much distinct sense of the politics of the police by offering an analysis and assessment of a politics of anarchism drawn from Rancière's work.

III. Defending Anarchism: Pure Politics

Perhaps I should remove all possibility of confusion at the outset of this section: it is not I who will be 'defending anarchism', but Todd May who does so in his recently published book, *The Political Thought of Jacques Rancière* (2008). Indeed, as I hinted at the beginning of this essay, while May's book offers a vibrant, engaged and always thought-provoking set of arguments in and around Rancière's writings, it seems a very oddly-titled work. Simply put, it does not set out to articulate 'the political thought' of Rancière; rather, it seeks to mobilize a particular reading of Rancière's work in support of a spirited defence of anarchism. (Hence the title of this section.) But I turn to May not merely because his book constitutes the entire reading list of English-language books specifically on Rancière's political thought, but because his particular approach to Rancière proves invaluable for clarifying the stakes of Rancière's concept of *la police*. Because May's appropriation of Rancière's thought for anarchist purposes requires a very determined and distinct interpretation of police, his argument helps me to work through what I've called 'the politics of the police'. Let me state the argument succinctly before unpacking it through my reading of May. May 'elevates' politics to a pure form of action, while reducing police to an *anti*-political and implicitly repressive order of domination and injustice. This leads, I argue, to an unproductive conception of 'the police' in the service of a limited theory of politics.

The steps to reach this conclusion prove subtle, since in so many ways May appears to be an exemplary reader of Rancière. Most praiseworthy is May's refusal to make Rancière into a philosopher; May sees clearly, and reminds his readers frequently, of the political stakes of the Rancièrean project. But on my reading, Rancière's politics are not the same as May's, and May is thereby often forced to creatively appropriate – or sometimes simply misread – Rancière in order to get to the anarchist conclusions that May had quite clearly decided on from the outset.[10] This divergence likely begins with May's account of 'the police', which, as mentioned above, proves notable precisely because May gives the police so much attention. May begins by emphasizing Rancière's own point, that the idea of a broadly understood 'police order' can be tied back to Foucault's lectures from the 1970s, where Foucault traces the genealogical origins of the term in seventeenth- and eighteenth-century European thought. May shows the extent to which Rancière's use of the term overlaps with Foucault's, while noting that Rancière develops the term quite differently. But when it comes to that development, May makes a very significant interpretive choice. At just this juncture, he writes: 'policing, as Rancière defines it, is deeply embedded in Western political philosophy' (2008: 42). Indeed, May contends that Rancière locates the first occurrence of such policing in Plato, and May explicates the concept of the police primarily through a summary of Rancière's interpretation and critique of the Platonic philosophy of order (May 2008: 42–3).

But this is a curious exegesis, since when Rancière himself introduces the term police, he defines it in a context *outside* the project of political philosophy. As I have already argued above, for Rancière, police names an order of intelligible bodies, a distribution and counting of the parts of society. Police is 'a symbolic constitution of the social' (2001: §19). Now, it is very much true that in both *Disagreement* and 'Ten Theses' Rancière goes on, later, to make a crucial argument about Platonic political philosophy and policing. *But the claim is not that Plato is an example of policing.* The claim is that Plato's *political philosophy* substitutes police for politics, that the structure of Plato's philosophical project operates precisely so as to identify politics with police. And this identification of the two amounts to the elimination of politics, as Rancière understands it.

Thus, *within the terms of political philosophy*, particularly in the Platonic project that Rancière names (as May rightly notes) 'archipolitics', the police is substituted for politics. But this substitution occurs as a part of, inside as it were, the philosophical project; nowhere does Rancière say that it is essential to the constitution of a police order as such. And this fact renders May's own definition of the police extremely problematic. Immediately after summarizing the critique of Platonic archi-politics, May comes to his most succinct statements on the police. He writes: 'in the end, the goal of policing *is precisely that of eliminating politics*' (2008: 43, emphasis added). Thus, this claim makes policing, by definition, a mechanism for the destruction of politics. Unsurprisingly, then, May proceeds to interpret Rancière's conception of politics as follows: the goal of politics is to eliminate the police. Politics, according to May, not only disrupts the police order (as Rancière clearly contends) but also says 'no' to that order in its entirety – something Rancière never asserts (May 2008: 49). Such a reading fits perfectly, of course, with an anarchist project in which true freedom and equality come only *from* the people and *after* the elimination of government.

But that is getting ahead of the story. Let me step back then and try to assess May's claim that the police order seeks the elimination of politics. This reading of policing is tied directly to May's understanding of archipolitics; he repeatedly refers to the latter as a 'form of policing' (e.g. May 2008: 43, 45). That is, archipolitics is one way that police tries to eliminate politics, meta-politics is another, and so on. But to put the relation between archipolitics and police in this way is to miss the entire brunt of Rancière's critique of the Platonic project. If the police order always and somehow naturally sought the elimination of politics, then there would be nothing especially problematic or even interesting about Plato. It is the fact that political philosophy seeks to replace politics with police that makes the Platonic (and Marxist, and Hobbesian, etc.) project so dangerous. The critique of political philosophy proves necessary, within Rancière's framework, because of the need to challenge, question and arrest this substitution. Rancière's entire approach to 'political philosophy', his effort to think politics outside its terms, therefore depends upon conceptualizing police as an order *distinct* from politics, but not as an order with an inherent drive to supplant politics.

By failing to take account of the difference between an empirically given police order and the mobilization of the police within the Platonic project, May turns politics and police into versions of matter and anti-matter: they can never actually meet except in some final, universe-altering confrontation, but they stand ultimately opposed to one another.[11] Hence May's claim that 'the goal of policing' *simpliciter* is the destruction of politics. Put directly, however, Rancière says no such thing about the police. Indeed, he explicitly rejects the notion of police or politics as pure forms in this way. After laying out the basic terms of politics as an activity antagonistic to and disruptive of policing, Rancière reminds his readers that politics remains inescapably twined with police. He writes: 'we should not forget either that if politics implements a logic entirely heterogeneous to that of the police, it is always bound up with the latter' (1999: 31; cf. Rancière 2001: §21).[12]

At this point one might accuse me of being either unfair to May (in the narrowness of my hermeneutic criticisms) or at least somewhat pedantic. I would respond by arguing that the stakes of these differences in conceptions of the police turn out to be quite high. They begin to emerge in May's reading when he develops his anarchist account of democratic politics. May's anarchist framework provides him with a structure in which to interpret some of the most complex, subtle, and/or vexing elements of Rancière's thought. Primary among these may be the fact that in taking almost everything we thought was politics and calling it police, Rancière opens himself to the question of when or where *his* politics happens. As I noted at the outset of this essay, Rancière offers a direct response, when he freely admits that politics occurs 'rarely' (1999: 17). But for most readers, especially political theorists, such an answer seems necessarily unsatisfying unless and until we provide one of two possible *supplements* to it: 1) we can supplement the response with an account of how to bring about such political moments; or 2) we can add to this answer a further elaboration of why and to what extent we should concern ourselves with phenomena that do not always add up to *political* moments.

The first option seems the obvious choice for May. Indeed, one of the ways in which Rancière's writings clearly do resonate with the project of anarchism is on this point. Whereas so many readers of Rancière balk at the notion of politics happening so little, May positively likes the fact that democratic politics is made rare on Rancière's account. Why? Because the rarity of politics resonates with the revolutionary project of anarchism. May wishes to define democratic politics as a process that 'enhances the lives' of those who engage in it. Democratic politics should be attractive to potential political actors for just this reason, and the fact that there are few historical examples of democratic politics, the fact that democratic politics is rare – all this only makes it *more attractive*. Why be a revolutionary anarchist if anyone can do it or if it has all been done before? May therefore wants to work within a space of political thought that calls on the revolution to come, that plans for it. That Rancière defines politics so as to make actual occurrences of it scarce poses no problems for May's political thought; rather, this dimension turns out to be an asset.[13]

For May, then, democratic politics comes into focus as a pure politics of the people. Anarchist thought depends upon maintaining a crucial distinction between government and the people. For example, May approvingly cites Kropotkin on communist anarchism: 'the name given to a principle of life and conduct under which society is conceived without government' (Kropotkin 1995 [1910], cited in May 2008: 83). Passages like this shed light on May's reading of Rancière's politics/police. Police takes the place of government in traditional anarchist thought, and politics plays the role of anarchist action. This leads to the essential twist that I have outlined above: police must not just be disrupted or re-ordered; it must be eliminated. Perhaps the most telling line in May comes early on, in his first and primary elucidation of Rancière's concepts of politics and police – that is, prior to his exploration of the history of anarchism as providing the 'roots' for Rancièrean politics. May turns from police to politics (just as Rancière does in *Disagreement*), arguing that 'politics . . . is not a matter of how distributions occur'. This is straightforward enough: politics is not police; it is not about ordering and distributing, not about the counting of those parts that already have a part. May, however, completes the logic in a striking move: 'distributions are what governments do, [b]ut *they are not what people do*' (2008: 47, emphasis added). This final claim fits perfectly well with the project of anarchism, but it does not fit at all into the broader frame of Rancière's project. In Rancière's terms we would have to say that, of course, distributions are things that people do. Rancière goes further, insisting that 'the police can procure all sorts of goods' (1999: 31). This, Rancière reminds us, does not mean that we should confuse police with politics, but it ought to give us pause when May claims that police stands opposed to people. Why does May feel compelled to make this seemingly unwarranted shift?

The answer, unsurprisingly, likely lies in May's commitment to anarchism. Anarchism, as May articulates it, requires a fundamental separation of spheres: anarchist politics must commit itself to the elimination of *all* injustice, the destruction of *all* orders of hierarchy. And this means, in addition, that anarchist politics must attempt to bring about a substantive equality. May forcefully defends a conception of anarchism as maintaining a radical commitment to equality. But again, none of this meshes very well with Rancière's understanding of politics or police. First, Rancière has himself actively resisted the idea of reducing his thought to anarchism.[14] More substantively, we can show that when Rancière argues, as I quoted above, that politics will *always* be 'bound up' with police, he continues as follows: 'the reason for this is simple: politics has no objects or issues of its own' (1999: 31). These are not isolated remarks; in later writings Rancière expands and develops this notion, precisely as clarification of his project. In a 2003 lecture, he argued: 'the opposition between politics and police goes along with the statement that politics has no "proper" object, *that all its objects are blended with the objects of police*' (Rancière 2003c: 4, emphasis added). Politics cannot be uncoupled from police; it only appears in this 'blended' form.

In contrast, May seeks a politics not only de-linked from police, but also fully self-referential and committed to the substantive ground of equality. Equality, for Rancière, is nothing like a substantive ground. Deranty puts it succinctly: 'equality is not an essence, a value or a goal' (Deranty 2003a: §1). Equality proves to be an *assumption* that can be *verified*, but it grounds nothing at all in Rancière's thought.[15] Yet because he insists on reading Rancière with and against the grain of distributive theories of justice, May feels the need to repeatedly ask Rancière for normative grounds (e.g. May 2008: 119). And while he remains very sensitive to Rancière's own understanding of equality as *not* providing such grounds, May still frequently implies that, perhaps equality serves this function in (a reconstructed) Rancièrean thought, after all (May 2008: 118).

Given that close readers of Rancière will tend to reject the foundationalist approach of Rawlsian or Habermasian normative political philosophy, the continued demand for normative grounds will strike some readers of May's book as odd. Rancière's conception of politics as dissensus, his understanding of subjectivization as disidentification, and his rejection of political ontology all seem to point away from the 'normative grounds' approach to political theory. And when Rancière argues famously in disagreement that 'parties do not exist prior to the declaration of wrong' he would appear to take the ground out from underneath the feet of foundationalists (1999: 39).[16] I argue that the need for normative grounds is not intrinsic to Rancière's arguments. Instead, this need is a *product* of May's own logic. May's project requires, what he calls, 'normative force' because of the unique way in which May comes to understand democratic politics itself. While May insists that democratic politics will always be connected to the world in some way, he defends a conception of politics that seems extremely inward-looking and self-referential. That is, democracy for May seems to be primarily about democratic actors. While politics might (or might not) change the world, its meaning, according to May, comes not from the world but from its agents. Thus, while politics has effects, May insists that we should not 'confuse having social effects with the existence of politics'. He continues with a striking formulation:

A politics may or may not effect change. It is not in the consequence but in the acting out of a presupposition of equality that politics occurs. [. . .] A democratic politics *is defined by the actions and the understandings of those who struggle*, not by the effects upon or actions taken by those the police order supports. (May 2008: 72, emphasis added)

Despite the fact that Rancière's own examples of politics all seem to involve new partitions of the sensible, the radical disruption and re-ordering of the police order – 'the essence of politics is to *disturb*' the police order, says Rancière – May insists here that the ultimate *definition* of democratic politics is found not just in the actions but in the *understandings* of democratic subjects. I have called this a 'self-referential' definition of politics, not because it is circular, but because it refers politics back to agents rather than to political effects.

It is just this dimension of May's argument that suggests a need for augmentation in the form of normative grounds. In other words, if politics only exists when agents struggle, then there needs to be some leverage, some motivation, some way to mobilize that struggle. The substantive commitment to equality provides that normative edge, on May's account. However, this redefinition of democratic politics as emerging out of the self-understanding of democratic actors has the curious but significant result of further denigrating the police. If politics refers only to itself, then police is only important as a foil for understanding politics. And May himself stresses this point when he insists that politics is not about changing police orders. Indeed, May echoes his lines from above, during his discussion of anarchism. He argues that anarchism does not strive for a change in government, a new form of government or a different set of people in power, but the overcoming of power. May first quotes Colin Ward, 'anarchism . . . doesn't want different people on top, it wants *us* to clamber out from underneath', and then goes on to insert the following: '(Compare this statement to Rancière's position that a democratic politics seeks to undermine police orders, not change or modify them.)' (May 2008: 96, quoting Ward 1982).

This seemingly innocent parenthetical requires serious comment. First, May's reference to 'Rancière's position' is actually an internal cross-reference within May's own text, since it is May himself, not Rancière, who argues that politics does not seek to change police orders (May 2008: 72; cf. May 2008: 43). But neither there nor at the moment of this parenthetical statement does May cite Rancière at all. And as I have shown, in Rancière's hands, politics has no autochthonous goal that it seeks of its own volition. Politics stands opposed to police, but always in *relation* to police. And this 'opposition' always manifests itself in the form of *transformed* police orders, not undone police orders. But, second, what I say here is surely no surprise to May, or any other reader of Rancière. Just three pages later, May writes: 'democratic politics . . . does not lead to a final state of justice but perhaps only to better conditions in a police order' (May 2008: 99). What accounts for the difference, and apparent contradiction, between these two quotations from May? The first appears as a parenthetical commentary on a summary of anarchist thought; the second emerges during an attempt to directly sort out Rancière's conception of politics from anarchist goals. In other words, May's attempt to make Rancière play the role of resource and support for anarchism leads May to stretchings and distortions of Rancière's thought that prove readily apparent to most readers of Rancière – including, at other points in his text, May himself.

In an effort to draw some conclusions from my critical interrogation of May's interpretation of Rancière, I would suggest then that in the hands of May's hermeneutics, the opposition between police and politics undergoes something of a Manichean transformation. Politics becomes a *pure* force, utterly and radically distinct from and in opposition to any and all police orders.[17] As an obvious but significant corollary, the concept of police is denigrated in May's hands: one utterly loses Rancière's sense of the police as 'neutral' or 'nonpejorative', and instead sees police as the evil other to politics. The police order is quite simply that which must be destroyed. While it remains inevitable, it must take the shape of the big Other precisely so as to motivate and mobilize the utopian anarchist vision of the future.

Indeed, May's reading resists any sense of a meeting point between the logic of politics and the order of the police: politics, May argues, surely stands opposed to police, but it becomes unclear how politics would ever *encounter* the police.[18] That is, like any Manichean view, May's rendering of the politics/police dichotomy precludes an active engagement between the two realms; the only form that battle can take is the ultimate battle, in which an anarchist utopia will replace all police orders once and for all. I should stress that this comes about despite May's own clear understanding that politics and police must meet in Rancière's thought. May argues that the democratic dissensus creates two worlds. However,

> if the worlds were entirely distinct, if they had no point of contact, every political struggle would be a fight to the death. Every democratic political struggle would reduce itself to a struggle between two competing visions, only one of which could prevail. There could be no democratic politics that wasn't entirely revolutionary. (May 2008: 112)

But this is precisely what happens within the terms of May's interpretation of politics and police. Police becomes pure domination and politics becomes purely revolutionary. Indeed, I would suggest that May articulates this problem so accurately precisely because it plagues his anarchist reinterpretation of Rancière. May recognizes that democratic politics does not work this way, yet May thinks that the Manichean separation of worlds is overcome by a sort of dialectical mediation of a third term: 'there is at least one common normative element in any nominally democratic society that binds those who struggle and those against whom they struggle. This common element [is] a commitment to equality' (2008: 112). May's misreading of politics and police (as radically separate) must therefore be supplemented by a misreading of equality (as substantive ground). But Rancière's own theory does not need a third term, since in Rancière's understanding, politics and police never form separate worlds; they are always and already 'bound up' with one another. Rancière says it directly: 'there is no "pure" politics' (Rancière 2003c: 2; cf. Chambers n.d.).

And it is in this binding, in this unavoidable meeting of the logic of politics with the logic of the police, that we may locate a viable and salient thinking of 'the politics of the police'. In the final section, then, I make the case for this rendering of police, and I counter May's anarchist vision of politics with a reassessment of a democratic politics that retains both impurity and impropriety.

IV. Returning to Democracy

My engagement with and critique of May's work sets the stage for the defence of my title that I promised earlier. How or why is 'the politics of the police' not merely oxymoronic? No doubt, my reading of Rancière has shown that politics is precisely that which stands opposed to and interrupts any order of the police, while police itself can never be understood as politics. And May's reading of Rancière pushes the opposition to its extreme, in that May winds up defending a vision of pure anarchist politics that would obliterate each and every police order, once and for all. However, it is precisely May's dialectical rendering of the police/politics difference that calls for a reassessment and rethinking of Rancière's own categories. That is, the fact that May ends up, as I showed above, coming to such non-Rancièrean conclusions while working from Rancièrean premises should lead us to a reinvestigation of those premises. I have tried to carry out such an investigation here by taking seriously Rancière's own understandings of *la police*, and by pushing his analysis further into an exploration of 'the politics of the police' – and doing so despite the potential risks involved.

Here I would close by delineating one other crucial dimension of *la police* and its politics and that is 'the politics of the police' in the most banal sense. In direct opposition to May, I want to argue that we must remain committed to and concerned with the politics of the police in the sense of changing, transforming, and improving our police orders. As Alex Thomson has very nicely put it, 'there is doubtless much to do in terms of developing better rather than worse forms of police' (2003: 11). When it comes to police we require a democratic vigilance, not a utopian dismissal. Rancière provokes his readers with his succinct assertion that 'we do not live in democracies'; instead, and as the only alternative, we live in police orders (2006b: 73). May reads these claims as a utopian call to someday fashion a pure democracy. He reads them as not merely a critique but a denigration of the world we do live in (a police order) in favour of the ideal of a true democracy. Obviously, I read Rancière very differently. On my reading, we do not live in democracies, *and we never will*. We never will, not because we will never achieve what we ought to achieve, not because of failures on our part, but because *that is not what democracy is about*.

Democracy is not utopia. 'To understand what democracy means is to hear the struggle that is at stake in the word' (Rancière 2006b: 93). But this is not a struggle that contains its own telos, and it is not a struggle merely for the sake of those who engage in it. Democracy does not create equality; it does not eliminate government. Democracy is, instead, 'the paradoxical condition of politics' (Rancière 2006b: 94). And as I have shown in detail above, a paradoxical politics is an impure politics. Democracy is both: 'democracy really means . . . the impurity of politics' (Rancière 2006b: 62). This explains why democratic politics necessarily produces, and will continue to do so, 'hatred of democracy' (Rancière 2006b: 94). None of this, however, changes the fact that democracies, in short, are not to be lived in. Rancière writes: 'there is, strictly speaking, no such thing as democratic government' (2006b: 52). Once again, May might take this as reason enough to reject all government, but I take it as reason to cultivate a democratic politics *more* not less attendant to the possibility of transforming the police order.

Democratic politics is that which emerges in such a way that it disrupts our given police order. Furthermore, I would contend, without complaining, that we will always live in police orders. Democratic politics proves to be a transformative force, one that requires cultivation, care and direction. Politics is therefore absolutely vital. At the same time, however, we cannot forget that 'nothing is political in itself', and while 'anything can become political' such becoming political *only* occurs when the logic of equality is made to meet the order of the police (Rancière 1999: 32). In the Rancièrean spirit of provocation, let me wrap up with something of an enthymeme. If we all live in police orders, and if '*[p]olitics acts on the police*', then the politics of the police (*la politique de la police*) must be central not only to political theory but also to our politics of ordinary life (Rancière 1999: 33, emphasis added).

Notes

For comments, criticisms, feedback, encouragement, enthusiasm and support related to earlier versions (both oral and written) of this essay, I would like to thank: John Altick, Paul Bowman, Rebecca Brown, Terrell Carver, Alan Finlayson, Andrew Schaap, Richard Stamp, Jeremy Valentine and all of the students in my Spring and Fall 2009 graduate seminars.

1. Sometimes it seems hard to tell what sort of thinker Rancière might be. For political theorists like myself it always proves tempting to read him as a political theorist, especially when focusing on his writings from the 1990s.

Yet Rancière repeatedly insists that he is not a political philosopher, just as he vociferously rejects the project of political philosophy. Rancière rarely discusses political theorists (especially not contemporary theorists), and his remarks are predominately negative.

2. The 'wrong', that which underwrites all politics, 'is the very impossibility of *arkhê*' (Rancière 1999: 13). Here I am taking Panagia's description of Rancière's *account* of politics and using it to describe Rancière's theory as practical intervention.

3. Rancière makes this point clear in a later lecture, when he says directly, 'I wrote the "Ten Theses on Politics" primarily as a critique of the Arendtian idea of a specific political sphere and a political way of life' (2003: 2).

4. See Foucault 1979; cf. May 2008: 41; and Muhle 2007. May and Muhle are the only commentators I know of who spend any time on the links between Rancière's concept of police and Foucault's work on governmentality. As I will argue below, while May notes the connection, he does not seem to give it any weight in his reading of Rancière. Muhle's unpublished work here proves to be a great resource for my own argument.

5. This translation comes from Muhle, who notes that the English translation of the 'Ten Theses' simply leaves out this final phrase. Muhle notes her surprise at this decision, before going on to make a very persuasive case for this final phrase as the most important part of the claim: since 'what politics does, is to make this supplement possible' (Muhle 2007: 4). I concur.

6. In the context of discussing the police in 'Ten Theses', Rancière goes on to explain that the partition of the sensible is what 'define[s] the modes of perception' that make that order visible and sayable in the first place. *Le partage du sensible* indicates not just the empirical givenness of an order; it tells us something about the very *intelligibility* of that order. Putting this in a language that Rancière himself might resist, we might say that any particular ordering of the world depends upon an ontologically prior *partition*. Rancière writes: 'the partition of the sensible is the cutting-up of the world and of "world"' (2001: §20). Hence, two points about such 'cutting up': 1) it suggests a partition (of the world) in that it simultaneously separates and joins; it excludes, and at the same time, it 'allows participation'; and 2) it refers to the sensible (the 'world') in that it determines what can be seen and what can be heard.

7. See Althusser 1972. I call the suggestion 'subtle', because even though 'state apparatus' is obviously an Althusserian term, Rancière neglects (or refuses) to cite Althusser on this point. In 'Ten Theses', on the other hand, in the context of rejecting the notion that the police primarily interpellates subjects, Rancière does cite Althusser (2001: §22).

8. This fact seems significant in light of the relative consistency of Rancière's thought across his more than 40 years of writing. Many of Rancière's key terms remain with him from his early archival work, through his writings on politics and philosophy in the 1990s, and all the way on to his work on the politics of aesthetics over the last 10 years. It is striking then that 'the police' does not appear in *On the Shores of Politics*, the collection of essays first published in 1992 and it hardly appears at all in *Hatred of Democracy*, originally published in 2005. Only in the two major political works published in the middle of the 1990s – *Disagreement* (originally 1995) and 'Ten Theses' (originally 1997) – does Rancière offer any serious attention to the concept of 'the police'. One might argue that *le partage du sensible* supplants *la police* in Rancière's more recent work, capturing the idea of a police order but on a broader level. But that only lends more credence to the idea that 'the police' serves a particular purpose in terms of Rancière's political intervention in the mid-1990s.
9. In this context, however, I would insist on not conflating Rancière's analysis of post-democracy with his articulation of archipolitics, parapolitics and metapolitics. The difference matters because it is a difference in both objects and levels of analysis. Rancière's analysis of archipolitics (for example) provides a critique of the project of political philosophy, whereas his analysis of postdemocracy provides a critique of contemporary politics. The latter therefore constitutes a political intervention in a sense different from the former. As I show in the text below, May sometimes elides these differences.
10. Another way of putting this would be to say that May did not discover anarchism through a reading of Rancière. Quite the contrary, May was already a committed, well-known and forceful defender of anarchist thought before he came to Rancière's writings and folded Rancière's thought into his own anarchist project. See May (1994).
11. Žižek (2004) outlines the paradox of this dialectical logic and accuses Rancière himself of falling prey to it (a false accusation according to my argument, as I show below). Alex Thomson (2003) had earlier worked through a similar logic in Rancière's work and arrived at more subtle and productive conclusions. See also Valentine (2005).
12. While I present this reading as a critique of May, he himself might freely admit to the difference between his position and Rancière's on this point. May departs from Rancière's notion that politics begins with a *wrong*, with what Deranty helpfully calls an 'ontological torsion' (2003a: §5). Explicitly flagging his claim as an argument *against* Rancière, May claims that politics 'is not necessarily antagonistic' (May 2008: 51–2). May must, in a way, mark this difference from Rancière, because Rancière's politics – as I explain

below – always remains impure, always occurs *in media res*. Whereas, in contrast, anarchist politics must be self-contained, self-referential and *sui generis*. May sees in this difference a need to tweak Rancière; I see in this difference the very reason not to read Rancière as May does.

13. May frames his second chapter – wherein he offers his detailed explications of politics and police and provides the majority of passages on which I rely in my reading here – with the story of citizen mobilization and actions in the wake of the death of a young African-American man who was killed when he was hit by a car driven by a white male student in Clemson, South Carolina. In the aftermath, May himself worked for 2 years as a community organizer with a group trying to improve relations between the police force and the African-American community. The group eventually ran two candidates for city council, both of whom lost (with low African-American voter turnout). In concluding the chapter, May notes that the group won certain concessions from the police force. But May's own assessment of the results of his two years of work is decisive: 'politics did not happen at Clemson' (May 2008: 75).

14. For example, see Rancière 2003: 1. On this point, compare Rancière's own discussion of anarchism in the recently published issue of *Anarchist Studies* (2008a).

15. Politics therefore proves to be the demonstration of the assumption of equality; it occurs if and only if there is an encounter between the logic of equality and the logic of domination. It is precisely the assumption of equality that makes possible this clash between heterogeneous logics; it is precisely the *verification* of equality that results from such conflict. This explains why equality must be understood in Rancière neither as a substantive good nor as an ideal telos. But this means, contra May, that politics does not occur because of equality, nor does politics achieve equality. All politics does – and this is not enough for May, though it is for me – is to challenge, to thwart, to disrupt or dislocate, and perhaps finally to change the police order. This argument also reveals another problematic dimension of the title to May's book: 'creating equality' has no part in 'the political thought of Jacques Rancière'.

16. For more on the significance of this claim to Rancière's project, particularly in relation to his notion of 'literarity', see Chambers (2005).

17. Žižek calls this 'ultra-politics' (2005: 71, 75).

18. While Žižek (2005) proposes this lack of encounter as a critique of Rancière and while Thomson (2003) delineates it as a potential trap for Rancière, it should be noted that an important body of commentators directly contests this line of reading, arguing instead that Rancière's politics can never be pure (see Muhle 2007; Panagia 2006; Rockhill 2004).

Works Cited

Arditi, Benjamin and Valentine, Jeremy (1999), *Polemicization: The Contingency of the Commonplace*, Edinburgh: Edinburgh University Press.
Arendt, Hannah (1958), *The Human Condition*, Chicago and London: University Of Chicago Press.
Chambers, Samuel A. (2003), *Untimely Politics*, Edinburgh: Edinburgh University Press.
Chambers, Samuel A. (2005), 'The Politics of Literarity', *Theory & Event*, 8 (3).
Chambers, Samuel A. (n.d.) 'Jacques Rancière and the Problem of Pure Politics', forthcoming in *European Journal of Political Theory*.
Dean, Jodi (2009), 'Politics without Politics', *Parallax*, 52 (July–September): 20–36.
Deranty, Jean-Philippe (2003a), 'Jacques Rancière's Contribution to the Ethics of Recognition', *Political Theory*, 31 (1): 136–56.
Deranty, Jean-Philippe (2003b), 'Rancière and Contemporary Political Ontology', *Theory & Event*, 6 (4).
Dillon, Michael (2003), '(De)void of Politics? A Response to Jacques Rancière's Ten Theses on Politics', *Theory & Event*, 6 (4).
Foucault, Michel (1978), *The History of Sexuality: An Introduction*, trans. Robert Hurley. New York: Vintage.
Ingram, James D. (2008), 'What is a "Right to have Rights?" Three Images of the Politics of Human Rights', *American Political Science Review*, 102 (4): 401–16.
May, Todd (1994), *The Political Philosophy of Poststructuralist Anarchism*, University Park: Pennsylvania State University Press.
May, Todd (2008), *The Political Thought of Jacques Rancière: Creating Equality*, Edinburgh: Edinburgh University Press.
Muhle, Maria (2007), 'Politics, police and power between Foucault and Rancière', unpublished paper presented at Jan Van Eyck Akademie, Maastricht, 8 November.
Panagia, Davide (2001), '*Ceci n'est pas un argument*: An Introduction to the Ten Theses', *Theory & Event*, 5 (3).
Panagia, Davide (2006), *The Poetics of Political Thinking*, Durham: Duke University Press.
Rancière, Jacques (1974), *La Leçon d'Althusser*, Paris: Gallimard.
— (1989), *The Nights of Labor: The Workers' Dream in Nineteenth-Century France*, trans. John Drury, Philadelphia: Temple University Press.
— (1991), *The Ignorant Schoolmaster: Five Lessons in Intellectual Emancipation*, trans. Kristin Ross, Stanford: Stanford University Press.

— (1994), *The Names of History: On the Poetics of Knowledge*, trans. Hassan Melehy, Minneapolis: University of Minnesota Press.
— (1995), *On the Shores of Politics*, trans. Liz Heron. New York: Verso.
— (1995), 'Politics, Identification, Subjectivization', in *The Identity in Question*, ed. John Rajchman. New York: Routledge: 63–72.
— (1999), *Disagreement: Politics and Philosophy*, trans. Julie Rose. Minneapolis: University of Minnesota Press.
— (2000), 'Dissenting Words: A Conversation with Jacques Rancière', interview with Davide Panagia, *Diacritics*, 30 (2): 113–26.
— (2001), 'Ten Theses on Politics', trans. Rachel Bowlby and Davide Panagia. *Theory & Event*, 5 (3).
— (2003a), 'Comment and Responses', *Theory & Event*, 6 (4).
— (2003b), *Short Voyages to the Land of the People*, trans. James B. Swenson, Stanford: Stanford University Press.
— (2003c), 'The Thinking of Dissensus: Politics and Aesthetics', unpublished paper from *Fidelity to the Disagreement: Jacques Rancière and the Political*, Goldsmith's College, University of London, September 16–17.
— (2004a), *The Flesh of Words: The Politics of Writing*, trans. Charlotte Mandell, Stanford: Stanford University Press.
— (2004b), *The Philosopher and his Poor*, trans. John Drury, Corinne Oster and Andrew Parker, Durham: Duke University Press.
— (2004c), *The Politics of Aesthetics: The Distribution of the Sensible*, trans. Gabriel Rockhill, London and New York: Continuum.
— (2004d), 'Who is the Subject of the Rights of Man?' *South Atlantic Quarterly*, 103 (2–3): 297–310.
— (2006a), *Film Fables*. New York: Berg.
— (2006b), *Hatred of Democracy*, trans. Steve Corcoran. London: Verso.
— (2007), 'What Does it Mean to be Un?' *Continuum: Journal of Media and Cultural Studies*, 21 (4), (December): 559–69.
— (2008a), 'Democracy, Anarchism and Radical Politics Today: An Interview with Jacques Rancière', *Anarchist Studies*, 16 (2): 173–85.
— (2008b), 'Misadventures in critical thinking'. Unpublished manuscript.
— (2008c), 'Aesthetics against Incarnation: An interview by Anne Marie Oliver', *Critical Inquiry*, 35 (1) (Autumn): 172–90.
— (2009a), *The Emancipated Spectator*, trans. Gregory Elliott, London: Verso.
— (2009b), *The Future of the Image*, trans. Gregory Elliott, London: Verso.
Rockhill, Gabriel (2004), 'The Silent Revolution', *SubStance*, 103, 33 (1): 54–76.
Thomson, Alex (2003), 'Re-Placing the Opposition: Rancière and Derrida', unpublished paper from *Fidelity to the Disagreement: Jacques Rancière and the Political*, Goldsmith's College, University of London, September 16–17.

Valentine, Jeremy (2005), 'Rancière and Contemporary Political Problems', *Paragraph*, 28 (1): 46–60.
Ward, Colin (1982), *Anarchy in Action*, London: Freedom Press.
Žižek, Slavoj (2005), 'The Lesson of Rancière', in *The Politics of Aesthetics*, ed. Gabriel Rockhill, New York: Continuum: 69–79.

On Captivation: A Remainder from the 'Indistinction of Art and Nonart'

Rey Chow and Julian Rohrhuber*

> What is a border or boundary? It is, first of all, the line that is drawn, let us call it its 'ridge'; its significance is one of definition. This boundary, this line, always has two sides. If I trace around me a closed contour, I keep myself in and defend myself against. One side of the line protects me and the other side excludes others.
> – Michel Serres (1997: 42)

> ... the greater part of 'thinking' consists of abductions of one kind or another.
> – Alfred Gell (1998: 15)

> charnière ... This word can be taken in the technical or anatomical sense of a central or cardinal articulation, a hinge pin ... or pivot. A charnière or hinge is an axial device that enables the circuit, the trope, or the movement of rotation. But one might also dream a bit in the vicinity of its homonym, that is, in line with this other artifact that the code of falconry also calls a charnière, the place where the hunter attracts the bird by laying out the flesh of a lure.
> – Jacques Derrida (1997: 64)

I. The Question of Boundaries in Relation to Art

Much of contemporary French thought is preoccupied with boundaries. The first and last epigraphs, taken respectively from Michel Serres's and Jacques Derrida's responses to Michel Foucault's first major work, *Folie et déraison: Histoire de la folie dans l'age classique* (*History of Madness*), are but two instances of a vast reserve of critical deliberations on this elusive topic, which has had enormous impact on the conceptualizations of knowledge production and circulation worldwide. Few discussions of knowledge production and circulation today can proceed without some attempt at addressing boundaries, if only (as is often the case) to reestablish and reinforce them.

Jacques Rancière's work may be approached similarly in light of these contemporary philosophical concerns with boundaries. One of Rancière's compelling notions about aesthetics, for instance, is that genuine art is what indistinguishes art and nonart: in such capacity for indistinction lies art's transformative power and potential to bring about a new humanity.[1] In many ways, the extensive spectrum of modern and postmodern art – from surrealism and cubism to pop art, documentaries, performance art, and the contemporary new media installations, reenactments and exhibits using human bodies as well as everyday objects – attests to this ongoing process of the morphing – and transgression – of proper artistic boundaries.[2] A classic example of such morphing and transgression, Marcel Duchamp's 'art' exhibit 'Fountain', we remember, features the mundane object of a urinal. (Indeed, the *tout-fait*/readymade, as exemplified by the bottle dryer, the bicycle wheel, the comb, the coat rack, and other found objects, is Duchamp's consciously good-humoured, avant-garde way of experimenting with boundaries, both in the sense of what may function as art and in the sense of how art may remain ambiguous.) Whereas in an earlier moment, theorists were fascinated with such boundary mutation in terms of the evolution in technology and belief (one thinks, for instance, of Walter Benjamin's (1969) oft-cited artwork essay of 1936, with its description of the interruption and decline of the aura – the magical, religious quality of the artwork bound to location and beholden at a distance – in the secular age of reproducible photographic and filmic images), Rancière's investment in the indistinction of art and nonart is consistent with his attempt to find a critical idiom that would represent the excluded others on the other side of the line, as alluded to by Serres, above – an attempt that is traceable to Rancière's break from Louis Althusser, his teacher, of whom he published a spectacular critique (*La Leçon d'Althusser*) in 1974.[3]

For many postwar French-speaking intellectuals, language has served as the privileged setting for the confrontations between various kinds of subjects (poets, leftist philosophers, workers, women, mental patients and colonized people), on the one hand, and, on the other, reason's claim to sovereignty: language is where the often perilous crossings of epistemic thresholds leave their material traces. Likewise may Rancière's rejection of Althusser be described as a relation to language, in the sense that it is a rejection not only of the master himself but also of the masterly pose (or dogmatism) of the language of theory and the language of institutionalized scholarly knowledge. Not surprisingly, one of the major influences on Rancière is Foucault's *The Archaeology of Knowledge* (1972).[4] Foucault's explorations of the subterranean discursive strata that underlie knowledge formation may, in retrospect, be understood as a type of research into what Rancière terms the silent witnesses of history, witnesses whose anonymity and wordless speech constitute a form of participation and partaking (in the French, *partage* – sharing). As in his work on madness, Foucault's special imprint here is that of an invitation to destabilize and declassify thought from within the apparatuses and institutions that give thought its constraining positivity and normativity. As Foucault puts it,

it is reflection, the act of consciousness, the elucidation of what is silent, language restored to what is mute, the illumination of the element of darkness that cuts man off from himself, the reanimation of the inert – it is all this and this alone that constituted the content and form of the ethical [in Western thought in modernity]. (1970: 328)

Rancière's attention to the questions of equality, justice, disagreement and commonality involved in the writing of history is recognizably akin to Foucault's politics and ethics;[5] likewise, we may surmise, is his argument about the indistinction of art and nonart, which is historically specific and inextricable from the emergence of such indistinction in modern French art and literature. Borrowing from Rancière's description of his own method, we may say that art, as much as democracy, is for him 'characterized by the fact of determining a specific experience without defining any border separating art from non-art' (Rancière 2009: 116). What interests him about any historical relation, including that pertaining to art, is 'the polemical nature that makes it an object of thinking, that situates it in a field of tensions' (116), and the possibility of constructing from the situation 'a dramaturgy of politics, conceived out of its limits' (119). (Note that the metaphor of staging is found in many of Rancière's discussions.)

At the same time, as in the case of Foucault's many interventions (in particular his interventions in the history of sexuality), once the forces of liberalization are set into motion, the questions of ontology, finitude and infinitude return, often with a vengeance. That is to say, once the vertical axis of metaphysical transcendence is displaced onto the horizontal one of empirical practices, the older questions of dominance and subordination, which may have been temporarily bracketed during that process of displacement, tend to persist and hover around the empirical practices in the form of epistemic limits. Rancière's endeavour to democratize art, we believe, is similarly haunted. For one thing, such democratization seems readily assimilable to the fashionable talk about 'flows' that is characteristic of our postmodern globalist culture, in which catchwords such as dispersion, circulation, migration and so forth have together produced a facile form of progressive thinking, capitalist and otherwise. Is the indistinction Rancière advances about art and nonart definitively different from such contemporary valorization of flows? How might it be perceived as definitively different?

As a first step in responding to these questions, it seems to us that a closer look at the notion of indistinction is in order.

II. How 'Madame Bovary, c'est moi' Becomes le Mot Juste: Medial Liberalization and Reflexivity as a Problematic in Art

In a good-humouredly ironic essay on the nineteenth-century novel *Madame Bovary*, Rancière argues that Emma Bovary, the heroine, has to be killed by Gustave Flaubert, the novelist, because she is unfaithful to the pure sensation that belongs in the then-new regime of art (Rancière 2008: 233–48). In mid-nineteenth-century France, as the social hierarchy of the *ancien régime* gave way to a new, democratic order of life, and as the border between art and everyday experience became porous – or so goes Rancière's argument – this story of a peasant's daughter and poor country doctor's wife is typical of the masses getting caught up in the excitement of 'the multitude of aspirations and desires, cropping up everywhere in all the pores of modern society' (2008: 236). Rancière, skillfully ventriloquizing and satirizing the attitudes of the learned classes of that time, including Flaubert's, sees Emma's predicament in terms of a common folk's way of pursuing democracy. Emma turns her fleeting sensations of pleasure (culled from romance novels, natural and architectural surroundings, and other mundane associations) into real things and people to be desired and possessed; she repeatedly seeks to solidify her daydreams in both sentimental and practical ways, in the form of extramarital affairs, beautiful clothes and jewellery, and fashionable furniture. Rather than condemning Emma for being deluded, Rancière traces in her behaviour the symptoms of what he calls a redistribution of the sensible, a process in which art and life have become ever more equivalent and interchangeable.[6] Emma's proliferating objects of desire are, as Rancière comments, serially replaceable and substitutable:

> When she has resisted her love for Leon, she thinks that she deserves a reward. She buys a piece of furniture. And not only any piece of furniture: a gothic prie-dieu. This is what respectable persons perceive as the law of democracy, the law of universal equivalence: anybody can exchange any desire for any other desire. (2008: 236)

In terms of the history of art and literature, Emma may thus be seen as practising a form of 'kitsch': her habits of mixing – and mixing up – art and nonart may be said to foreshadow the high modernist principle of juxtaposition/collage, a principle that is alternately manifest in literary writing (consider what T. S. Eliot, in his study of the affinities between the metaphysical poets and modernist writers such as himself, alludes to as the violent yoking-together of the most heterogeneous ideas) (Eliot 1975: 60),[7] in painting (consider Salvador Dali's way of gathering distinct mundane objects in dreamlike proximity), and in early film (consider Lev Kuleshev's montage experiments whereby unrelated images were assembled in different sequences, each generating a disparate narrative).

According to Rancière, Flaubert, too, was infected with Emma's disease of democratic equivalence and equality (2008: 237). As a novelist, Flaubert understood that 'there is no border separating poetic matters from prosaic matters, no border between what belongs to the poetical realm of noble action and what belongs to the territory of prosaic life' (2008: 237). Hence, perhaps, Flaubert's well-known confession, 'Madame Bovary, c'est moi!' Rather than handling the equivalence between art and nonart in Emma's vulgar manner, however, Flaubert comes to terms with it by developing a distinctive style – one that specializes in precision and exactitude, and in enjoying sensations as pure sensations, disconnected from the sensorium of ordinary experience and from the chains of individuality (2008: 241) – so as to foreground the specificity and purity of art itself. Style, in other words, is 'the way in which the writer disappears, the way in which the writer tries to reach a kind of impersonal view' (Rancière 2008a: 189). For Flaubert, Rancière writes, the task of literature, as a new regime of writing, consists in none other than inscribing the difference between these two ways of making art similar to nonart (2008: 243). *Madame Bovary* is, in this respect, 'the first antikitsch manifesto' (2008: 240).

Rancière's reading asks us to think of *Madame Bovary* as the scene of a disagreement (to borrow an important term from him), a disagreement that takes the form of divergent, or irreconcilable, approaches to the same words – such as democracy and equality – and that results, in this case, in a death sentence for Emma. Despite his identification with the heroine, the artist must kill her off in order that (his) art may live. Flaubert's signature dedication to *le mot juste*, then, needs to be understood as the outcome of a struggle for domination – a kind of violence, in fact – which Rancière implicitly restores to Art, with a capital A. Although Flaubert has won, this violence means that Art will henceforth survive only as an eccentric (off-centred) practice with its own rules and criteria, often at the expense of universal communicability and accessibility. With a form of 'speech' that is increasingly fastidious, solipsistic, self-referential and intransitive, and a potency achieved only through a persistent withdrawal from the world,[8] the emergence of Art as such thus stands as one of the ironic historical effects of the liberalizing of the boundaries between art and life. Art is now a form of self-imposed quarantine: if Emma soils art with life, a circle has to be drawn around her (and her type of personal behaviour).

The example of Flaubert highlights what, in today's terminology, we would call medial reflexivity. Once Art takes on a specificity of its own, the question of boundaries becomes complex: boundaries are no longer simply the demarcations externally imposed but must involve as well differentiations internal to the artwork itself. When rethought in terms of medial reflexivity, the putative killing of Emma can be understood as part and parcel of a process by which an artistic medium (in this case, novel writing) becomes self-conscious, in the sense of having a heightened awareness of its own activity, capability and limits. On this point, some classic examples come to mind by way of contrast. Gotthold Ephraim Lessing's analysis of *The Laocoön*, in which a visual medium (sculpture) and a linguistic medium (poetry) are said to operate each on the awareness of their own semiotic limits as well as capacities, would be one instance of such reflexive self-observation. Friedrich Schiller's analysis of the distinction between naïve and sentimental poetry (on the basis of the poet's becoming-conscious of a loss, the loss of the plenitude that is nature) would be another. As Rancière points out, the implicit assumption underlying such classical discussions of aesthetics is that there *can be* an appropriateness or correspondence between content and form – that the appropriate medium, deemed suitable for a particular kind of subject matter, still exists – whereas such an assumption has been rendered meaningless by the anti-representational nature of modern avant-garde art, for which there is, simultaneously, no longer a form that is definitively appropriate to a particular type of content and no longer any medial constraint/limit to what can be represented.[9]

Although we do not have the space to offer a fully fledged discussion of medial reflexivity here, it is noteworthy that Rancière's reading of *Madame Bovary* in effect places the novel in an interesting discursive interstice, in which an older notion of artistic/medial reflexivity (or self-understanding), still operating on the premise of formal constraints, must now give way to the disappearance of such constraints and, with them, the possible disappearance of any harmonious correspondence between medium and subject matter. Faced with the liberalization of the limits previously imposed on art, medial reflexivity becomes, in Flaubert's hands, reconfigured as a new particularity, *le mot juste*, which, as a kind of medial agency, is defined as much by its political ineffectualness/impotence to change the world as by its stylistic singularity. Despite being chronologically closer to our time, much of the hyper performativity of contemporary conceptual artworks may be seen as genealogically akin to Flaubert's handling of artistic/medial reflexivity, whereby art, in defiance of a thoroughly instrumentalist world, folds completely upon itself with its own (narcissistically rebellious) set of semiotic gestures, including a consciously reiterated display of – and often ironic play on – its conditions of possibility, conditions under which art's autonomy is constantly assailed by other dominant social forces such as commercialism. Accordingly, as everything in the world has become construed in terms of exchangeability and market value, art needs, by default, to make its mark of distinction in the form of uselessness. Formulated in these terms, modern artistic/medial reflexivity tends always to be a matter of dis-ease (with the world), a self-consciousness of its own futility and social inconsequentiality. Rancière's advocacy of the indistinction of art and nonart, it seems, has crystallized such dis-ease (itself an ongoing historical situation) by bringing it up to date.[10]

For Rancière the politics of *contemporary* art is constituted by a fundamental undecidability among contradictory attitudes shown by various aesthetic paradigms, all of which bear witness to a common world.[11] This emphasis on the world as common means that Rancière tends to be equivocal on the question of mediality. Even as he speaks sympathetically to the impersonality of style (the quarantining of art from the messiness of the personal and the subjective), as exemplified by Flaubert, for instance, he is (in contrast to proponents of technical medium specificity such as

Friedrich A. Kittler) in favour of an expansive rather than restrictive approach to the medium as such: 'a medium cannot be reduced to a specific materiality and a specific apparatus. A medium also means a milieu or a sensorium, a configuration of space and time, of sensory forms and modes of perception' (Rancière 2008a: 185).[12] Hence, also, his equivocal reading of Flaubert: 'Flaubert writes "against" Madame Bovary and the "democratic" confusion of art and life, but, at the same time, he writes from the "democratic" point of view which affirms the equality of subjects and intensities. It is this tension that interests me' (Rancière 2003: 205).

At this juncture, we believe it would be productive to shift gears and broaden the parameters of our discussion by introducing another type of discourse, cultural anthropology, so as to probe further the ramifications of Rancière's provocation. This shift to cultural anthropology enables a certain 'unthought' (to use a phrase from Foucault) to come into view,[13] not only because the cultural frame of reference for thinking about art and politics is extended beyond France and Europe but also because, in a comparable democratic movement towards indistinction and social equity, another type of border and hierarchy unexpectedly reasserts itself.

III. The Trap as Artwork

Cultural anthropologists have long observed that non-Western societies' practices of art can be quite different from those familiar to Euro-American audiences, who are by convention more accustomed to a specific distinction between art and nonart. James Clifford's critique, in *The Predicament of Culture* (1988), of the dichotomization between art museums and ethnographic museums in the West, and Michael Taussig's account, in *Mimesis and Alterity* (1992), of the artful creativity of non-Western cultural rituals are but two prominent examples published in recent decades. Indeed, the signs are that the field of cultural anthropology itself is undergoing a remarkable discursive transformation in regard to the status of artistic practices (Fischer 2009).

The work of British anthropologist Alfred Gell provides an instructive point of intersection with the issues at hand. In *Art and Agency* (1998), a series of essays defining what constitutes an anthropology of art, Gell challenges, and rejects, the universalizing tendencies of Western aesthetics on account of its Eurocentricity and ideological presumptions, including its acceptance of a purely institutional notion of art.[14] In contrast to an aesthetics that serves Western art in the form of a cult, Gell proposes a general anthropology of art on the basis of relationships between participants in social systems of various kinds. In his words, this would be an 'action-centred approach to art' that is 'preoccupied with the practical mediatory role of art objects in the social process' (Gell 1998: 6). Such action, he argues, is itself uncentred, and places of 'the agent' and 'the patient' (or the recipient) may swap. Importantly, then, 'Nothing is decidable in advance about the nature of this [art] object' (Gell 1998: 7) but, as is characteristic of anthropologists' way of solving problems about the apparent irrationality of human behaviour, the point is that of 'locating . . . behaviour . . . in the dynamics of social interaction, . . . a real process, or dialectic, unfolding in time' (Gell 1998: 10).

To underscore the distributed nature of agency (1998: 22) at play within such situations, Gell invokes the interesting notion of abduction – a term used, as he reminds us, by logicians and semioticians to designate the inference of meanings that are not established or provable, but hypothetical and derived from a particular case under consideration (1998: 14–16). By stressing abduction, Gell intends to depict the contingency of agency in situations in which agency can only be grasped as effect, as the outcome of interactions between agents who/which are seeking to realize their life projects through their relations with others: 'the spaces of anthropology are those which are traversed by agents in the course of their biographies, be they narrow, or, as is becoming increasingly the case, wide or even world-wide' (1998: 11). These agents may fit into classical categories of personhood, such as artist, recipient, a portraited person or the patron who instigates the work, but they may just as well be technical objects, ancestors, spirits or hybrid entities. In their function of being an index to one or the other kind of agency, *artifacts* are pivotal in that they bring about (and not result from) differences between inwardness (mind) and externality (what is physical or social) (Gell 1998: 126 ff.). This is why abduction is a remarkably well-chosen term, poised as it is between the experience of personhood and the impersonality of causation. In any given situation (what Gell calls a 'causal milieu'), agency is ultimately the trace of an anomaly, an aberrant cause. Rather than being attributable, unambiguously, to semiotic conventions or laws or nature, agency is what must be inferred or abducted (into being/existence) (Gell 1998: 20).

Gell's democratic approach to art resonates most suggestively with Rancière's in the essay 'Vogel's Net', in which he argues against the Hegelian differentiation between art and artifacts, as recalled by art historian Arthur Danto, whereby art's superiority is seen as residing in its superfluous, non-instrumental value (Gell 1999: 187–214). In a way that echoes Flaubert's stylization, as discussed above, this differentiation may be paraphrased as follows: art is more because it is less – more artistic (read: superior) because it is less utilitarian (read: vulgar). To deconstruct Danto's age-old aesthetic assertion as one steeped in elitism, Gell introduces a cross-cultural scenario, by observing that the so-called artifacts in certain 'primitive' societies have in common with Western avant-garde art the key attribute of obscuring the more stable distinction between art and everyday objects. This observation allows Gell to argue that such artifacts are, de facto, art, which is now defined not so much by sensuous beauty as by conceptuality and reflexivity. Whereas Rancière articulates art's alterity to the working or lower classes, the masses, the country as opposed to the metropolis and so forth, Gell does so by way of life worlds beyond the bounds of Euro America and Western aesthetics. Notwithstanding their different cultural frames of reference, however, the two authors obviously share an ethico-political interest in the liberalizing of the boundaries of sensibility, identity, and agency in the modern world.

Even so, the most intriguing part about Gell's argument is not exactly the point about the indistinguishability of art and artifacts. It is rather the key example he picked to illustrate such indistinguishability: the trap, a device for capturing animals. (Just to repeat, Gell's point is that as an artifact, the trap is really a kind of – that is, equivalent to – conceptual art.)

The trap is, to all appearances, the opposite of freedom: its 'art' or cunning lies in an aggressive potential to take another being captive and bring it into submission. It is the state of arrest and closure, coinciding with the prey's loss of mobility and autonomy, that makes the trap a trap. If the artwork is reconceptualized in the cross-cultural – and globally sensitive – manner that Gell proposes, with its attendant conceptuality and reflexivity, and if such reconceptualization, much like some of Rancière's formulations, is aimed at a certain social emancipation (the emancipation from the rigidity of classification and hierarchical distinctions, and above all from the stable differentiation of experiences), how come it is the trap that occupies such a strategic place in this emancipatory thinking? What exactly is the status of the trap in relation to art?

As an example of the emancipation of the distinction between art and artifacts, the trap in Gell's text makes it imperative to ask: whose/what emancipation are we talking about? Whose/what mind, consciousness, or thought is being liberated in the conceptual flow between art and nonart? Is it that of the designer of the trap, that of the philosopher who discerns its cunning, or that of the trap itself? Yet such conceptual mobility and fluidity would not be possible (that is, realized) without the prey's abduction/participation. It is only in the prey's entanglement and, finally, its embodied state of captivity that the intent/intelligence of the trap's design is fulfilled and becomes intelligible.

What begins as a democratic attempt on the part of the cultural anthropologist to dissolve the distinction between art ('Western') and everyday objects ('non-Western') has, in other words, reintroduced into the scene a crucial type of distinction – the hierarchy between the hunter and the prey, a hierarchy that underwrites the zone of contact as a site of cruelty, domination, subordination and asymmetrical power dynamics. The non-Western example Gell picked to instantiate a radical epistemic break with conventional Western aesthetics, it appears, is precisely what threatens to throw his ethical project off course, intercepting (abducting!) it from its erstwhile movement towards cultural equality.[15]

Albeit salutary, then, the philosophical and social scientific attempts to realign art with freedom (especially in the form of the artwork/artifact that renders the distinction between art and nonart indistinguishable) tend to run into a paradox, one that revolves around the (knotty figure of the) trap in the terms outlined. This paradox leads us to conjecture that *what remains of art* in the age of medial liberalization is perhaps less a relation to freedom as such than a relation to capture/captivity, a field of discursivity that, as we will go on to suggest, has an arguably irreducible linkage to art and literature. (Let us note that even when making its appearance in a supposedly nonartistic and nonliterary realm such as cultural anthropology, the trap returns us in uncanny fashion to a literary form – Western tragedy, to be exact – as Gell's passing comments illuminatingly indicate.)[16]

IV. The Artwork as Trap, and the Force of Captivation

At one level, what the trap conjures, together with what Gell alludes to as the abduction of the indexes of meaning in processes of social interaction, is of course none other than the tradition of literary and artistic representations of phenomena of capture and imprisonment, phenomena that have long inspired authors across cultures. The memorable image, described by

Henry David Thoreau, of the American muskrat repeatedly chewing off a paw if the paw is caught, until it can no longer walk because it has chewed off all its paws this way, is simply one among many examples of a literary fascination with entrapment and its thematic associations of escape, resistance, endurance, sacrifice, and survival (Thoreau 2004: 66). Another example might be Vladimir Nabokov's *Lolita*, which, according to the author, had its germ in a news item about an ape in the Paris Zoo. When encouraged to draw a picture, the ape, it was said, drew the bars of his cage (Pettman 2006: 66).[17] In our time, Foucault's influential discussions of confinement – in the form of the institutionalized compartmentalization of madness, criminality, education, sexuality, reproduction and so forth – may also be understood as contiguous with a longstanding philosophical preoccupation with entrapment as a type of limit experience, which for Foucault culminates not in spaces of darkness (as in the dungeon) but in spaces of visibility (as in Bentham's Panopticon).[18] Foucault's summary statement on panopticism is that 'visibility is a trap' (Foucault 1975: 200). The examples of Thoreau, Nabokov, Foucault and other writers and artists suggest that the trap is, arguably, an archetypal epistemic/representational device, a *dispositif* (in Foucault's terms), perhaps, that has been central to what may be called a parapoetics (McCaffery 2008: 161–79). In the years since September 11, 2001, as incidents of arbitrary arrest and torture, forced detention, unjust execution and other varieties of physical coercion become routines of the global order of terror, the ramifications of the trap have acquired ever more profound degrees of poignancy.

At the same time, this marked semiotic kinship between the trap and art/literature should not be restricted to the level of represented content. In terms of discursive formations, what the figure of the trap accentuates is a structure of unevenness – an uneven distribution of forces, to be precise – whose injurious effect is, by definition, *borne by the prey* (the recipient of the trap's negative impact). The trap is an index to a type of social interaction in which one party takes advantage of another by being temporally preemptive, by catching the other unawares. This time differential between the hunter's and the prey's contacts with the trap, it follows, is an implicit division of labour, one that rewards the former's (premeditated) action of deceiving, disabling and disempowering the latter. To talk about the trap as a clever device, an intelligent artifact, a sophisticated conceptual artwork and so forth, is to talk about this process of one-upmanship. This fundamental structure of unevenness is the reason the trap, as much as being an archetypical device for portraying suffering, can also be a source of comic relief. Duchamp's readymade 'Trébuchet'/'Trap' provides an excellent case in point: a coat rack lying on the floor, which the artist kicks every time he walks past it, is transformed into avant-garde Art by being nailed permanently to the floor. The *showing* of the visual object is henceforth encoded with a narrative *telling* how it all happened over time: the artist, initially in the position of an unsuspecting fool who repeatedly stumbles on the coat rack, in the end masters the situation/makes his escape by deliberately staging the process of trapping and thus turning the joke back on the coat rack itself, which is now, literally, stuck.[19] Whether in the form of tragedy (with a kind of heroism defined through suffering and endurance) or comedy (with a kind of heroism defined through slapstick humour and ironic distance), however, the trap tends to be treated as a unified discursive plane, one that is organized strictly by the binary, mechanistic determinism of openness and enclosure, and oriented towards the interest of the hunter – that is to say, the winner – when, ontologically and epistemically speaking, no such discursive unity exists.

To put this in more formal terms: the trap, by virtue of its binary operation (open/shut), is a line of pressure, constraint and blockage. Nevertheless, once the trap snaps shut and a prey is caught, the trap's formal structure of obstruction and inhibition sets into motion a new process that is, potentially, indeterminate. Like the *charnière* mentioned by Derrida in the third epigraph at the beginning of the present essay, the trap may therefore be analogized/approximated to a hinge or pivot, around which multiple planes rotate in perpetual slippage from one another, in such ways as to conjoin mobility with enclosure, and alterity with capture. How so?

The missing link is the prey's experience of *being* captured: how to *count* this experience without simply collapsing it back into the intent/intelligence of the trap's design, which is complete only when the prey gets caught? For, once caught, the prey's existence renders the trap more than just the elegant design understood from the sovereign command perspective of the hunter, who can henceforth no longer monopolize the terms of the interaction. The hunter's carefully conceived, pre-emptive plan, as embodied in the open trap, is now folded into an other space/time that comes into being through entrapment, while the prey's past and present actions take on, belatedly, a new, additional significance as self-entanglement. Gell's aforementioned allusion to tragedy (note 16) is an attempt to account for this temporal knot of suspense and *anagnorisis*.

This discursive excess, at once inarticulate and indispensable, at once outside and informing the economy of the trap's instrumentalist functioning, is what makes the trap such an inexhaustibly evocative object for literary and artistic contemplation. Such discursive excess means that a supplementary plane of articulation, the plane of articulation of an other, ensnared in but not coinciding with the hunter's, philosopher's, or conceptual artist's, and oscillating between the shock of ensnarement and the pain of possible annihilation, now slides into place to rupture, from within, the trap's aforementioned, presumed discursive unity. Entangled, vulnerable and delirious, this supplementary discursive plane comes into being – 'appears' – only as the trap snaps shut, yet has the potential of tilting the trap towards a radically heteronomous affective assemblage, one in which a reactive relation to the world – in the form of being caught, being struck, being touched, being infected and so forth –, which is situationally entwined with but also phenomenally disjointed and discontinuous from an active one (as in catching, striking, touching, infecting, and so forth), is a primary, rather than simply derivative, sensation.

In the English language, this heteronomous affective assemblage (rather than the straightforwardly mechanistic, open-and-shut determinism that allows the trap to function) is invoked whenever we speak of being 'captivated' in the sense of being lured and held by an unusual person, event or spectacle. To be captivated is to be captured by means other than the purely physical, with an effect that is, nonetheless, lived and felt *as* embodied captivity. The French word *captation*, referring to a process of deception and inveiglement by artful means, is suggestive in so far as it pinpoints the elusive yet vital connection between the state of being captivated and art.[20] But the English word *captivation* seems more felicitous, not least because it is semantically suspended between (capture as) an aggressive move and an affective state, and carries within it the force of the trap in both active and reactive senses, without their being organized necessarily in a hierarchical fashion and collapsed into a single discursive plane.[21] As an experience formed through a collaboration of intensities, sensuous and imaginary as well as rationalist, captivation seems – or so we'd like to propose – to have a privileged relationship to art and literature, in ways that are irreducible to other frames of interpretation.

In this light, Rancière's reading of *Madame Bovary* begins to assume an interestingly opaque quality. The ingenuity of Rancière's analysis lies in his endeavour to restore to the degenerate (adulterous, frivolous, selfish, irresponsible, immoral . . .) character of Emma a kind of agency. Indeed, reading with Rancière, we may say that Emma's scandalous behaviour is a kind of muted speech or silent witnessing, which is symptomatic of an indifference 'to the system of social differentiations defining what the daughter of a peasant can feel, think and do' (Rancière 2009: 121), an indifference that should be given its share/place in history. Such a reading would be consistent with Rancière's formulations of 'emancipation': 'a set of practices guided by the supposition that everyone is equal and by the attempt to verify this supposition' (1992: 58). Rancière names the politics of emancipation a 'heterology': 'the politics of emancipation is the politics of the self as an other, or, in Greek terms, a *heteron*. The logic of emancipation is a heterology' (1992: 59). While we find Rancière's reasoning persuasive, our disagreement with him is over the nature of otherness/ heterology in regard to Emma's behaviour. By referring to Emma as a peasant's daughter and a poor country doctor's wife, Rancière implies that such otherness/heterology should, ultimately, be articulated to class, and yet his class-oriented assessment seems ambiguous. If what Emma personifies is indeed class emancipation as such, why does Rancière need to devote so much space to rationalizing how she *has to* die for Flaubert's art to succeed, as though such emancipation contains in it a surplus of signification that has to be reabsorbed (either accounted for or wiped away)? What is it about Emma's emancipatory trajectory that seems so unsettling, that it is not enough to accept her death as suicide, as the novel has presented it, but necessary to reframe it with a categorical imperative – as something that demands a violent solution, an *act* of killing by her author, as though the latter recognized in her something of a dangerous equal/rival, who must be cautiously warded off?[22]

Whereas for Flaubert, the indistinction of art and life means that even the most lowly aspects of life may be turned into – that is, refined and purified as – Art, Emma's 'problem' is that she readily yields, physically and mentally, to pleasures of the unproductive and non-purifiable kind – romance novels, fleeting sensations and idle aspirations. Much as their difference is amply registered by Rancière, it is also what constitutes the opacity of his analysis: Flaubert might have been as much a captive as Emma is to the menacing new social condition of the indiscriminate equivalence of things, but, like a good, hard worker from the ranks of (what Rancière calls) the reactionary bourgeoisie, he (re)directed his captivity to a new purpose, the purpose of an exquisite art, whereas Emma's response to this new social condition is that of a steadily intensified madness until her life is completely ruined.[23] In living in such a manner as to dramatize the border/threshold between fantasy and reality, Emma is much less the conventional proletarian[24] seeking class emancipation than a proto-mass culture consumer who abandons herself to the lure of inanimate, fictional objects, which are her vital sources of happiness.

Emma's emancipation, if it can be so called, is not only a matter of her wanting to convert fantasies into life (as Rancière suggests); rather, it is also that she prefers daydreaming to life itself, and that she wants to live continuously *entertained*, even at the expense of her own and her family's wellbeing, by those spectral objects, those absent presences that are part fantasy, part sensation and part reality. (To 'entertain' is, etymologically, to hold between, in a manner that resonates with the phenomenon of captivation.) Having endless desires; having desires in endlessly repeated and serialized forms: *this* is Emma's heterology and project of self-transformation and self-invention. In a manner that anticipates the behaviours of both the perpetrators and the victims of the global financial crisis of the 2000s (the unregulated investment bankers, subprime mortgage lenders, and home purchasers with zero down payments), Emma plunges headlong into disaster because, we might say, of her over-imaginative claims – claims that are based exclusively on the imagination and increasingly detached from/independent of material reality – so much so that suicide becomes her only viable form of debt repudiation (the only way she can declare bankruptcy). But suicide is also a form of intransitive speech: like Flaubert's Art, it is about severing the ties to the sentiments, to the messiness of life itself, by drawing an absolute line between the imaginary world and the social world. If Flaubert drew the line with self-discipline and hard work, Emma draws the line with her own life. She, too, is an artist, and perhaps not only a kitsch artist (as Rancière writes) but also a hunger artist; her Art, too, is crafted with precision and exactitude, though not of words but of death.[25]

Much as Rancière's discussions prompt an understanding of Emma's story as one about class, therefore, something about the story does not quite fit such a reading, which somehow cannot account for the excessiveness of captivation – with its combination of pleasure and unfreedom – except, perhaps, by reducing it to false consciousness. Obviously, Rancière recognizes the unsatisfactory nature of that language of an anachronistic, orthodox Marxist analysis,[26] but even as he is invested in being affirmative of Emma's transgressive behaviour, he seems to have stopped short of probing the significance of Emma's experience of being captivated to its logical conclusion. By reinscribing Emma's perverse solutions to *ennui* in a kind of heterology that is, nonetheless, rooted in class, and by reverting the agency of her final self-performance to her author/creator, Rancière is, of course, not mistaken; it is simply that he has not gone far enough. Borrowing his own concept, might not we see in Emma's final self-performance precisely a redistribution of the sensible – in the extreme form of a cessation of the senses, of non-sense?[27] In not granting Emma authorship/ownership of her suicide, and in transferring that authorship/ownership – that deed, as it were – to Flaubert and recoding it as an act of *his* artistic resistance, has not Rancière inadvertently further muted Emma's muted speech?

But Rancière should probably not be held responsible for what is a much larger problematic about art in modernity. Unlike other types of social transformation that bear clear, progressive designations such as 'class struggle', 'decolonization', 'women's lib', 'gay rights' and 'transgender', the state of being captivated has no such collective name recognition based in identity politics even though it is a situation in which an undeniable relation to alterity unfolds. How to describe a form of solidarity that is not with other members of one's class, race, nation or gender but – in what may be the real scandal of Flaubert's tale – with the spectres of thought, abstraction, fiction and illusion? Like a virulent parasite that has gradually overtaken its host,[28] Emma's state of captivation – and the pleasure and unfreedom that accompany it – brings into play the entire supplementary discursive domain that tangles up the open/shut determinism of the trap with its own creative-cum-destructive momentum. As the *imbalance* between the claims/demands made by those spectres, on the one hand, and so-called reality, on the other, accrues to the point of no return, captivation spirals into catastrophe. Captivation, then, is the deranged remainder that is unassimilable to the metanarratives of freedom that underlie both capitalist consumerism (in which an autonomous subject makes choices from an endless proliferation of material goods) and socialist revolution (in which an autonomous subject emancipates herself from the constraints imposed by class, race, colonialism, gender, and so forth). Even while inextricably enmeshed with these two dominant discourse networks, captivation poses the question of art and politics not in the form of an integration with such networks but in the form of a disjunction, an encounter – and interrogation – of an insistently ontological import.

That is to say, the state of captivation brings to the fore questions of being – of origination, freedom, finitude and infinitude: Where do I come from, where am I heading towards, when/where will I end? By whose script and design do I exist? What does it mean to have a life of my own? Is there more to I than I? As they confront us with the abyss of existence, these open-ended, because ultimately irresolvable, questions have conventionally lent themselves to purposes of mass rationalization and indoctrination, purposes that, as Louis Althusser has shown, are readily appropriated/ abducted by, and sutured with, ideological state apparatuses such as the church, the state, the family, the police, the school, the military, and so forth. For Althusser, the ontological as well as sociopolitical reward for accepting the interpellation by such apparatuses is the shelter of coherent identification, which shields and protects one from the openness of the abyss. When realized on a collective scale, identification ensures the indefinite reproducibility of a particular type of society (as for instance, the modern, postindustrial, secular, bourgeois society of Western Europe) and its infrastructure.[29] Is captivation simply a variant of interpellation? We will respond to this question by way of a brief discussion of a contemporary film. (For reasons of space, we will have to limit ourselves to those aspects of the film that are most salient to our discussion.)

V. Capturing the Lives of Others ...

Like *Madame Bovary*, the film *Das Leben der Anderen/The Lives of Others* (2006; directed by Florian Henckel von Donnersmarck) offers a provocative staging of captivation, in a social context quite distinct from the nineteenth-century French countryside. The story takes place in East Germany during the period before the fall of the Berlin Wall and German reunification. Wiesler, an ambitious Stasi interrogator with expertise in coercing confessions, is ordered by his superiors to eavesdrop on the writer Georg Dreyman and his lover, Christa Maria Sieland, a well-known stage actress, in whom a high-ranking Stasi official, Hempf, has a sexual interest. At the level of the plot, then, the trap appears readily in two closely linked but by no means subtle manners: first, as the secret police state itself, which imprisons its citizens in a universal network of surveillance; second, as the particular eavesdropping operation installed in Dreyman's apartment building to capture the details of his and his lover's lives. By today's media standards, the eavesdropping operation is a rather simple setup, which 'bugs' the apartment and transmits the sounds to a tape recorder, while the recorded contents are interpreted and reported by typewriter onto paper documents to be filed in the Stasi bureaucracy. (These documents will become available to the public after German reunification, which is how Dreyman eventually discovers the truth.) In so far as it serves to objectify the seamless, pervasive and omniscient workings of the police state, the figure of the trap can be thought of as the most crucial, albeit silent, mediator in this story.

Dramatically, in the minimalist, audial medium in which the lovers are taken captive, another scene begins to unfold. The poetry reading, music, intimate conversations, lovemaking, social gatherings and other happenings in Dreyman's apartment, received by Wiesler in the form of intermittent sounds, gradually exert a magical hold on him. Instead of monitoring his prey with the sadistic detachment of an all-knowing captor, Wiesler undergoes a transformation in which his victims begin to assume a new kind of significance, affecting him as though they were the fictional characters in a radio play. Drawn *beside himself* into this other, imaginary world, Wiesler tries participating in it vicariously, by gestures of appropriation and mimicry: he re-enters and looks around in Dreyman's apartment, touches Dreyman's bed, and steals Dreyman's copy of Brecht's poems for his own reading. Such attachment to this other world culminates at the critical juncture when Dreyman's clandestine activity of writing articles for the West is about to be exposed. The Stasi, having been alerted by Sieland (through a coerced confession) to a doorsill where Dreyman hides his typewriter, plans to break into his apartment and arrest him on charges of treason. At great peril to himself, Wiesler pre-empts this planned exposure by removing the typewriter just in time. With the Stasi unable to arrest him, Dreyman survives as a writer. Eventually, upon learning the truth by reading his own file in the former East German government archives, Dreyman dedicates a new book to Wiesler, identifying the latter simply by his former Stasi work number, HGW XX17. By then, Wiesler has become a low-level postal worker.

Wiesler's transformation easily lends itself to an anticommunist reading, according to which this film would be laudable on account of its reaffirmation of a universal humanism: by daring to abandon his sinister assignment and to rescue a writer who courageously criticizes the secret police state, Wiesler regains his humanity, vindicates good morals, makes the world a better place, and so forth. The logic of this anticommunist reading is consistent with the celebration of the fall of the Berlin Wall as a triumph of Western enlightenment in the barbarous East, the celebration of the reunification of the German nation, and other such teleological narratives. The details of the film, however, tell a different story, especially if we approach it from the perspective of the trap.

Trapping in this instance is, significantly, enacted in a series of mimetic efforts. Like Wiesler's attempt to appropriate and mimic bits of Dreyman's life, the injunction to tape-record and transcribe by typewriter amounts to a methodical process of copying. But once the activity of copying begins – that is, once the state-sanctioned, instrumentalist trapping procedure is in force – a radically distinct discursive plane begins to assume existence *side by side* with the oppressive agenda of the state, in such a way as to bring about a reversal of the positions of captor and captives, a reversal that coincides with a mutation of the very medium of surveillance and capture. Sound, intended officially for the purpose of recording and copying, now breaks off from itself into a different audial pathway: in the process of being heard by Wiesler in a reduced form, with most of the accompanying empirical 'reality' subtracted, sound becomes instead an aperture for interventional creativity.

Like a musical conductor or stage director, Wiesler proceeds to reassemble and rewrite the official score/script/plot. Not only does he intercept Sieland's plan to continue to meet with her abuser, Hempf, and not only does he hide what Dreyman is writing – an article about artists and suicides in East Germany, which eventually appears in *Der Spiegel* – by fabricating details of a nonexistent, politically uncontroversial play; he also alters the position and role of one little prop – Dreyman's typewriter. From its original status as the incriminating piece of evidence sought by the Stasi, this writing tool has now turned into a false lead, *a new object whose significance lies in the fact that it is missing*. This gesture of alteration, by which the thing that is at once the good writer's vital means of protest and the evil state's desired means of persecution vanishes into a useless deception, unveils itself as a void, successfully obstructs the Stasi's procedure in an innovative politics, one that erupts simultaneously as an artwork, in the midst of the most oppressive of political situations.

This, then, is how captivation may be distinguished from Althusser's formulation of interpellation: rather than putting its stresses on a cohering and overdetermined process of identification with the ideological state apparatuses, captivation, as a type of receptivity, is at once involved and devolved – and separate. Its reciprocation of the hailing of alterity, in other words, takes the form not of an obedient conformity with an absolute structure of domination, which allows one to find and anchor oneself in a rewarding relation to such a structure (as in Althusser's argument), but rather in the form of a loosening, and losing, of that self, often in 'non-productive' processes such as daydreaming and art.[30] In the slipping-away of the shelter that is identification emerges that heteronomous affective assemblage, as mentioned in our foregoing discussion, whereby politics returns not to government but (possibly through the voiding of a particular political agenda, as in this film) to anarchy, the condition of having no *arkhê*.[31]

This loosening/loss of the self, moreover, is not the result of crossing an external border or overcoming a constraint; it rather occurs from within the limits imposed by the situation, which ambiguates between Wiesler's role as audience and his role as actor. Wiesler's isolation – staged in his opaque looks, his lonely movements, and his restricted access to the world which he is to oversee – blocks the possibility of a total overview. Yet it is precisely in the midst of such a blockage that Wiesler metamorphoses into the dreamer-artist of an unanticipated political situation, in which his captives/victims are given a new existence as the imaginary objects he seeks to set free. In this entanglement of politics and art, captivation brings with it a terrifying kind of freedom. Stripped of the identification that is the protection of the state, the bureaucracy and the hierarchy of officialdom, Wiesler ends up living the life of a modest, now nameless messenger, a 'nobody'.

In so far as Wiesler is neither the intellectual/writer nor the professional actor (the conventional agents of literature and art, even in a communist state, as represented by Dreyman and Sieland), his captivation may ultimately be seen as a form of self-distraction-cum-self-destruction. Whereas Emma Bovary commits suicide, Wiesler annihilates himself by enmeshment in a foreign universe, a universe in which he is the other, in which he has no speech of his own except that of being captivated. Interestingly, this speechlessness of the other is exactly the place where *Das Leben der Anderen* becomes a rejoinder to Rancière's compelling notions of equality and democracy. As Rancière writes, such notions are not so much about the liberation of thought per se as about the restoration to the world around us of a collective agency, a common 'speech' that is otherwise mute, anonymous and unacknowledged.[32] As history is typically a record composed by the victors, the challenge to us is to be able to hear, to listen for such common speech.

Our analysis could have ended at this point, but we would like to introduce one more complication, even though a full discussion of it will have to be deferred. The trap also functions in an important manner in relation to the actress Sieland, Dreyman's lover, who is throughout the film referred to as an artist. In focusing attention on Wiesler's transformation by captivation, the film has simultaneously cast Sieland in the position of an abject female, who, despite her artistic talent, is held captive to her body, which serves both to inaugurate and to conclude the plot that revolves around the male characters (Hempf, who desires her and forces her into an affair with him; Grubitz, who supervises the eavesdropping operation; Dreyman, who loves her, is aware of the affair, but somehow continues to believe that he himself is an exception to the state's surveillance; Wiesler, whose captivation changes his own life). Of all the male characters, Wiesler is closest to Sieland in his capacity for self-sacrifice and self-annihilation; at the same time, if Wiesler's ingenious removal of the typewriter saves Dreyman, it also seals Sieland's tragic fate. As the Stasi officers arrive to make their planned arrest of Dreyman, Sieland flees the apartment in guilt (we surmise) as she believes that her betrayal of her lover is about to be revealed, only then to be fatally hit by a truck rushing by. If she had stayed behind, the fact that the typewriter is missing would have meant that the Stasi would return to punish her for lying and step up its harassment. In Sieland's case, all exits have been blocked, and her death is in effect a suicide.

In a disturbing parallel to Emma Bovary and Flaubert, therefore, here is a situation in which, to paraphrase Rancière, a woman artist 'has to be killed' as the socio-historical conditions of her lifeworld become entangled with the makings of the male author's creative work, which in this case applies both to Dreyman's article about artists in East Germany who commit suicide and to Wiesler's dream-art rescue of his characters from the persecution of the state. Furthermore, it applies to the plot of the film (that is to say, director von Donnersmarck's story), for which the killing is arguably an easy escape, conserving the narrative centre of gravity in the male protagonists.

Traversed by the multiplicities of homosocial (in particular, male homosocial) as well as heterosexual bonding, the discursive planes rotating around the trap are potentially endless – and often incommensurate. Whose captivation counts in the end, and whose captivation counts *as art?* – that of a male, a female, or . . .? Are not group identities as such, including sexual identities and their many variants, ultimately also traps? These questions of agency may never be fully answered, but the implications of their unfolding should be part of any in-depth consideration of the indistinction of art and nonart.

Notes

* With thanks to Chris Cullens for her helpful suggestions on the first draft of this essay.
1. See in particular 'The Distribution of the Sensible' (Rancière 2004); 'Politics and Aesthetics: An Interview' (conducted in 2002), (Rancière 2003: 191–211); 'Problems and Transformations in Critical Art/2004' (Rancière 2006: 83–93); 'A Few Remarks on the Method of Jacques Rancière' Rancière 2009: 114–23).
2. For a helpful introduction to conceptual art, see the essay 'Ideas, Systems, Processes' in Marzona and Grosenick (2005: 6–25). For an influential discussion, see also Bourriaud (2002).
3. See Rancière's account of his relations with Althusser in 'Politics and Aesthetics: an Interview' (2003: 194–96); see also Peter Hallward's introduction to the same interview, 191.
4. 'If, among the thinkers of my generation, there was one I was quite close to at one point, it was Foucault. Something of Foucault's archaeological project – the will to think the conditions of possibility of such and such a form of statement or such and such an object's constitution – has stuck with me' (Rancière 2003: 208–9). See also Rancière's description, in Foucauldian terms, of how he approached the question of the worker in Marxism after 1968: 'Being a "worker" wasn't in the first instance a condition reflected in forms of consciousness or action; it was a form of symbolization, the arrangement of a certain set of statements or utterances. I became interested in reconstituting the world that made these utterances [énonciations] possible' (2003: 196).
5. See the many discussions in Rancière's works such as *The Ignorant Schoolmaster: Five Lessons in Intellectual Emancipation* (1991), *The Names of History: on the Poetics of Knowledge* (1994), *Disagreement: Politics and Philosophy* (1999), and *The Philosopher and His Poor* (2004).
6. See also his amplification of this point in Rancière 2009.
7. Eliot is quoting Samuel Johnson, who remarks of poets such as Donne, Cleveland and Cowley that 'the most heterogeneous ideas are yoked by violence together'.

8. In *The Order of Things*, Foucault discusses the historical emergence of literature in modern Western Europe in similar terms, as a type of language that becomes increasingly self-referential and intransitive (1970: 294–300).
9. Rancière, 'Are Some Things Unrepresentable?' (in Rancière 2007: 109–38). See also his comments in 'Why Emma Bovary Had to be Killed' (2008: 237). An interlocutor who springs to mind here is Clement Greenberg, who defended the adequacy of certain art forms precisely in terms of an avant-garde notion of medium specificity, emphasizing in particular the anti-sculptural, two-dimensional character of painting. In other words, art is art because it is self-referential, because it is an investigation and purification of itself (its medium specificity) (Greenberg 1940: 296–310).
10. For an important earlier discussion of this ongoing historical situation and the controversy over the status of art in modern European society, see Peter Bürger, *Theory of the Avant-Garde* (1984).
11. See his comments in 'Problems and Transformations in Critical Art' (Rancière 2006).
12. By contrast, Kittler has written, for instance, that '[a] medium is a medium. Therefore it cannot be translated. To transfer messages from one medium to another always involves reshaping them to conform to new standards and materials' (1990: 165).
13. See the section 'The Cogito and the Unthought' in Foucault, *The Order of Things* (1970: 322 and following).
14. By 'institutional', Gell refers to views according to which art is simply what circulates as art; that is, views that do not consider what artistic meaning may be immanent to the work. For an informed discussion, see Dickie (1984).
15. The arguably unresolved sketch of what Gell terms an extended mind, which makes up the second part of *Art and Agency*, shows that this issue is indeed, to use his own words, 'unfinished business' (1998: 80–1).
16. At one point, Gell compares different trapped animals to 'tragic heroes' such as Faust and Othello. 'The fact that animals who fall victim to traps have always brought about their downfall by their own actions, their own complacent self-confidence, ensures that trapping is a far more poetic and tragic form of hunting than the simple chase. The latter kind of hunting equalizes hunters and victims, united in spontaneous action and reaction, whereas trapping decisively hierarchizes hunter and victim. The trapper is God, or the fates, the trapped animal is man in his tragic incarnation' (1999: 202).
17. Pettman offers an illuminating analysis of the important allusions to spider webs in Nabokov's novel.
18. For a study of the theme of incarceration in French literature, see Brombert (1978).

19. For an informative discussion of this and other readymades of Duchamp's, see Molesworth (1998: 51–61).
20. For an astute discussion of *captation* in the contexts of economics and sociology, in particular in relation to strategies for marketing commodities, see Cochoy (2007: 203–23). Cochoy argues that in the situation of consumerist publics, *captation* has the task of controlling a fleeting target and thus must devise strategies that suggest possibilities of exit, flight and freedom. For scholars who have studied the phenomena of commodified literature (including pulp fiction and television soap operas), Cochoy's analysis may not come across as groundbreaking, but what is noteworthy is the fact that when he needs to explain the intricacy of *captation*, he turns specifically to narrative fiction – in this case the story of Little Red Riding Hood (see pages 212 and following) – both in terms of what narrative actions can signify within the story, and in terms of fiction itself as a device adopted by the literary author for purposes of captivating the reader.
21. Although he offers very sensitive formulations of captivation, Gell tends to preserve the hierarchy between the active and the reactive senses, as for instance in the relation between the artist and the spectator. This is evident in the rather negative terminology he uses to describe the spectator's condition of being trapped (or awe-struck) when confronted by the artist's virtuosity: 'fundamental inequality', 'demoralization', 'inability', '"blockage" in cognition', 'defeat', and so forth (Gell 1998: 68–72). And, while he introduces themes of paradoxical recursion and exchange of places between captive and captor, with artworks attaining a certain universality in their function as 'thought-traps', 'impeding passage' (1999: 213) and becoming agents in a distribution of personhood (a distribution whereby agents may be as entangled as patients/recipients), Gell nonetheless retains the notion of a 'primary agency' (as the source of intentional action), which he only indirectly, and perhaps incompletely, deconstructs in his analysis of the extended mind (1998: 221–58). What seems missing from his otherwise extraordinary work is a theorization of the *state* of being trapped (or awe-struck) – that is to say, of captivation as an experience that exceeds an *ex post facto* analysis of power relations, and that exceeds the type of formalization that is based strictly on cognition/mind.
22. For an interesting discussion of *Madame Bovary* in terms of mimetic desire, see Girard (1965: 63–4; 148–9).
23. Foucault's essay 'Madness, the Absence of Work' (1997: 97–104) would be a relevant intertext to read alongside Emma's lack of productivity. Towards the end of his essay on *Madame Bovary*, Rancière briefly invokes 'hysteria' as a possible key to the literature (by authors such as Flaubert, Marcel Proust and Virginia Woolf) in which human bodies suffer from a disease provoked by the 'excess' of thought (see Rancière 2008a: 246 and following).

24. Rancière's definition of the proletarian, it should be noted, is etymologically specific: 'a certain way of being at one and the same time inside and outside the symbolic order of the distribution of social identities' (1992: 80). See also his elaboration of the links between 'proletarian' and processes of subjectivization and identification on 60 and following.
25. The reference here is, of course, to Franz Kafka's remarkable short story 'A Hunger Artist', in which what the artist, who lives in a cage, keeps performing (or putting on display) until death is, arguably and allegorically speaking, his craving – an insatiable metaphysical demand, a bottomless existential abyss that can never be filled.
26. See, for instance, his remarks on the worker, as cited in note no. 4, above.
27. Rancière is in fact quite sympathetic to this line of thinking, which he associates with the theme of the self-destructive will and a race towards nothingness in some examples of nineteenth-century literature; see his remarks in (2003: 208).
28. For a philosophical discussion of parasitism as a type of origination, see Serres (1982).
29. See Althusser (1971: 127–86).
30. A helpful text here is Alain Badiou's Althusserian reading of the apostle Paul's interpellation by the event of Christ's resurrection. Instead of losing himself in the experience, Paul found/anchored himself successfully by establishing the institution of the Christian church and empire; his subjective upsurge thus became a coherent part of a biopolitics of government through religious conviction. See Badiou (2003).
31. See Rancière (1992): 'politics is not the enactment of the principle, the law, or the self of a community. Put in other words, politics has no arkhê, it is anarchical' (59).
32. See in particular Rancière's comments in (2003).

Works Cited

Althusser, Louis (1971), 'Ideology and Ideological State Apparatuses (Notes towards an Investigation', in *Lenin and Philosophy and Other Essays*, trans. Ben Brewster, New York: Monthly Review.

Badiou, Alain (2003), *Saint Paul: The Foundation of Universalism*, trans. Ray Brassier, Stanford: Stanford University Press.

Benjamin, Walter (1969), 'The Work of Art in the Age of Mechanical Reproduction', in *Illuminations*, ed. with an intro. Hannah Aredt, trans. Harry Zohn, New York: Schocken, 217–51.

Bourriaud, Nicolas (2002), *Relational Aesthetics*, trans. Simon Pleasance and Fronza Woods with the participation of Mathieu Copeland, Dijon: les presses du reel.

Brombert, Victor (1978), *The Romantic Prison: the French Tradition*, Princeton: Princeton University Press.
Bürger, Peter (1984), *Theory of the Avant-Garde*, trans. Michael Shaw, foreword Jochen Schulte-Sasse, Minneapolis: University of Minnesota Press.
Clifford, James (1988), *The Predicament of Culture: Twentieth-century Ethnography, Literature, and Art*, Cambridge, MA: Harvard University Press.
Cochoy, Franck (2007), 'A Brief Theory of the "Captation" of Publics: Understanding the Market with Little Red Riding Hood', trans. Couze Venn, *Theory, Culture & Society* 24 (7–8): 203–23.
Derrida, Jacques (1997), '"To Do Justice to Freud": The History of Madness in the Age of Psychoanalysis', in *Foucault and His Interlocutors*, ed. and intro. Arnold Davidson, Chicago and London: University of Chicago Press.
Dickie, George (1984), *The Art Circle: A Theory of Art*, New York: Haven.
Eliot, T. S. (1975), 'The Metaphysical Poets (1921)', in *Selected Prose of T. S. Eliot*, ed. with an intro. Frank Kermode, New York: Harcourt Brace Jovanovich; Farrar, Straus and Giroux.
Fischer, Michael M. J. (2009), *Anthropological Futures*, Durham and London: Duke University Press.
Foucault, Michel (1970), *The Order of Things: An Archaeology of the Human Sciences*, trans. Alan Sheridan, London: Tavistock.
— (1972), *The Archaeology of Knowledge*, trans. Alan Sheridan Smith, London: Tavistock.
— (1975), *Discipline and Punish: The Birth of the Prison*, London: Vintage.
— (1997) 'Madness, the Absence of Work', trans. Peter Stastny and Deniz Sengel, *Foucault and His Interlocutors*, ed. and intro. Arnold Davidson, Chicago and London: University of Chicago Press.
Gell, Alfred (1998), *Art and Agency: An Anthropological Theory*, Oxford: Clarendon.
— (1999), 'Vogel's Net: Traps as Artworks and Artworks as Traps', *The Art of Anthropology: Essays and Diagrams*, ed. Eric Hirsch, London and New Brunswick: Athlone.
Girard, René (1965), *Deceit, Desire, and the Novel: Self and Other in Literary Structure*, trans. Yvonne Freccero, Baltimore and London: Johns Hopkins UP.
Greenberg, Clement (1940), 'Towards a Newer Laocoon', *Partisan Review* 7 (July–August 1940): 296–310.
Kittler, Friedrich (1990), *Discourse Networks 1800/1900*, trans. Michael Metteer, with Chris Cullens, foreword David E. Wellbery, Stanford: Stanford University Press.
Marzona, Daniel and Uta Grosenick [eds] (2005), 'Ideas, Systems, Processes', *Conceptual Art*, Köln: Taschen, 6–25.

McCaffery, Steve (2008), 'Parapoetics and the Architectural Leap', in *A Time for the Humanities: Futurity and the Limits of Autonomy*, ed. James J. Bono, Tim Dean, Ewa Plonowska Ziarek, New York: Fordham University Press.
Molesworth, Helen (1998), 'Work Avoidance: The Everyday Life of Marcel Duchamp's Readymades', *Art Journal* 57 (4) (Winter): 51–61.
Pettman, Dominic (2006), *Love and Other Technologies: Retrofitting Eros for the Information Age*, New York: Fordham University Press.
Rancière, Jacques (1991), *The Ignorant Schoolmaster: Five Lessons in Intellectual Emancipation*, trans. with an intro. Kristin Ross, Stanford: Stanford University Press.
— (1992) 'Politics, Identification, and Subjectivization', *October* 61 (Summer 1992): 58–64.
— (1994), *The Names of History: on the Poetics of Knowledge*, trans. Hassan Melehy, foreword Hayden White, Minneapolis and London: University of Minnesota Press.
— (1999) *Disagreement: Politics and Philosophy*, trans. Julie Rose, Minneapolis and London: University of Minnesota Press.
— (2003), 'Politics and Aesthetics: An Interview' (conducted in 2002), trans. Forbes Morlock, intro. Peter Hallward, *Angelaki: Journal of the Theoretical Humanities* 8 (2) (August 2003): 191–211.
— (2004), 'The Distribution of the Sensible', in *The Politics of Aesthetics: the Distribution of the Sensible*, trans. with an intro. Gabriel Rockhill, London and New York: Continuum.
— (2004a), *The Philosopher and His Poor*, ed. Andrew Parker, trans. Andrew Parker, Corinne Oster, and John Drury, Durham and London: Duke University Press.
— (2006), 'Problems and Transformations in Critical Art/2004', trans. Claire Bishop, assisted by Pablo Lafuente, in *Participation* (Documents of Contemporary Art Series), ed. Claire Bishop, London: Whitechapel; Cambridge, MA: MIT Press, 83–93.
— (2007), *The Future of the Image*, trans. Gregory Elliott, New York and London: Verso.
— (2008), 'Why Emma Bovary Had to be Killed', *Critical Inquiry* 34 (Winter): 233–48.
— (2008a), 'Aesthetics against Incarnation: An Interview by Anne Marie Oliver', *Critical Inquiry* 35 (Autumn).
— (2009), 'A Few Remarks on the Method of Jacques Rancière', *Parallax* 15 (3): 114–23.
Serres, Michel (1982), *The Parasite*, trans., with notes, by Lawrence R. Schehr, Baltimore and London: Johns Hopkins University Press.

— (1997), 'The Geometry of the Incommunicable: Madness', in *Foucault and His Interlocutors*, ed. and intro. Arnold Davidson, Chicago and London: University of Chicago Press.

Taussig, Michael (1992), *Mimesis and Alterity: A Particular History of the Senses*, New York and London: Routledge.

Thoreau, Henry David (2004), *Walden* (1854), Princeton: Princeton University Press.

Politics without Politics

Jodi Dean

I.

In some left political theory, democracy is an aspiration that occupies a place once held by communism. One might think of Chantal Mouffe's and Ernesto Laclau's work on radical democracy, accounts of deliberative democracy influenced by Jürgen Habermas's theory of communicative action or the pluralism espoused by William Connolly. These proper names, however, point to more than the specific proposals of specific theorists. They highlight a general underlying supposition that despite all our problems with democracy, democracy is the solution to all our problems. Whether expressed as the idea of an empty place where things can be otherwise or in terms of a set of procedures that incorporate already the keys to revising and reforming political practice, democracy, it seems, is our only political option. As Margaret Thatcher said of capitalism, there is no alternative. For the left, democracy is our last, best hope.

Democracy, though, is inadequate as a language and frame for left political aspiration. Here are two reasons why; there are others. First, the right speaks the language of democracy. It voices its goals and aspirations in democratic terms. One of the reasons given for the United States' invasion of Iraq, for example, was the goal of bringing democracy to the Middle East. Similarly, leftists in the United States urge inclusion and participation, and so do those on the political right. The right complains about the exclusion of conservatives from the academy and God from politics. They, too, try to mobilize grass-root support and increase participation. There is nothing particularly left, then, about inclusion and participation. These are elements of democracy the right also supports. This right-wing adoption of democratic ideals prevents the left from occupying the position of a political alternative to the right – if left positions are the same as right ones then the left isn't an alternative. Slavoj Žižek describes this situation where one's enemy speaks one's language as 'victory in defeat' (2008: 189). When one's enemy accepts one's terms, one's point of critique and resistance is lost, subsumed. The dimension of antagonism (fundamental opposition) vanishes.

A second reason democracy is inadequate as an expression of left aspiration is that contemporary democratic language employs and reinforces the rhetoric of capitalism: free choice, liberty, satisfaction, communication, connection, diversity. Like any media savvy corporation, democratic activists want to ensure that voices are heard and opinions registered. Corporations and activists alike are united in their preoccupation with awareness: people need to be aware of issues, of products, of products as signs of issues. In this concrete sense, Žižek is right to claim that attachment to democracy is the form our attachment to capital takes (2002: 273; 2008: 184). In the consumption and entertainment-driven setting of the contemporary United States, one's commitments to capitalism are expressed as commitments to democracy. They are the same way of life, the same daily practices of 'aware-ing' oneself and expressing one's opinion, of choosing and voting and considering one's choice a vote and one's vote a choice.

More than inadequate as an expression of left political aspiration, democracy names left castration ('I know, but nevertheless'). Because the left presents itself as appealing to and supporting democracy, it fails to take a stand, to name an enemy. Instead of drawing a line and saying what it is against, what it excludes, left political theory in the contemporary United States advocates inclusion, universality, multiplicity, the plurality of modes of becoming and ethical responsiveness.[1] The dilemmas arising out of such advocacy have vexed left politics for some time now as the politically correct encounter situations where inclusion comes up against its limits. Politics embracing cultural diversity and progressive approaches to gender and sexuality do not fit easily together when what is taken to be a distinct culture rests on patriarchy or homophobia. Likewise, opposition to religious fundamentalism can rub up against secularizing projects of Western imperialism. In such instances, an ideal of inclusivity is clearly inadequate: not every position is compatible with every other.

Left embrace of democracy denies democracy's limits. It wants to hide itself from the ways democracy necessarily depends on and requires exclusion. Insofar as left political theory adopts democracy as its primary aspiration, it disavows the fundamental antagonism conditioning politics as such. For the left (in the United States and in parts of the European Union), democracy thus takes the form of a fantasy of politics without politics (like fascism is a form of capitalism without capitalism): everyone and everything is included, respected, valued and entitled. No one is made to feel uncomfortable. Everyone is heard and seen and recognized and has a place at the table (George Lakoff (2008) identifies Barack Obama as a key figure in the new politics, which is precisely this 'politics' of unity, empathy, and understanding).

The criticisms of left embrace of democracy I raise here are part of a broadly shared frustration with and on the contemporary left. Indeed, left complaining or whining might even be the primary mode of left theorizing today. We wallow in misery, in the deadlock in which we find ourselves. But whereas my emphasis is on democracy as the name of left deadlock, of the fantasy of politics without politics, others view the current problem as a crisis of de-democratization (Wendy Brown) or de-politicization (Jacques Rancière). As Rancière makes clear in his writings from the 1990s, elements of the depoliticization thesis resonate with mainstream political discussions of the end of ideology, the rise of consensus politics, and even the neoliberal withering away of the state, that is, the revisioning of the state as just another contractor of economic services – we were told that the era of big government was over. Financial crises that manifest themselves in the United States in 2008 and led to what the Bush administration presented as a necessary 700 billion dollar bailout of banks and institutions 'too big to fail' quickly made this notion seem quaint and unconvincing. Nonetheless, the theme of depoliticization has been a pronounced one in the United States and Europe since the collapse of the Soviet Union. It makes sense, then, to consider this theme more closely, interrogating its suppositions and their applicability in the contemporary setting. If the diagnosis of de-democraticization and de-politicization is correct, then left politics should seek more democracy, should attempt re-politicization. But if I am right about the contemporary democratic deadlock, then a politics that reasserts democracy as the solution to all our problems will continue to entrap us in the same old circuits of defeat. It will fail, moreover, to attend to the politicizations already conditioning the current conjuncture.

In *On the Shores of Politics* (1992), Rancière offers a version of the end of ideology thesis that affiliates this end with a kind of triumph of democracy (a triumph he criticizes). Democracy, Rancière writes, is 'no longer perceived as the object of a choice but lived as an ambient milieu, as the natural habitat of postmodern individuality, no longer imposing struggles and sacrifices in sharp contradiction with the pleasures of the egalitarian age' (Rancière 1992: 22). Such lived democracy is habitat rather than struggle; it is the setting in which we find ourselves rather than a position requiring sacrifice and decision. As habitat, democracy is not itself political. Although this 'becoming modest' of the state appears as a quintessentially modern adoption of the 'same modes of management, communication, and consultation as the business enterprise' (1992: 106), depoliticization, Rancière argues, is actually the 'oldest task of politics' (19). Politics itself brings about depoliticization. Indeed, 'politics is the art of suppressing the political' (11). Rancière's arguments here are elegant and persuasive. They result, however, in an analysis that hinders our ability to think clearly about the current conjuncture. Rancière accounts for the cause of depoliticization, politics itself, but he can't explain the specificity of the present combination of neoliberalism and democracy as ambient milieu. Contemporary depoliticization, then, is but another appearance of the same old problem of politics.

In *Disagreement* (1999), Rancière attends to some of these specificities. He claims that 'the state today legitimizes itself by declaring that politics is impossible' (1999: 110). The present is thus marked by more than politics' paradoxical essence – the suppression of the political. It is characterized by the explicit acknowledgement of depoliticization as the contemporary state's legitimizing ideal. Accordingly, Rancière identifies several elements of contemporary post-politics as they confirm the impossibility of politics and hence legitimize the state: the spread of law, the generalization of expertise and the practice of polling for opinion (Rancière 1999: 112). Polling, for example, renders the people as 'identical to the sum of its parts' (105). 'Their count is always even and with nothing left over', he writes, 'And this people absolutely equal to itself can always be broken down into its reality: its socioprofessional categories and its age brackets' (105). It is worth noting that Rancière's emphasis on law repeats the 'juridification' thesis Habermas offered already in the 1980s. For Habermas, the problem was law's encroachment on the lifeworld. Excess regulation risked supplanting the communicative engagement of participants in socio-political interaction. For Rancière, the problem is a legal resolution of conflict that forecloses the possibility of politicization.

The arguments for post-politics and de-democratization are at best unconvincing and at worst misleading to a left seeking to undo 30 years of neoliberalization. The claim that we are in a post-political time, that politics has been foreclosed, excluded, prevented from emerging, is childishly petulant. It's like the left is saying, 'if we don't get to play what we want, we're not going to play'. The failure of left politics to win, or even score, is equated with a failure of politics as such, rather than acknowledged in the specificity of left defeat. Leftists assume that our lack of good ideas means the end of the political. If the game isn't played on our terms, we aren't going to play at all. We aren't even going to recognize that a game is being played. To this extent, the claim for post-politics erases its own standpoint of enunciation. Why refer to a formation as post-political if one does not have political grounds for doing so? If one already has such grounds, then how exactly is the situation post-political? If one lacks them, then what is the purpose of the claim if not to draw attention to or figure this lack for the sake of political struggle?

Given the successes of the right, moreover, the claim that we live in a post-political time doesn't ring true. In the United States, the right has worked actively to reframe the constitution according to a theory of the unitary executive, to reverse the steps taken towards racial equality by undercutting *Brown v. the Board of Education*, to facilitate the redistribution of wealth to the top one percent of the population, to undermine the Geneva conventions as well as *habeas corpus*, to empower unwarranted state surveillance of the population, and to install a narrow, extreme, version of fundamentalist Christian doctrine into scientific discussions of evolution and climate change so as to disable any supposition of a common world or reality for which we might share responsibility. These are political achievements. To emphasize post-politics prevents us from understanding them as such.

Far from affirming the identity of the people with itself, as Rancière argues, contemporary polls reveal a fundamental split, a fundamental uncertainty, and the excess of politics over attempts to identify the people with 'the calculations of a science of the population's opinions' (Rancière 1999: 105). Since the 2000 U.S. presidential election, ultimately decided by the U.S. Supreme Court, conventional wisdom has affirmed a divide between red and blue states. Polls reveal this split. They express not indecision or variance among groups understood as parts of a whole but instead a fundamental division. Former president Bill Clinton's quip following the election to the effect that 'the people have spoken; we just don't know what they said' is thus misleading. What was clearly spoken was the division in the country. Likewise, polls taken daily, even hourly, during the long U.S. presidential campaign of 2008 *differ* from each other; consumers of political news ingest numbers that *differ* from each other, call each other into doubt, and render the very categories of polling unstable. The gap between polls and electoral outcomes, the failure of exit polls accurately to predict the votes tallied (an issue in both the 2000 and the 2004 elections) and the politicization of this gap as corruption, crime, theft and the racist disenfranchisement of African-American voters express a politics irreducible to the 'postdemocratic metapolitics' Rancière associates with the triumph of consensus.

While it may well have been a compelling account of France in the 1990s, Rancière's version of post-politics is inapplicable to the United States post-9/11. From the present vantage point, Rancière's critique of the spread of law as a primary form of depoliticization appears as a neoliberal argument against governmental oversight and for privatization. Not only does it fail to acknowledge the collapse of regulation in the financial sector, but it also occludes forms of public/private partnership, the rise of private security forces, and contemporary practices of surveillance wherein state agencies rely on private databases. Rancière's dismissal of law, administration and expertise thus cannot serve as a basis for a critique of the neoliberal state's abolition of oversight and neglect of basic governance. I should add that it is also incompatible with the acknowledgement of the widespread scepticism towards science and expertise and the concomitant cultivation and embrace of amateur, ordinary and common opinion, a phenomenon Žižek associates with a general decline in symbolic efficiency (Žižek 1999: 322). Over the last decade, the United States has witnessed the supplanting of expert knowledge by gut instinct, by religious faith, by capacities to know simply by seeing or feeling, and by the rejection of detail and complexity as elitist, unnecessary and unwarranted. In this setting, techno-legal regulation and administration would be an improvement.

Nonetheless, there are two ways that post-politics is a useful descriptor. Post-politics names a specific problem in left political theory: the fantasy of a politics without politics. Such a fantasy animates Michael Hardt's and Antonio Negri's multitude as well as Giorgio Agamben's coming community. It appears as well in the U.S. left's embrace of new social movements and identity politics. Understood in terms of the fantasy of a politics without politics, the problem of post-politics then becomes not one of governance, not one of consensus politics and opinion polls, but rather one linked to the left embrace of identity as the primary term and terrain of political struggle. In accepting an empirical account of identities (an acceptance we can date to the 1980s and 1990s), left endeavours towards inclusion and recognition ended up naturalizing rather than politicizing markers of identity. We treated identities as sociological rather than political categories and hence as unable to figure universal claims. For example, a term like 'people of color' fails to function as a universal but designates instead exclusion from the category 'white'. It works sociologically as an empirical description rather than politically as a claim to universality. To be clear, this failure of identity categories to function politically is not always and everywhere the case. It is not a necessary outcome of identity politics. Nonetheless, it is widespread and it works against the building and invigorating of a contemporary left.

A second way the concept of post-politics can be useful is as an accentuation of the depoliticization of democracy. In the current conjuncture, to argue for democracy is to argue for more of the same. It is vehemently to demand what is already present, accepted, agreed on. To appeal to democracy is to appeal to the process in place. To this extent, democracy does not establish another stage (to use Rancière's formulation for disrupting a particular regime of appearance). It does not open onto the universal or mobilize a segment of society as society. Such mobilization was possible when democracy named an opposition, whether to oligarchy or absolutism or fascism or colonialism. In these instances, to stand for democracy was to stand against another order constituted against democracy. These days, though, when right and left agree on democracy, when democracy is the underlying supposition, when it provides the basic vocabulary of law and politics, to emphasize democracy is simply to invoke our 'ambient milieu', to try to have politics without politics.

Before proceeding, I should acknowledge my uncertainty regarding my lack of confidence in democracy. Perhaps my doubts stem from the wrong concept of democracy. Or perhaps they oscillate between concepts, ultimately relying on no concept whatsoever. There are at least three sites a theory of democracy might designate:

1. democracy might designate a site of resistance, struggle or opposition;
2. democracy might designate a system of governance, order or rule;
3. democracy might designate a society, culture or spirit (ambient milieu).

Which of these three is correct? Derrideans would say the fourth one: democracy is always to come and hence necessarily exceeds the three aforementioned sites. But this answer is just another version of 'I know but nevertheless'. Democracy remains an ideological fantasy covering the failures, excesses and obscenities of real existing democracy. The Derridean response thus returns me back to where I started: democracy as the solution to the problems of democracy or the democratic capture of left aspirations to equitable and sustainable distributions of resources, labour and its products.

Derridean democracy to come and the post-politics, post-democracy thesis are two sides of the same coin. They are two aspects of democratic time, past and or future, but not now (Žižek might say that their relation is that of a parallax; we can see democracy from each perspective but not from the two perspectives simultaneously). Consider a chant repeated at hundreds and thousands of protests over the last decade: *What do we want? Democracy! When do we want it? Now!* This chant works as a protest because it is clearly impossible. What would happen if the response were 'Okay, protestors, you've got your democracy. Now what are you going to do?' Imagine the executive branch of the U.S. government walking off the job, handing their codes and files and top-secret stamps to the throngs outside their gates, the protestors wondering what to do with their puppets, signs and bongos as they fragment into affinity groups and try to decide what their goals and priorities are. The protestors are not really demanding democracy now. Their demand is not meant to be met.[2]

Democracy has already arrived – as language of right and left, governance and electoral politics, ambient milieu. This is what democracy looks like, real existing democracy. To avoid the trauma of the real, of getting what we wished for, leftists move from actuality to possibility (from what we have to what could be), a move, incidentally, perpetually denied socialist critics of real existing socialism.

But this move from actual to possible democracy doesn't quite work. It misses its own movement or moving, the torsion that the shift from actual to possible entails. Žižek's description of the temporal anamorphosis (distortion) of *objet petit a* is appropriate here:

Spatially, *a* is an object whose proper contours are discernible only if we glimpse it askance; it is forever indiscernible to the straightforward look. Temporally, it is an object which exists only qua anticipated or lost, only in the modality of not-yet or not-anymore, never in the 'now' of a pure, undivided present. (Žižek 1993: 156)

This description applies to democracy. Democracy is anticipated or lost, but never present. When one looks at the present, all one sees is a gap, perhaps manifested by multiple attempts to fill it, as in the various definitions of democracy as resistance, governance or ambient milieu. There can be past democratic ideals – nostalgic fantasies of Athens, town meetings, our days in the resistance – or there can be hope for the future, justification of present acts in terms of this future, but there isn't responsibility now. So disavowing democracy's arrival, democracy now, contemporary left fantasies of democracy animate its diagnoses of post-politics and inspire its rejections of law, regulation and the state.

In the account I've offered thus far, democracy appears as an obscure object-cause of desire, something that can never be fully attained or reached without ending the desire for it. But this is only one aspect of *objet a*. The other is its status in drive, not as something lost but as a hole or gap, not as an impossible lost object but as loss itself. Drawing from Lacan, Žižek construes drive as fixation, not as the thing onto which one is fixated (Žižek 2006: 62). In drive, enjoyment comes from missing one's goal, from the repeated yet ever failing efforts to reach it that start to become satisfying on their own. Drive circulates around an object, generating satisfaction through this very circulation. Perhaps paradoxically, then, drive is at the same time disruptive. Fixation cuts into and derails the regular course of things, what is taken for the conventional patterns of everyday life, assessments of benefit and risk, pragmatic realism, and the organic attempts to secure the conditions of life. It's a traumatic kernel in the reality of the symbolic order itself.

This drive dimension better describes democracy for the left; it is our circling around, our missing of a goal, and the satisfaction we attain through this missing. It accounts for the attachments and repetitions to which we are stuck, even as this very stuckness undermines our possibilities for political efficacy. Democratic drive, then, is another way of conceiving democracy as ambient milieu, a way that highlights the circulation we can't avoid, but which at the same time can't be understood as giving us what we want even as it gives us something else instead, some kick of enjoyment. We protest. We talk. We complain. We undercut our every assertion, criticizing its exclusivity, partiality and fallibility in advance as if some kind of purity were possible, as if we could avoid getting our hands dirty. We sign petitions and forward them to everyone in our mailbox, fetishizing communication technologies as the solution to our problems. We worry about conservatives even as we revel in our superiority – *how can anyone be so stupid?* We enjoy.

If drive involves circling around and fixating on a loss, hole or gap, how should the hole around which democracy circulates be understood? For it is neither the empty place of power, nor a missing and impossible unity, nor a master signifier ready to be articulated into a signifying chain, conceptions that all rely on a logic of desire. In *Disagreement*, Rancière considers the beginnings of politics in terms of 'an original twist that short-circuits the natural logic of "properties"' (Rancière 1999: 13). This twist, torsion or interrupted current, he argues, is the wrong of a fundamental dispute that causes politics to occur. The smooth space of the natural order confronts a gap or hole. So there is not a natural order but a twisted one. There is a not a smooth flow or set of natural relations and identities; there is a hole distorting the whole, belying the fiction or fantasy of the whole thing or order.

The hole of this original torsion is a missing conjunction, a missing link between people and government that political theory tries at best to express and at worst to occlude (government of the people, by the people, for the people, over the people). The torsion of politics means that the people and the government are not present at the same time (even Rousseau had to gloss his fantasy of the unrepresentable sovereignty of the people with a nod to Corsica). Where the people are present, there is chaos, disruption. Where government is present, then the people are not. Insofar as the people can never be fully present – some don't show up, didn't hear what was going on, were mislead by a powerful speaker, were miscounted from the outset – their necessary absence is the gap of politics.

The torsion of wrong, Rancière adds, makes each class different from itself (Rancière 1999: 18). A class doesn't simply persist doing its part in a larger complete whole. Political groups such as classes are not functional components of a prior order, an assumption as depoliticizing as it is foundational to political theory. Insofar as they are split within the whole and within themselves, the many cannot be politically. Polls try to make them appear through a count, which is always a kind of miscount and distortion. The many, though, is only political through and as one, few or some: one represents us to ourselves as many; few make possible and organize, provide themes and ideas; some do all the work (business types present this as the 80/20 rule). The people are always non-all, not simply because the many is open and incomplete but because it cannot totalize itself. The rule of a leader, party, or even the law compensates for or occupies the hole of the missing conjunction between people and government (Žižek 2002: 187–9).

Hence Rancière in *Disagreement* separates political activity into two parts, two opposed yet entangled logics of politics and the police (Rancière 1999: 28). We might think of these two parts as a division between legitimacy and order; each has what the other needs and/or wants, something that remains inaccessible, out of reach, something that would destruct if attained. To split politics into itself and the police is a way of saying there is no pure politics; there is more than upheaval; there is rule and ruling requires limits. In Rancière's terms 'politics acts on the police' (1999: 33).

Žižek adds the insight that cutting through both aspects of politics is the difference between rule and its obscene supplement, the difference between the letter of the law and the shadowy, nightly law on which it rests (Žižek 1999: 234–5). We invoke this obscene dimension when we speak of dirty politics, dirty tricks and dirty cops, of those who are willing to get their hands dirty. Žižek refers to the famous line from Saint-Just: 'nobody can rule innocently' (1999: 221). This is another way of saying that there is no pure politics, no innocent position. Politics' primal scene, as it were, is its confrontation with compromise, failure, exclusion, the means necessary to get things done.

Different discursive formations provide the fantasies occluding (and securing) this obscene fact. The master's version: there is one who can rule innocently. Fantasies of the master forever seek to find this One. The democratic response replaces the one with all (as if such an all were possible without its constitutive exclusion): everybody can rule innocently. The perverse response: I'm willing to make myself into an instrument of the dirty work. Rancière has yet another response. He fully accepts that there is no innocent position (this is his notion of the police), but adds that this is not a problem because anybody can rule.

That anybody, anybody at all, can rule is, for Rancière, the scandal of democracy. Democracy is the scandalous actuality of the contingency of the political. Via Žižek, I understand 'contingent' to describe something that cannot be wholly grounded in its conditions of possibility (Žižek 1993: 157). That which is contingent is possible; it could have been otherwise. Possibility, though, is not the same as contingency: what happens contingently could have not happened although it did. But why does Rancière associate contingency with democracy? Why is democracy another word for the contingency of the political? In the remainder of this chapter, I take up this question of contingency, focusing on changes in Rancière's discussions of politics and equality from *On the Shores of Politics* to *Disagreement*. My interest here is in the way Rancière's arguments provide insight into the failure of democracy as a political form. Politics exceeds its narrative capture in and as democracy. As he attempts to equate politics and democracy, Rancière brings to expression the deadlock of democratic drive.

II.

I've presented post-politics and democracy-to-come as two sides of the same coin. I've suggested that the gap separating and connecting them be thought in terms of the closed circuit of drive rather than the openness of desire. So understood, democracy is not what we seek but never reach, not a name for political desire as such, but instead a term for the capture of political aspiration in the circuit of drive. Democracy is a remnant from the nineteenth and twentieth centuries we have yet to escape. Differently put, if democracy names a political desire that is never fulfilled, then it is accompanied by a political drive wherein democracy is what we fail to escape. In this dimension of drive, democracy designates our political stuckness.

In *On the Shores of Politics*, Rancière presents politics as the depoliticizing response to democracy and equality as the counter-factual supposition to be repeatedly inscribed in and on the community. There is politics, he argues, because there is democracy. Politics responds to democracy. Understanding why requires the introduction of the notion of equality.

Rancière construes equality in terms of the creation of a space of appearance: 'the egalitarian polemic invents an insubstantial community completely determined by the contingency and resolve of its enactment' (1992: 87). In the setting of material hierarchy, of a factual inequality wherein the few have much and the many have little, a claim to equality is spoken; it is contingently and forcibly introduced into the setting. Equality is posited and with it the demand that inequality be explained. This egalitarian polemic enables the people to appear, not as an actually existing empirical group but as a supposition of reason and community. It contrasts with the facts of actual inequality and produces a shared rationality by effecting a division between how things appear and how they can be made, forcibly, to appear. The postulation of a shared meaning, Rancière argues, 'assumes a symbolic violence both in respect of the other and in respect of oneself' (1992: 49). Politics results from this specifically democratic mobilization of appearance. It responds to the inscription of equality into facticity by trying to suppress it.

In *Disagreement*, Rancière changes this formulation of politics as a depoliticizing response to equality as he focuses on the confrontation equality stages. The opposition between democracy and politics becomes an opposition between politics (understood as democratic) and the police. Politics is no longer the force of depoliticization; rather, it is an activity antagonistic to policing (the other side of the antagonism constitutive of the political).

I read the opposition Rancière introduces in *Disagreement* as internal to the political, as a division within politics between two perspectives linked by the gap between them (a parallax gap wherein the same object appears slightly different when looked at from the perspective of each division). Politics, then, is the manifestation of this gap or division. Examples of the division between politics and the police in the history of political thought appear as divisions between legislation and execution, between constituent and constituted power, and between the people as sovereign and as subject. In Rancière's version, politics occurs in the meet-up between two heterogeneous processes – the process of the police and the process of equality. The police is 'an order of bodies that defines the allocation of ways of doing, ways of being, and ways of saying [. . .] it is an order of the visible and the sayable' (Rancière 1999: 29). Rancière uses the term politics to designate 'whatever breaks with the tangible configuration whereby parties and parts or lack of them are defined by a presupposition that, by definition, has no place in that configuration – that of the part of those who have no part' (1999: 29–30).

Each aspect of political activity, politics and police, makes something appear. Politics – through the egalitarian inscription – disorders appearance, making something appear different from the way it appeared before. As an ordering or arranging, a counting, an assigning of place, the police, too, makes something appear differently. The clash of politics in the gap and confrontation of two heterogeneous logics, then, is a clash not between how things are in reality or between reality and appearance, but in their modes of appearance or representation.

The part of no part thus does not designate the objectivity of an empirical group excluded from the political domain. It's not another way of referring to a politics of identity by locating a marginalized other. For Rancière, political subjectification is not political identification, rather it is the inscription of a name, a disidentification and the registration of a gap (Rancière 1999: 36). He explains that there are 'political modes of subjectification only in the set or relationships that the *we* and the *name* maintain with the set of 'persons', the concrete play of identities and alterities implicated in the demonstration and the worlds – common or separate – where these are defined' (1999: 59). Political subjectification stages polemical scenes, paradoxical scenes that bring out the contradiction between two logics. Indeed, it stages the very contradiction between police logic and political logic (Rancière 1999: 41). This contradiction is thus internal to politics; it is politics. Accordingly, it makes most sense to think of the part that is not a part as precisely such a gap: a gap in the existing order of appearance between that order and other possible arrangements, the space between and within worlds. The Lacanian term for the part of no part would then be *objet petit a*, an impossible, formal object produced as the excess of a process or relation, a kind of gap that incites or annoys, the missingness or not-quite-rightness that calls out to us.

A benefit of considering the part of no part as *objet a* is its accentuation of the fact that this part is not a substantial part, not an empirical designator such that exclusion is the exclusion of people and their inclusion necessarily a political good. For example, religious fundamentalist might be a name of the part with no part in a liberal order. To include that part would distort and disrupt the order predicated on the exclusion of fundamentalist religion. Moreover, if one views the contemporary political terrain as a global one, as constituted through the elimination or subsumption of an outside (Hardt and Negri's view), then understanding the part of no part as *objet a* can enable the theorization of the holes and gaps constitutive of the shape this global terrain takes. Finally, to treat the part of no part as *objet a* brings out the fact that the democratic narrativization of the gap or torsion of politics is but one possible narration. There are others, others that might and should be rejected or accepted but that will continue to incite, annoy, thwart and produce us. Acknowledging these torsions will not make them go away. But it might enable us better to comprehend and tactically address ways that we enjoy being politically stuck.

I've argued that the part of no part be understood as *objet a* and that the division between politics and the police be read as an internal division within politics. If this division is not internal to politics, then Rancière's position falls into a kind of hysterical pure politics of resistance (see Žižek's critique in *The Ticklish Subject*). Much of his discussion in *Disagreement* suggests such a pure politics, particularly insofar as Rancière insists that politics is essentially democratic and that it is democratic because it consists in the confrontation between the police logic and egalitarian logic. For example, he views politics has happening 'very little or rarely', only when the mechanisms of majesty and management are 'stopped in their tracks by the effect of a presupposition that is totally foreign to them yet without which none of them could ultimately function: the presupposition of the equality of anyone and everyone, or the paradoxical effectiveness of the sheer contingency of any order' (1999: 17). I turn, then, to Rancière's account of equality and its association with contingency.

As I have already mentioned, in *On the Shores of Politics*, the inscription of the egalitarian signifier into a factual situation makes the 'community of equals appear as the ultimate underpinning of the distribution of institutions and obligations' (Rancière 1992: 91). The declaration of equality makes the artifice of power visible as such. It makes a given arrangement of power appear as contingent, unnecessary, as something that has been created and could be otherwise. *Disagreement* develops this contingent dimension of equality such that equality means the sheer contingency of social order. Rancière describes the empty freedom the Athenians presented to philosophy as 'the equality of anyone at all with anyone else: in other words, in the final analysis, the absence of *arkhê*, the sheer contingency of any social order' (1999: 15). What is given isn't necessary; it didn't have to be this way. It could have been otherwise. Politics occurs when a given order of the police (or partition of the perceptible) is confronted with its own contingency.

Rancière's emphasis on contingency is not convincing on its own (without an accompanying discussion of possibility and necessity). It's more akin to a fantasy. *Like Cinderella, I could really be a princess! I coulda been a contender, a rock star. I still could!* Žižek argues that fantasy, 'in its most basic dimension, implies *the choice of thought at the expense of being*: in fantasy I find myself reduced to the evanescent point of a thought contemplating the course of events during my absence' (1993: 64). What Rancière presents as contingency is a fantasy that holds out the possibility of 'anything at all' as a way of accommodating a situation without confronting the reality of the constraints in producing it, the determinations of socio-economic systems and practices. Such a fantasy is ultimately a fantasy of my own non-existence in the situation I confront, as if somehow I was outside of and apart from the situation's determinations. Leaving aside the historical question of whether democracy in Athens really meant that anyone could rule, anyone at all – the determinations of gender and slavery suggest otherwise – a reading of politics as rooted only in its own contingency is too close to a state of nature or view from nowhere to be useful for thinking through the challenges of contemporary politics. What possibilities does a given actualization abandon or even foreclose? Simply to say that such an actualization was contingent rather than necessary neglects this question and obscures the persistence of necessity under the fantasy of what could have happened.

The claim that the situation could have been different fails to provide leverage towards making the situation different. Few today argue that our arrangements and institutions are natural or inevitable. For example, social conservatives in the United States readily accept that the family is a social construct and a fragile one at that. Hence, they offer policies designed to shore up a specific patriarchal vision of the nuclear family. They don't think sexual identity is fixed; thus, they sponsor programmes that try to make gay people straight. When democracy is our ambient milieu, contingency's revelation of artifice, of the fact that things might be otherwise, loses any efficacy it might have had in setting where order was justified as natural.

More troubling, though, is Rancière's rendering of contingency specifically as *equality*. Rancière's idea is that insofar as the political order is not given by nature, not determined, it rests on an underlying contingency; its foundation is its lack of foundation (Rancière 1999: 16). Politics occurs as an interruption, the interruption of a freedom that 'makes real the ultimate equality on which society rests' (16). The question, then, is the status of this equality. A foundation in equality is not the same as the contingency of inequality; underlying a contingent inequality could well be multiple contingent inequalities or the possibility of equality. Rancière seems to be saying that something about equality is Real, more than an inscription and the production of a common space of disagreement. He suggests, in other words, that equality is not only an aspect of the symbolic order but also a distorting of or gap within that order. When equality appears it appears within the order of the police. Politics forces it to appear and so changes this order, but the appearing remains within the order of the police. The order of the police is a condition for equality's appearance.

Rancière describes the equality he has in mind as that of any speaking being with any other speaking being. The logic of equality, he says, is a logic that dispels the count and distribution of the order of the police; it 'disrupts this harmony through the mere fact of achieving the contingency of the equality, neither arithmetical or geometric, of any speaking being whatsoever' (1999: 28). Not surprisingly given this supposition of communicative competence on the part of speaking beings, Rancière considers the necessary suppositions of understanding in language. His account differs from Hábermas's primarily on the matter of consensus (*Disagreement* has an extended critique of Habermas on a number of grounds including Habermas's distinction between poetic and argumentative language, his shift away from a third-person perspective, and his account of performative contradiction). For Habermas the supposition of understanding means that we have to suppose an orientation to agreement. Rancière disagrees. He argues that understanding is rooted in a supposition of equality and this supposition leads to disagreement.

Consider a command. To follow a command, the commanded must comprehend what the command is and understand that the command is meant to be followed or observed. The implication of this supposition of understanding, Rancière tells us, is that even hierarchy is premised on an underlying equality. He writes: 'equality is an assumption that another understands what I'm saying' (33). In the setting of what Žižek tags the decline of symbolic efficiency, this assumption of understanding is rather far-fetched. Our present political-mediological setting is one of dissensus, incredulity and competing conceptions of reality. Most of the time it seems like no one understands much of anything anyone says. As Žižek points out, Donald Davidson designates the background assumption that everything another says is not completely wrong the 'principle of charity'. It's a presumption of underlying agreement on which disagreement rests. Davidson argues that 'charity is not an option [. . .] charity is forced on us; whether we like it or not, if we want to understand others, we must count them right in most matters' (cited in Žižek 2000: 114). The decline of symbolic efficiency points to the withering away of this principle of charity: less and less are people today forced to presume charity or understanding. There are strong material-technological explanations for this withering away. Not only are communication technologies charitable in our stead, making connections with other machines, but the interconnecting of ever more people lets us find enough of those who share our convictions that we don't have to believe. In fact, we can imagine a contemporary post-linguistic argument to the effect that equality is the assumption that nobody understands what anyone else is saying, an assumption of shared incomprehension (but an incomprehension that connects nonetheless), a kind of incommensurability that morphs into its opposite. Insofar as equality can be just as easily viewed in terms of incomprehension as it can be viewed as a supposition of understanding or principle of charity, Rancière's argument for equality is unconvincing.

Nonetheless, what is important for Rancière is the equality that underpins understanding. He explains:

> To say that there is a common speech situation *because* an inferior understands what a superior is saying means that a disagreement, a provisional confrontation must be set up between two camps: those for whom there is an understanding within understanding, that is, that all speaking beings are equal speaking beings, and those who do not think so. The paradox is that those who think there is an understanding within understanding are for that very reason unable to take this deduction any further except in the form of a disagreement, since they are bound to show a result that is not at all apparent. (Rancière 1999: 49)

Rancière's argument is a nice twist on the idea of performative contradiction (and I have in mind here Habermas's use of this idea). Typically, the idea of a performative contradiction emphasizes an incompatibility between the content of an utterance and the conditions that make its uttering possible (Lacan discusses this as a difference between the enunciation and the enunciated). In introducing the performative contradiction, one forces the speaker to consider what she has to assume not just to make her point but to speak at all. Rancière's version of this idea employs a response to the claim of performative contradiction that says, 'So what? I still disagree' (a response that drives Habermasians crazy). He highlights the side of the one accused of contradicting herself (her conditions of speech), attributing to her an obstinacy or resistance in the face of full awareness of contradiction. This obstinacy, moreover, is what sets politics in motion. The stand-off makes politics necessary.

More specifically, then, Rancière takes the fact of understanding and says that from this fact one can assume that speaking beings are equal or one can assume that speaking beings are unequal. Those who insist that speaking beings are equal cannot rely on logic or reason to persuade their opponent (who doesn't accept them as equal). But their insistence can nonetheless stage the disagreement between them and their opponent; it can make the division between them appear. The one who asserts that understanding means that speaking beings are equal has to prove what is not apparent. He has to demonstrate what does not appear to be the case. He has to make equality appear in a setting of apparent inequality. The stage of political conflict, then, is constituted through positing an equality of speaking beings in a setting of inequality, through making this common stage appear via disagreement. Rancière's example is the worker who proceeds counterfactually as if there were a shared world of argument, even though there is not one, even though the owner of capital does not recognize or does not want to recognize this common world.

So politics appears through the disagreement of speaking beings, through a clash or gap produced in the encounter between their worlds and their words, a clash Rancière describes as a staging of the contradiction between the egalitarian logic and the logic of the police. The assertion of egalitarian logic is contingent; one might assert equality or one might not. But here's the rub: *disagreement* is what makes the stage of political conflict appear. Equality is one contingent vehicle for disagreement. Equality can serve as such a vehicle because it is counter to the conditions in which it is claimed (hierarchical conditions); hierarchy, however, is only one potentially politicizable condition of a given participation of the perceptible. The Real attached to equality, then, is the gap, missingness, or not-quite-rightness that the claim to equality makes apparent; it's the Real of a disjuncture. More precisely, *objet a* attaches to equality as the gaze that perceives the gap effected by the distortion of the Real (see Žižek 1993: 66).

Rancière's emphasis is on the disagreement between those who claim the equality of speaking beings and those who deny it. Such disagreement is not essential to equality but can be made to appear through other counterfactual claims. We can imagine the inscription of liberty as a claim to freedom in conditions of unfreedom; or the converse: a claim of unfreedom in conditions of freedom. One says an unfettered market in commodities is freedom. The other responds: I disagree. We can imagine the inscription of ownership in the commons, a claim to private property in conditions of common goods. One says: this is mine. The other responds: I disagree. And we can imagine claims of belonging in conditions of fear and exclusion. The one says: I am one of you. The other says: I disagree. Each of these instances of liberty, ownership and belonging stages a conflict within a given partition of the perceptible and attempts to make an alternative partition appear. But none is the same as the egalitarian inscription and none is strictly speaking democratic. There are non-democratic stagings of disagreement. And because there are non-democratic stagings, politics is not necessarily democratic.

In fact, more problematic than Rancière's reduction of politics to the clash between the egalitarian logic and the logic of the police is a further entanglement that the instances of liberty, ownership, and belonging highlight, namely, the implication that the police is necessarily counter to democracy and democracy necessarily counter to the police. The order of the police may well involve a rule of law that seeks to preserve and protect certain liberties, common or public spaces, and practices of belonging. Contesting this order can involve taking the position of the part of no part and making the violence and contingency of the order's partition of the perceptible appear. Insofar as such contestation is contingent, its effects are neither necessary nor necessarily democratic. Again, we might think here of instances of a fundamentalist (whether religious, ethnic, or market) rejection of its democratic foreclosure; the fundamentalist occupies the place of what a democratic partitioning must exclude and makes this exclusion appear in its contingency and violence.

If the dominant order presents itself as democratic, if the order of the police is the order of democracy, then only non-democratic stagings of disagreement can be political since only they set up a contrast with the conditions of their utterance. Far from exclusively democratic, politics can be fascist, anarchist, imperial, communist. Such stagings are holes, gaps, torsions in the contemporary setting, sites that annoy and excite. Rancière narrativizes the introduction of gaps as necessarily democratic and laments the contemporary post-political conditions of impossibility for their emergence. My argument is that gaps emerge; they are political, and contemporary democracy organizes enjoyment as an effect of circling around these gaps. Rancière's narrativization, then, is better understood as an image of the capture of politics in the circuits of democratic drive. The contemporary setting is not one of simple opposition between post-political consensus and the eruption of irrational violence (an eruption Rancière views as a return of the archaic). Rather, it involves the satisfaction of the democratic drive as its aims remain inhibited.

A consideration of the gaze may help clarify my idea here. Rancière emphasizes the way the disagreement over the equality of speaking beings stages a conflict and enables the appearance of the contingency of the prior partition of the perceptible. Disagreement depends on a prior thwarting of the aim, equality. Rather than achieving the goal of equality, then, disagreement produces satisfaction, I'll call it a political satisfaction, by staging the lack of equality. Although it might seem paradoxical that one's aim is not agreement to one's demand – the demand for equality – the paradox occurs only in the register of desire. Understood in terms of drive, the bending or distortion or change in the aim such that the failure to reach it provides enjoyment makes sense. The aim of equality is sublimated in the drive to make one's disagreement with inequality appear. One gets satisfaction by appearing in one's disagreement. This provides its own partial enjoyment and in fact can only continue to provide it so long as there is inequality, so long as the ostensible aim in staging the disagreement isn't reached.

Rancière's account of the staging of disagreement, rather than figuring the political as such (the political confrontation between politics and the police) exemplifies the sublimation of politics in democratic drive. As drive, democracy organizes enjoyment via a multiplicity of stagings, of making oneself visible in one's lack. Contemporary protests in the United States, whether as marches, vigils, Facebook pages or internet petitions aim at visibility, awareness, being seen. They don't aim at taking power. Our politics is one of endless attempts to make ourselves seen. It's as if instead of looking at our opponents and working out ways to defeat them, we get off on imagining them looking at us. And since, as Lacan reminds us in Seminar XI, the object of the drive is of total indifference (1998: 168), the disagreement one imagines oneself being seen as staging is irrelevant.

Egalitarian or elite, anarchist or communist, any political gap will provide a charge sublimated as it is within the democratic drive. We want to make ourselves seen as political without actually taking the risk of politics.

Notes

1. Hence the signifying importance of the Holocaust as the exception, the one undeniable thing that must be clearly condemned. Of course, even this seemingly clear instance of 'that which must be condemned' can be and is increasingly becoming cloudy as with movements towards acknowledging the suffering of the German people during the war or in Hollywood films that consider the 'good Nazis'.
2. A reader on my blog countered with the claim that 'this is what democracy looks like' is a more common protest chant. He argues that this is an assertion of a present democracy as disruption. I disagree. In the United States protests are not disruptive in the least. They are occasions for families to march together, for vendors to supply t-shirts and bumper stickers, for cops to photograph activist groups. They are licit and momentary, guarantees and supports of the system they ostensibly contest.

Works Cited

Lacan, Jacques (1998), *The Seminar of Jacques Lacan. Book XI. The Four Fundamental Concepts of Psychoanalysis*, ed. Jacques-Alain Miller; trans. Alan Sheridan, New York: Norton.

Lakoff, George (2008), 'Much More than Race: What Makes a Speech Great', posted to Open Left on March 24, 2008. Available at http://www.openleft.com/showDiary.do?diaryId=4751.

Rancière, Jacques (1992), *On the Shores of Politics*, trans., Liz Heron, London: Verso.

— (1999), *Disagreement*, trans. Julie Rose, Minneapolis: University of Minnesota Press.

Žižek, Slavoj (1993), *Tarrying with the Negative*, Durham, NC: Duke University Press.

— (1999), *The Ticklish Subject*, London: Verso.
— (2000), *The Fragile Absolute*, London: Verso.
— (2002), *Revolution at the Gates*, London: Verso.
— (2006), *The Parallax View*, Cambridge, MA: The MIT Press.
— (2008), *In Defense of Lost Causes*, London: Verso.

Out of Place: Unprofessional Painting, Jacques Rancière and the Distribution of the Sensible

Ben Highmore

One way of characterizing the challenge that Jacques Rancière poses is to see his work as a refusal to 'know your place', to see it as a refusal to endlessly reconfirm and re-establish the places that have been set for workers or, for that matter, for left-wing intellectuals. 'Knowing your place' might well be one of the abiding questions of the engaged intellectual: 'how is it that the worker knows his or her place?' The answers supplied have tended to posit a form of internalization (of power relations) as the solution to this riddle: for Louis Althusser, for instance, the inculcation of ideology is performed by a subject identifying as the object of a police enquiry; for Bourdieu it is the inevitable result of a profound and constitutional pedagogy.[1] But what if these solutions were not the answer to the riddle but another aspect of its seemingly effective performance? In designating the place for workers (as those that 'know their place') and intellectuals (as those that understand how it is that workers 'know their place') aren't the likes of Althusser and Bourdieu complicit in staking out a certain distribution of proper places? Or, more fundamentally, doesn't their work perform the very thing it sets out to unmask (in this Althusser takes the role of the police inspector and Bourdieu the role of the class instructor)?

Rancière begins elsewhere. His challenge begins when we ask: what happens when a worker or an intellectual refuses to know their place? What happens, for instance, when an educator no longer teaches what they know, but starts to teach from a position of shared ignorance? What happens when a worker refuses to follow the path ascribed to them as either good worker or revolutionary worker, and instead opts for bohemia, for dreams, for painting or poetry? In following these seemingly more wayward trajectories, Rancière concocts an approach to the social that is alive to its 'distribution of the sensible'. For Rancière the distribution of the sensible is 'the system of *a priori* forms determining what presents itself to sense experience. It is a delimitation of spaces and times, of the visible and the invisible, of speech and noise, that simultaneously determines the place and stakes of politics as a form of experience' (2004b: 13). This phrase, 'the distribution of the sensible' (*le partage du sensible*) takes us into the heartland of Rancière's approach to politics and art. Synoptically it is the uneven carving-up of the sensorial world. By continually starting from specific instances of the orchestration and re-orchestration of the sensorial, Rancière provides a form of aesthetic attention that alters our understanding of, and our approach to art and politics. In privileging moments of aesthetic impropriety (in politics as much as in art), Rancière writes critical histories that examine breaches in the distribution of the sensible and that uncover the virtual equality that is ushered in when the distribution of the sensible is disrupted, and when a redistribution of the sensible is possible.

In this essay I want to explore the opportunities and problems that arise from Rancière's work, particularly in relation to his choice of the 'distribution of the sensible' as the insistent object of study. I will look at a concrete example of a possible breach in the distribution of the sensible: a 1938 exhibition that included a number of artworks by mineworkers from the Ashington colliery (in the North-East of England) called 'Unprofessional Painting' (as we will see much will hang on the term 'unprofessional'). But to get there I need to spend some time quickly outlining the force of Rancière's aesthetic approach to the social.

I. The Distribution of the Sensible

In an essay from 2005 Jacques Rancière announces his project in the following way: 'it is not a matter of art and taste; it is, first of all, a matter of time and space' (2005: 13). He is writing about aesthetics, but he could just as easily have been writing about politics:

Politics, indeed, is not the exercise of, or struggle for, power. It is the configuration of a specific space, the framing of a particular sphere of experience, of objects posited as common and as pertaining to a common decision, of subjects recognized as capable of designating these object and putting forward arguments about them. (2009a: 24)

The formulation acts like a warning: you thought aesthetics was about taste or what counts as art, but you are getting ahead of yourself, you need to take some steps back. You thought politics was all about power or struggle but you need to start from a more concrete encounter with the social.

The social, for Rancière, is the orchestration of times and spaces, of sense and non-sense. It is the sensual, material realm that demarcates what is visible and what remains invisible, what gets heard as speech and what remains noise (who is heard and who is not). On another register (one less explored by Rancière) it parcels out the whole realm of sensuous, passionate life: proper and improper emotional responses, the allocation of disgust and delight to smells and sights; and so on. But this 'distribution of the sensible' is reliant on a temporal geography that will underwrite it: here, in this place, at this time, you will count as a problem to be solved; but at another time and place you will just be invisible. Take for example the speech of someone recounting their life story in a psychiatrist's office and that same speech being heard in a job interview. What is an appropriate and understandable discourse in one place becomes inappropriate disclosure (and unlistenable-to) in another. The cultural materiality here is not a hierarchy of established values that might be representative of a class or a culture (or the conventions of a social scene), it is the physical space of the doctor's office and the interviewing room, the segment of time that it fills (the 50-minute hour, for instance), and the way they connect and disconnect with the orchestrations of other spaces and times.

Rancière's doctoral thesis, which was published in France in 1981 as *La Nuit des prolétaires* (translated and published in English in 1989 as *The Nights of Labor: The Workers' Dream in Nineteenth-Century France*), established a set of awkward examples that have continued to vivify his thinking and reveal the centrality of understanding the social world as the distribution of times and spaces. In the book he follows the lives of worker-poets and worker-philosophers in the 1830s and 1840s many of whom are converts to the utopian socialism of Saint-Simon. The lacemakers, seamstresses, cabinetmakers, joiners, printers, and floor-layers that Rancière introduces us to, do not unite in fraternal solidarity demanding the recognition of the 'dignity of labour'. Far from it, they know that hard manual labour robs them of what they most want: freedom. Instead of desiring better conditions, they desire the languid existence of bourgeois leisure: time to think, time to write. So they graft during the day, and live their bohemian lives at night.

For Rancière it is a significant discovery: the history of workers doesn't correspond to the historical mission laid out by doctrinaire Marxists. More crucially it lays the foundations for Rancière's political aesthetics. In the social setting of *The Nights of Labor* the worker is faced with an orthodox distribution of time, money, rest and leisure, where 'good workers' (seen by both the left and the right) exert themselves on the work of others during the day and replenish themselves by sleep during the night. To know your place as a worker is also to know your partition of time: a time for work, a time for rest. By stealing back the hours of night for another form of existence (another form of labour), the worker-poets don't simply intervene in the production of poetry, they intervene in the distribution of allotted time. And this intervention, for Rancière, is the condition of politics:

Politics occurs when those who 'have no' time take the time necessary to front up as inhabitants of a common space and demonstrate that their mouths really do emit speech capable of making pronouncements on the common which cannot be reduced to voices signalling pain. (2009a: 24)

These worker-poets are performing politics by reusing the nights that are meant for proletarian sleep, by making themselves at home in a medium that is not theirs (poetry, philosophy), and dreaming of a life that they weren't born to. Politics, in Rancière's idiosyncratic use of the term, is

whatever shifts a body from the place assigned to it or changes a place's destination. It makes visible what had no business being seen, and makes heard a discourse where once there was only place for noise; it makes understood as discourse what was once only heard as noise. (1999: 30)

Against the dominant usage of the term 'politics', that would see it as a theory of parties and policies, Rancière trenchantly allows it only one meaning: the enacting of a disruption in the parcelling out of allocated space, time and sense. The workers' dreams make no sense in the prescribed landscape of *proper* social relations. Rancière will describe his subsequent enquiries as emanating from this capturing of night by the worker-poets: 'substituting a topography of the *re*-distribution of the possible and a multiplicity of lines of temporality for the order of time prescribing the impossible has been a red thread in the process of my research' (2005: 23). The possible is the workers' dream deemed as impossible by a temporal ordering that would offer workers no time and no dreams. It is only by behaving improperly, of disrespecting propriety, that a new distribution of the sensible is possible. It is this concentration on the distribution of time and space, and the possibilities for reconfiguring it, that link Rancière's approach to politics to his approach to art. Indeed, in as much as art performs a possible alteration of the distribution of the sensible, it becomes the privileged example of meta-politics.

In his many writings on aesthetics Jacques Rancière takes to task the usual slicing up of art historical periods. Rather than settle for the one-thing-after-another of art's 'isms' (futurism follows impressionism which is followed by surrealism, and so on), or of the epochal designations of 'realism' followed by 'modernism' and then on to 'postmodernism', Rancière suggests another route that both follows the historical patterning of periodization while also flouting its logic of substitution. Central to his account of art is the emergence of what he calls the 'aesthetic regime of art': the form of art emerging at the end of the eighteenth century that fundamentally reorganizes the sensorial realm. His example comes from the writer Stendhal. Looking back on his late eighteenth-century childhood in provincial France Stendhal recounted that the noises that marked his childhood were 'ringing church bells, a water pump, a neighbour's flute' (Rancière 2009a: 4). Stendhal would, of course, go on to be one of the major authors of literary realism. For Rancière the crucial item on Stendhal's list is the water pump: it is the inclusion of this that demonstrates the way that the aesthetic regime of art is founded on an indifference to a hierarchy of significance (the water pump is as glorious as the cathedral organ and the church bells) and on a concomitant sensual pedagogy (the material recognition of the water pump as a potentially glorious noise). Thus the literary registering of the everyday constitutes a 'new writing made up of sensory micro-events, that new privilege of the minute, of the instantaneous and the discontinuous', which is coterminous with a 'new education of the senses informed by the insignificant noises and events of ordinary life' (2009a: 10, 6). The republican ethos of Stendhal's French childhood provides the sensorial education that will allow the erstwhile insignificant sounds of water pumps to become significant, and this education will be an aesthetic one, enacted by a range of different elements including literature. What marks this example out as particularly significant for Rancière is not because it demonstrates the point where 'water pumps' are added to the list of things that can be considered significant and worthy of a writer's attention. It is because at the moment when a 'water pump' challenges the regime of the worthwhile (what Rancière calls, somewhat confusingly, the 'representative regime of art'), a door swings open showing the whole sensate world as (potentially) worthy of attention.

For Rancière art is always social in as much as it always describes a sensorial realm, and is always involved in 'constituting forms of common life' (2009a: 26). Stendhal's writing not only demarcates an orchestration of sensual life, whereby what had been considered insignificant becomes newly significant, it allows new collective and democratic experiences to come into being on the grounds that older forms of significance have been disorganized and superseded. This is the aesthetic regime of art and it simultaneously names an indifference to any established hierarchy of iconography, while it also establishes a new form of identification of art as art. But rather than this latter assertion heralding the autonomy of art (the autonomy of art from social necessity), it does precisely the opposite: it ties art to the communities of those prepared to recognize it as such. Take, for instance, the case of painterly abstraction. Traditional art history might understand the difference between an abstract painting and a naturalistic rendering of a scene of ordinary life as the radical refusal of the former to enter into the business of representation. For Rancière both forms of naturalism and abstraction partake in a redistribution of the sensible that establishes ordinariness and equality as their tacit but insistent leitmotif:

> for abstract painting to appear, it is first necessary that the subject matter of painting be considered a matter of indifference. This began with the idea that painting a cook with her kitchen utensils was as noble as painting a general on a battlefield. (2004b: 54)

Abstract paintings function to constitute 'forms of common life' by their invitation to a community of painters and onlookers that anything is a possible subject of art. And this, in a different way, is also true of the painting of a cook. What both share is their negative response to a regime of art where everything had its place in a pecking order of value:

> What is the kernel of the aesthetic revolution? First of all, negatively, it means the ruin of any art defined as a set of systematisable practices with clear rules. It means the ruin of any art where art's dignity is defined by the dignity of its subjects – in the end, the ruin of the whole hierarchical conception of art which places tragedy above comedy and history painting above genre painting, etc. To begin with, then, the aesthetic revolution is the idea that everything is material for art, so that art is no longer governed by its subject, by what it speaks of; art can show and speak of everything in the same manner. In this sense, the aesthetic revolution is an extension to infinity of the realm of language, of poetry. (2003: 205)

The aesthetic revolution in art is meta-political in both its redistribution of sensual matter (what is worthy of notice, what is paintable, sayable) and in its positing of a community of those who might recognize a new redistribution of sensible matter.

Such an approach to aesthetic work is without doubt valuable: not only does it reconfigure a host of tired demarcations of 'movements', but more importantly it also connects art to life in an urgent and vital way. Yet it also poses a number of questions that might return us to older questions of the relationship between art and life in their material entanglements. For instance, if the painting of a cook rather than a king opens up art to the equality of matter, then how are we to think of this sign of equality? Is it actual or virtual? A probability or a possibility? And what are the limits of its potential redistribution? If a cook is worthy of the painter's eye, is this same attention to be aimed at everything? Is there nothing that either falls below the horizon of visibility or else provokes taboos in relation to visibility and points to the limits of indifference? (For instance same-sex and interracial desire or young people's sexuality are hardly a matter of indifference to newspaper columnists and censors.) If a disruption occurs that potentially allows everything to be deemed worthy of attention then how long does this equality last before 'a cook' just becomes part of a new list of acceptable images? And, lastly, what sort of communities might be fashioned under this sign of equality, that also participate in other 'distributions of the sensible' that might be connected with other material spaces and times (not least the spaces and times that are signalled by such designations as 'professional' and 'unprofessional')? To pursue this last question (and that is all I can do here) it is worth looking at a concrete and complex example of a community of painters.

II. Unprofessional Painting

The exhibition 'Unprofessional Painting' opened on 8 October 1938 at the Bensham Grove Educational Settlement in Gateshead-on-Tyne. It then travelled to the Wertheim Gallery (London), to the Peckham Health Centre and Fulham Town Hall (both in London), and on to the Mansfield Art Gallery (Glasgow). The exhibition consisted of around 50 paintings and about a dozen sculptures by the Ashington Art Group as well as paintings by other so-called Sunday painters. The exhibition was organized by

Robert Lyon, a lecturer in painting at Durham University (who was also the group's tutor) and Julian Trevelyan and Tom Harrisson, both of whom were involved with the recently formed social experiment Mass-Observation.[2] The Ashington Art Group had its beginnings in 1934 as part of a self-organized education club associated with the colliery and facilitated by the Workers Education Authority (the WEA). Members would ask the WEA to supply tutors who would deliver a lecture course on their specialist topic (evolution, for instance). In 1934 the topic was 'Art Appreciation' and Robert Lyon, their lecturer for the course, started off by showing black-and-white slides of Italian Renaissance painting. It quickly became clear that this approach was failing to engage the interests of the audience (who were predominantly mineworkers). After some discussion it was suggested (by Lyon, it is presumed) that 'appreciation' of art might be arrived at by practical activities (lino cuts, wood cuts and later by painting).

By 1938 the group had become an enthusiastic painting collective (who, crucially, put money from painting sales into a communal fund). When the Mass-Observation team visited the colliery town, the art group were an established force that had been the subject of various newspaper articles and radio programmes. The 'pitmen painters' painted a world of work and leisure, of domesticity and public life in and around Ashington: football games, colliery buildings and machinery, dogs, pigeon crees, allotments, pithead baths, committee meetings, mining incidents and injuries, local characters, and so on. For Tom Harrisson two related aspects of the paintings were crucial. First: the lack of perspective in the paintings (or rather lack of conventional 'single-point perspective') was seen as being truer to ordinary life than the technically proficient work of engaged social realists such as the Euston Road school of left-leaning artists (William Coldstream, Lawrence Gowing, and so on). Second: the artists were seen as imbuing their subject matter with an urgent and authentic materiality:

It is easy to forget that every factory, slag heap and villa, was built by man. But it is not easily forgotten by the bricklayers, joiners or spinners. So when Harry Youngs, who holds the iron for the blacksmith to strike in the shop at the bottom of the pit shaft, and has but two fingers on one hand, sees a pit pony, it is more than lovely; it is his living his life.[3]

The sense of authenticity that was ascribed to the Ashington miners' paintings by the press and by the likes of Tom Harrisson was connected to the enthusiasm that various avant-gardist tendencies had for untutored and 'naive' work in general. The work of the Cornish fisherman, chandler and artist Alfred Wallis, for example, had recently been championed by artists like Ben Nicholson and Barbara Hepworth. Wallis' paintings rendered the Cornish coast or a journey to Newfoundland on bits of timber using industrial paints, and in a manner that was closer to a medieval mapping of space and significance, than forms of naturalism that had been practised since the renaissance.

Such untutored work could be seen as performing avant-gardist 'practices of negation'. The phrase is T. J. Clark's and it is his way of grouping together the varied interests of cutting-edge modernist and realist artists since Courbet. For Clark 'a practice of negation' was an innovation in painting 'whereby a previously established set of skills or frame of reference [...] are deliberately avoided or travestied, in such a way as to imply that only *by* such incompetence or obscurity will genuine picturing get done' (1985: 55). The examples that Clark offers include:

Deliberate displays of painterly awkwardness, or facility in kinds of painting that were not supposed to be worth perfecting. Primitivisms of all shapes and sizes. The use of degenerate or trivial or 'inartistic' materials. Denial of full conscious control over the artefact; automatic or aleatory ways of doing things. A taste for the margins and vestiges of social life; a wish to celebrate the 'insignificant' or disreputable in modernity. (1985: 55)

Clark's description of avant-garde 'practices of negation', which corresponds, to some degree, to Rancière's 'aesthetic regime of art', would explain the value of the art of Wallis or the Pitmen Painters *for* the professional avant-garde artist. Here, then, were untutored artists using inartistic materials (household paints, bits of cardboard), painting subject matter that was considered insignificant not just artistically but also socially; painters who were also positioned in a distinctly marginal relationship to the centrality of the metropolis.

For Julian Trevelyan, a surrealist artist and one of the Mass-Observation team, the work of the Ashington Miners, as well as work by various Sunday painters that he was getting to know, put the very project of avant-gardism in jeopardy:

These, and other Sunday painters that I now met, filled me with doubt about the value of professionalism in painting; they expressed themselves with so much more 'sayfulness' (a favourite word of Tom Harrisson) than most of the exhibitors at the London Group or the Royal Academy; they had had to forge for themselves their own language, and the need to do so must have been very strong in the first place. (1957: 91–2)

No doubt 'sayfulness' is a coded way of establishing the value of authenticity, but it seems clear that for an art practice that attempts to negate the values of tutored art then the work of those who haven't actually been tutored is bound to fashion the kinds of work that the tutored can only envy.

Yet from the perspective of the Ashington miners it is equally clear, of course, that what is being painted is not a negation either in its subject matter or in its style of rendering. Dogs and work, for instance, aren't painted as examples of the 'insignificant' or 'the margins of life' but as central and significant aspects of life. Similarly 'painterly awkwardness' is not achieved by shrugging off technical proficiency in the name of the aleatory and the automatic, but by never having access to technical proficiency in the first place. The staging of the Unprofessional Painting exhibition, then, could be seen as a clash between two 'distributions of the sensible' that result in a mutual misunderstanding based on a common object of value (the paintings). The explanations of the paintings' value would no doubt be different depending on whose perspective is followed, yet both seem to allow the aesthetic regime of art to establish the possibility that anything and everything might be a subject for art.

During the middle weekend of the Gateshead exhibition a debate was organized around the proposition that 'Anyone Can Paint'. In the end the motion was carried by 40 to 20, but it seems clear that the mix of responses was characterized by mutually incompatible values. For instance one of the speakers who voted against the motion was 'George Downs, who sells women's underwear in the Caledonian Market' who, although he had a few pictures in the exhibition, knew that not everyone could paint as he 'has been trying to paint for years' but 'still couldn't'.[4] For the *Daily Express* 'professional painters need have no jealousy' in regard to an exhibition like Unprofessional Painting, as it would simply increase interest in the sort of work that professional avant-garde artists were then doing. The exhibition similarly re-established a distribution of the sensible around the very value of professionalism by ascribing prices for the various artworks according to whether the 'artists' were represented by a gallery or not (£50 for a painting by the postal worker and artist Louis Vivin and £2 for a painting by an Ashington miner). Vivin (who had recently died) transmogrified from a professional postal worker to a professional artist. The Ashington painters remained 'pitmen' painters – professional proletarians who painted.

The exhibition 'Unprofessional Painting' could be seen to establish a disagreement or a dissensus at its core. This dissensus revolves around not just whether 'anyone can paint' but the delegation of professionalism. The people that gathered in Gateshead were professionals but their professions were clearly distinct: a mix of those whose professions were first and foremost proletarian and those who had the luxury to be writers, painters, journalists. Yet this gathering in a place, where everyone involved has a set of common concerns (albeit concerns that point in different directions) and a set of common objects, offers an image of community without a shared identity. For Rancière the community-making function of the art of the aesthetic regime is not producing identity-driven communities but communities organized around dissensus and dis-identification:

I do not take the phrase 'community of sense' to mean a collectivity shaped by some common feeling. I understand it as a frame of visibility and intelligibility that puts things or practices together under the same meaning, which shapes thereby a certain sense of community. A community of sense is a certain cutting out of space and time that binds together practices, forms of visibility, and patterns of intelligibility. (2009b: 31)

The extent to which the group that gathered at Gateshead to discuss whether 'anyone can paint' were a community of sense is, I think, an open question. To some degree it seems clear that various parties were talking past each other, and that their relationship to the aesthetic regime of art were of different degrees. Yet it also seems apparent that congregating around this space and time was a virtual equality that if it didn't become operative was at least glimpsed.

Rancière reminds us that there has always been music, dancing, picturing, and so on, but what we call 'Art' has only been in existence for the last 200 years. 'Art', in this sense, is coterminous with the aesthetic regime of art, it is art that declares its autonomy from the world of social necessity, and in so doing reveals its (necessary) relationship to the social (in Kantian terms it reveals that its social purpose is its purposelessness). Yet one of the characteristics of the aesthetic regime of art is the way that it includes previous regimes of art within its folds: 'the temporality specific to the aesthetic regime of the arts is a co-presence of heterogeneous temporalities'; 'at a given point in time, several regimes coexist and intermingle in the works themselves' (2004b: 26, 50). In the case of the Unprofessional Painting exhibition one of the shared aspects of its aesthetic regime was a desire to imagine a return to a time before 'Art', a time when there was always music, dancing, picturing, a time when this was an ordinary part of life. For Trevelyan 'the Ashington Group was part of a movement which would make painting as common an art as music once was'.[5] The aesthetic regime of art incorporates the desire for its dissolution as its crucial characteristic.

The aesthetic regime of art is not an image of utopia: it is animated not simply by the political disruption of the sensible and the opening up of the sensate world to the proposition of equality. It is also animated by what, in another context, Rancière calls police logic. This is the force that marshals the sensible to the orchestration of an uneven and interested distribution. Rancière has the measure of how crucial the term 'professional' is in the breaching and redistribution of sensorial orchestrations. Writing in *Disagreement* about the trial of the revolutionary Auguste Blanqui in 1832 Rancière recalls the details of the exchange between the judge and Blanqui:

> Asked by the magistrate to give his profession, Blanqui simply replies: 'proletarian'. The magistrate immediately objects to this response: 'That is not a profession', thereby setting himself up for copping the accused's immediate response: 'It is the profession of thirty million Frenchman who live off their labor and who are deprived of political rights'. The judge then agrees to have the court clerk list proletarian as a new 'profession'. Blanqui's two replies summarize the entire conflict between politics and the police: everything turns on the double acceptance of a single word, *profession*. For the prosecutor, embodying police logic, profession means job, trade: the activity that puts a body in its place and function. It is clear that proletarian does not designate any occupation whatever, at most the vaguely defined state of the poverty-stricken manual labourer, which in any case, is not appropriate to the accused. But, within revolutionary politics, Blanqui gives the same word a different meaning: a profession is a profession of faith, a declaration of membership of a collective. (1999: 37–8)

The dissensus at Gateshead figured the term 'professional' as the 'elephant in the room' – the strikingly obvious aspect that no one was talking about. It organized whether you were called a painter or a 'Pitmen' painter. Yet 'unprofessional' was not simply a marker of class it was also a profession of faith that pulled in multiple directions not least towards the possibility that 'everyone can paint'.

III. Conclusion

As an art historian or art critic Jacques Rancière is out of place. Indeed he claims to have little expertise in the area, falling into writing about art just because people asked him to. The invitations to write came mainly from an art community who had found something in his book

The Ignorant Schoolmaster that connected with their own situation, their own desires. But what would be the measure of Rancière's contribution to art history? In relation to the art historical business of characterizing different forms of art and periodizing the *longue durée* of art history, Rancière's approach is not startlingly new. His characterizing of the 'aesthetic regime of art' often seems to invoke an understanding of the long history of 'the modern' that is often taken-for-granted in art historical and 'lit-crit' circles. For instance his insistence that the aesthetic regime is constituted by an endless inauguration of 'the splendour of the insignificant' in visual art and literature is a common assessment of the rise of the novel and the emergence of 'the painting of modern life'. John Dewey, for instance, could claim in 1934 that 'the novel has been the great instrument of effecting change in prose literature. It shifted the centre of attention from the court to the bourgeoisie, then to the "poor" and the labourer, and then to the common person irrespective of station' (1980 [1934]: 189). The point here is not that it is Dewey rather than Rancière who could be seen as originally minting this insight, rather that even in 1934 you didn't really need to argue your case for a claim like this. Similarly Rancière's elaborate demarcation of different regimes of art is both suggestive and limited. In plotting out a movement from an ethical regime to a representative regime and on towards an aesthetic regime of art (which can also include within it aspects of the other two regimes) Rancière's schema is no more or less convincing than other macro histories of art: it fits where it touches. Indeed Christa and Peter Bürger's historical sociology of art and literature, which plots out the functional transformation of literature across a similar time period, and which finds similar functional breaks as Rancière (though to quite different ends), is in many ways a much sturdier edifice.[6]

The value of Rancière's work does not lie here but in the way he puts art and politics out of place. The value of being out of place is not to carry on 'business as usual' but to alter the realm of the sensible. And it is here that Rancière's phrase 'the distribution of the sensible' works to enliven our commerce with art and with the sensual and sensorial world more generally. From one perspective it might seem that Rancière hugely overestimates the social currency of art by making it his prime example of where such a distribution of the sensible is figured, but in doing so he takes art (and non-art) out of the realm of the taken-for-granted (where everything is in its place). Perhaps it is in his claim that art is a form of meta-politics where the overestimation of art results in constraining the real productivity of pursuing the 'distribution of the sensible'. The metapolitics of art links him, in my mind at least, to German critical theory (particularly to Walter Benjamin) and Rancière's assessment of the role of the art of the aesthetic regime can read like an amalgam of Adorno and Benjamin:

Aesthetic art promises a political accomplishment that it cannot satisfy, and thrives on that ambiguity. That is why those who want to isolate it from politics are somewhat beside the point. It is also why those who want it to fulfil its political promise are condemned to a certain melancholy. (2010: 133)

In the end, though, it is not such thoughts that seem most compelling for taking art to a new place. It is as sensible matter that connects to other sensible matter that allows art to become improper and to share some space with the larger world of sensible matter.

In treating art as sensible matter Rancière connects artworks to communities of people in ways that are compelling and materialist: 'Human beings are tied together by a certain sensory fabric, a certain distribution of the sensible, which defines their way of being together; and politics is about the transformation of the sensory fabric of "being together"' (2009c: 56). There are myriad ways forward from this work that would include not just rethinking what we do with art, but also thinking about the aesthetic dimension of our social worlds more generally. It might mean, for instance, that we need to look much more seriously at the sensual and sensorial dimensions of our social worlds. If Rancière offers nothing else he at least offers us a way of taking aesthetics away from a world of fussy deliberations about 'art and beauty' into a lively social world animated by the full range of passions.

Notes

1. Louis Althusser's influential description of ideological identification is central to his 1969 essay 'Ideology and Ideological State Apparatuses (Note towards an Investigation)' (Althusser 1971). Pierre Bourdieu's homology between education and social positioning is most extravagantly described in *Distinction: A Social Critique of the Judgement of Taste* (Bourdieu 1992 – first published in France in 1979). Rancière's reply to Althusser is given in *La Leçon d'Althusser* (1974); his reply to Bourdieu can be found in *The Philosopher and his Poor* (2004a – first published in France in 1983).

2. This very short account is reliant on Trevelyan's autobiography *Indigo Days* (1957) and William Feaver's *Pitman Painters: The Ashington Group 1934–1984* (1993), as well as on Lee Hall's play (which is based on the same material) *The Pitmen Painters* (2008). It should be noted that there is scant material from the painters themselves about their work though Feaver quotes from various interviews he conducted when researching his book. For material on Mass-Observation, cf. Hubble (2006) and Chapter 6 of Highmore (2002).
3. Tom Harrisson cited in 25 September 1938, *The Sunday Sun* (reproduced in Feaver 1993: 79).
4. *Daily Express*, 18 October 1938, in Feaver (1993: 82).
5. *Daily Express*, 18 October 1938, in Feaver (1993: 82).
6. Cf. Bürger and Bürger (1992). This point is also made by Gail Day in her 'The Fear of Heteronomy' (2009), which offers a trenchant critique of Rancière's lack of attention to avant-gardism.

Works Cited

Althusser, Louis (1971), 'Ideology and Ideological State Apparatuses (Note towards an Investigation)', in *Lenin and Philosophy and Other Essays*, trans. Ben Brewster, London: New Left Books: 127–86.
Bourdieu, Pierre (1992), *Distinction: A Social Critique of the Judgement of Taste*, trans. Richard Nice, London: Routledge.
Bürger, Peter and Bürger, Christa (1992), *The Institutions of Art*, trans. Loren Kruker, Lincoln: University of Nebraska Press.
Clark, T. J. (1985), 'Clement Greenberg's Theory of Art', in *Pollock and After: The Critical Debate*, ed. Francis Frascina, London: Harper and Row: 47–63.
Day, Gail (2009), 'The Fear of Heteronomy', *Third Text*, 23 (4): 393–406.
Dewey, John (1980 [1934]), *Art as Experience*, New York: Perigee Books.
Feaver, William (1993), *Pitman Painters: The Ashington Group 1934–1984*. Manchester: Carnet Press.
Hall, Lee (2008), *The Pitmen Painters*, London: Faber.
Highmore, Ben (2002), *Everyday Life and Cultural Theory*, London: Routledge.
Hubble, Nick (2006), *Mass-Observation and Everyday Life: Culture, History, Theory*, Basingstoke: Palgrave.
Rancière, Jacques (1974), *La Leçon d'Althusser*, Paris: Gallimard.
— (1989), *The Nights of Labor: The Workers' Dream in Nineteenth-Century France*, trans. Donald Reid, Philadelphia: Temple University Press.
— (1999), *Disagreement: Politics and Philosophy*, trans. Julie Rose, Minneapolis: University of Minnesota Press.

— (2003), 'Politics and Aesthetics', interview with Peter Hallward, *Angelaki*, 8 (2) (August): 191–211.
— (2004a), *The Philosopher and His Poor*, trans. John Drury, Corinne Oster and Andrew Parker, Durham: Duke University Press.
— (2004b), *The Politics of Aesthetics*, trans. Gabriel Rockhill, London and New York: Continuum.
— (2005), 'From Politics to Aesthetics?' *Paragraph*, 28 (1): 13–25.
— (2009a), *Aesthetics and Its Discontents*, trans. Steven Corcoran, Cambridge: Polity.
— (2009b), 'Contemporary Art and the Politics of Aesthetics', in *Communities of Sense: Rethinking Aesthetics and Politics*, ed. Beth Hinderliter, William Kaizen, Vered Maimon, Jaleh Mansoor, and Seth McCormick, Durham: Duke University Press: 31–50.
— (2009c), *The Emancipated Spectator*, trans. Gregory Elliott, London: Verso.
— (2010), *Dissensus: On Politics and Aesthetics*, trans. Steven Corcoran, London: Continuum.
Trevelyan, Julian (1957), *Indigo Days*, London: MacGibbon and Kee.

The Wrong of Contemporary Art: Aesthetics and Political Indeterminacy

Suhail Malik and Andrea Phillips

In 2009, after attempting to settle upon an organizing principle for an online participatory archive of contemporary art, the editors of *e-flux* web journal concluded 'that no objective structure or criterion exists with which to organize artistic activity from the past twenty years or so' (Aranda et al. 2009). Recognizing the ubiquity and persistence of the term 'contemporary art', the editors remark that it is the 'unanswerability' of its 'self-evidence' that gives the horizon for art's production and reception over the period. In the first of two ensuing *e-flux* journal issues dedicated to the question 'What is Contemporary Art?' a number of well-known historians, artists, curators and critics were asked to respond to this paradox wherein contemporary art is without definition or criteria yet is recognizable. Hal Foster (2010) summarizes the tenor of agreement among the contributors by stating that 'the category of "contemporary art" is not a new one. What is new is the sense that, in its very heterogeneity, much present practice seems to float free of historical determination, conceptual definition, and critical judgment'. While such a recognition of contemporary art regularly leads to a dismissal of its capacity to engage in effective forms of political critique, it is exactly the condition of 'heterogeneity' more precisely, art's indefiniteness *and* identifiability – that, in sharp contrast, Jacques Rancière establishes to be art's political specificity. Rancière lucidly identifies the paradox at work here in his notion of 'art in the aesthetic regime' – that which 'asserts the absolute singularity of art and, at the same time, destroys any pragmatic criterion for isolating this singularity' (2004b: 23). For Rancière, aesthetics is the condition for art's horizonless dispersion to nonetheless be the specific and cogent operation of a coherent logic of art. Contrary to any lament of the loss of art's critical or political endeavours, it is this logic that for Rancière manifests a politics that is more radical and more principled with respect to equality than the normative criteria and methods exemplified well by Foster's determination of a critical art.

Assuming a consistency between Rancière's conceptualization of politics in the mid-1990s, primarily in *Disagreement* (first published in French in 1995), and his characterization of the politics of contemporary art in the mid-2000s, we seek here to identify what the claimed politics for art in the aesthetic regime might be. This requires the elaboration of a torsion in Rancière's thinking of aesthetics, specifically through an examination of the fate of the 'wrong' that is the operation of politics in the earlier work and its connection to the later writings on art. This leads us in turn to understand Rancière's cogent articulation of a logic of art as being not only entirely fitting to the current terms of contemporary art's affirmation and distribution but also to expose the limitations of the politics occasioned in and by such art.

The basic schema of Rancière's logic of art is that of an originary complexity: the non-identity of art to itself and the identification of this non-identity, which aesthetics provides in its relation to art. Aesthetics does so because, following Schiller's *Aesthetic Education* (Rancière 2009a: 27ff.), it affirms the 'free play' between the production of art (*poiesis*, form-making) and its 'reception' by a passive sensibility (*aisthesis*, matter) such that the two 'stand [. . .] in immediate relation to one another through the very gap of their ground' (Rancière 2009a: 8). Contrasted to both the representative regime of art, in which *poiesis* and *aisthesis* are pegged to one another by a common account that gives these dimensions of art a systematic integrity, or the ethical regime of art, in which images are considered only with regard to a truth or communal meaning outside of the art itself (Rancière 2004b: 20–12; 2009a: 28), each of which fill in or close the gap between *poiesis* and *aisthesis*, in the aesthetic regime there is no art in general, no unity or coherence but only the singularity or particularity of art affirming the paradoxical consistency of aesthetics. It is this paradox that allows art to be identified at all: aesthetics is 'a way of thinking the paradoxical sensorium that *made it possible to define* the things of art' in and as the exappropriation of its own production (Rancière 2009a: 11, emphasis added). Without aesthetics art would disappear into the particularity of its each time unique inventions (and the singularity of art would vanish with it). Aesthetics is then the name of the paradoxical identification of the non-identity of art. If there is to be something called contemporary art, aesthetics and art are indissociable. Hence, Rancière's formulation of 'art in the aesthetic regime' or what is here called 'aesthetics-art'.

The schema of aesthetics-art is concisely presented in Rancière's formulation that 'art is art insofar as it is also non-art, or something other than art' (2009a: 36). Here, Rancière distinguishes what we call aesthetics-art from forms of art that through their content and form (location, use of signifying materials, etc.) propose a deliberative social and/or political agenda typical of a historical notion of 'critical art' that Rancière deftly characterizes as 'set[ting] out to build awareness of the mechanisms of domination to turn the spectator into a conscious agent of world transformation' (2009a: 45). Rancière's examples of this 'critical art' range across modernism, from John Heartfield to Martha Rosler, Kryzstof Wodizcko and Hans Haacke. Such work is premised upon the assumption that the viewer is incapable of recognizing the relations between image circulation, power and capital (for example) and seeks to lead her or him to recognize (better yet) the horrors of the world (war, capital, misogyny, xenophobia, etc.). Instead of activating a 'suspension of relations of domination' (Rancière 2009a: 53) – an aim that would seem inherent in the critical ambitions of such work – such art in fact does nothing to suspend the 'relations of domination'. Quite the opposite. For Rancière, aesthetics-art takes a different tack and has different effects. It shifts the focus of an analysis of art's politics away from its internal or socially-driven claims towards its structural capacity to *instantiate* a politics, effecting a different relation with the spectator of art than historical models of critical art. The free play between *poiesis* and *aisthesis* in aesthetics-art sustains a 'tension' between, on the one hand, a logic that maintains the separation of art from other kinds of sensory experience – all the more to have political effectivity through its autonomy from the domination of life by capitalism and so on – and, on the other, a logic that pushes art towards 'life' in which it becomes fully integrated as an effective and direct form of activity (Rancière 2009a: 46). The tension between these two logics 'combin[es] these two powers' and 'involves [. . .] heterogeneous logics': ensuring its 'political intelligibility' by borrowing from its tendency to indistinction, or non-identity, while its identity proposes a distinction from other kinds of production (Rancière 2009a: 46).

In *The Emancipated Spectator* Rancière uses a particular installation by Josephine Meckseper to illustrate his argument. The work, an untitled piece shown in one of the main cultural venues of the second biennial of contemporary art in Seville in 2006, comprises photographs taken of the protests that accompanied the announcement of the invasion of Iraq in 2003. These photos are accompanied elsewhere in the city by a vitrine of objects – perfume bottles, advertising notices, pieces of packaging, etc. – placed in a shop front that bring to the viewer's attention the ways in which the critical culture that sought to disestablish the society of the spectacle in the late 1960s has itself been spectacularized and commodified. Meckseper's work uses vitrines, images and unadulterated (although re-arranged) commodities to 'escape the limitations of radical aesthetics and get into the more complex, seductive sides of power' (Gillick 2008). Differently from the earlier photomontages of Martha Rosler, whose art is identifiably 'critical' along the lines advocated by Foster, with Meckseper's art the viewer also recognizes her own complicity in the image bank itself, and in this respect it is typical of the rhetorical strategies of contemporary art. While the viewer is still told what she does not want to see – 'the participation of your supposed gestures of revolt in this process of exhibiting signs of distinction governed by commodity exhibition' (Rancière 2009b: 29) – she is also shown what she does not know how to see: her participation in the commodification of revolt, that the 'march is itself a march of image consumers and spectacular indignations' (2009b: 28). The doubling in Meckseper's work with the spectator's informed or 'emancipated' position distinguishes it from the previous generation of critical art artists: it is the *absence* of a structuring narrative controlling the reception or delivery of these images in relation to the vitrine of objects that makes it exemplary of aesthetics-art.

Whatever politics this art has is generated not from its ostensible subject matter alone but from 'the short circuit and clash that reveal[s] the secret concealed by the exhibition of images' (2009b: 29). Such a 'clash' instantiates a politics for Rancière for two main reasons:

1. The free play between *poiesis* and *aisthesis* means that aesthetics-art has no order(ing) between these aspects. Maintaining the free play between *poiesis* and *aisthesis* is in Rancière's terms a politics because it disarticulates the police order (1999: 28–31). The latter is the most general notion of the organization of power, places, ways of being and

doing; the system of distribution and legitimization, however formally or informally implemented, that is a 'governing of th[e] appearance' of bodies which Rancière famously calls the partition of the sensible.[1] It is exemplified most cogently for Rancière by Plato's organization of politics in which the *logos* is not just the sonorous emission itself *qua* speech but also 'the *account* that is made of speech', most pointedly, that a sound *is* speech and not just noise or animal grunt (1999: 22–3). In the police order, the two dimensions of the *logos* – speech and its account – are pegged. In these terms, the representational and ethical regimes are kinds of police orders for the arts (and there are, Rancière notes, better and worse police orders). For Rancière, 'whatever breaks the tangible configuration of parties governed by a presupposition' of such partitions is politics (1999: 29) – and this is exactly what the admission of the free play of the aesthetic regime does in maintaining the scission between the two dimensions of the *logos* for art. More generally, politics disorders the police order and has 'no place in that configuration' (Rancière 1999: 29–30); it does not assume anything of that partition or power.

2. The free play between *poiesis* and *aisthesis* for aesthetics-art admits an equality between them and so of the active intelligence and passive sensibility by which they are respectively characterized. In affirming such an equality, aesthetics-art observes the principle of equality that is for Rancière 'solely' what occasions politics (1999: 31) in that it is equality that is instantiated by 'whatever breaks the tangible configuration' of a police order. That the principle of equality is the occasion of politics is understood in more familiar terms when it is rendered as the bringing together of community and non-community together, or what Rancière phrases the 'assertion of a common world' (1999: 55). If community is in part constituted through what it takes to be legitimate communications which are its own (its *logos* as the account of what speech counts) then the assertion that 'speaking beings are equal because of their common capacity for speech' is a version of the principle of politics since it 'redistributes the way that speaking bodies are distributed in an articulation between the order of saying, the order of doing, and the order of being' (Rancière 1999: 55). For aesthetics-art, the disestablishment of the account of the *logos* or the more general sensorium by the repartition of the sensible is assured not only by the 'free play' and 'gap' between *poiesis* and *aisthesis* but also by the absence of any

narrative that binds these two aspects of the work to one another in any inevitable way.

A politics of aesthetics-art along these lines can be elaborated by referring to Thomas Hirschhorn's installations and sculptures. These works range in scale and site but are recognizable by his use of signature 'everyday' materials such as plastic sheeting, tin foil, newspaper, parcel tape and cheap wood, and by their overload of information – visual, textural, architectural. In particular, the artist's 'monuments' produced from the late 1990s, each located in traditionally poor districts of the cities whose festivals commission them, enlisting local people to work on their construction and maintenance, and each dedicated to a philosopher – Spinoza (Amsterdam, 1999 and 2009), Deleuze (Avignon, 2000) and Bataille (Documenta, Kassel, 2002) – are widely regarded as sites of potent contradiction in debates about contemporary 'political' art, not least in their forceful if schematic meshing of those who live in the areas in which the monuments are situated with the contemporary art milieu who seek them out as part of their circuit of interests. Contrary to initial readings of the *Monuments*, Hirschhorn dismisses the idea that his work needs to be activated through some sense of community participation. Speaking of the *Bataille Monument*, commissioned for Okwui Enwesor's *Documenta XI*, and sited in a Turkish area of Kassel a taxi-ride away from the main sites of the exhibition, Hirschhorn says:

Rather than triggering the participation of the audience, I want to implicate them. I want to force the audience to be confronted with my work. This is the exchange I propose. The artworks don't need participation; it's not an interactive work. It doesn't need to be completed by the audience; it needs to be an active, autonomous work with the possibility of implication. (2004: 25)

Hirschhorn's articulation of the concept of an active work resembles Rancière's notion of a politics generated not only by the free play between the art's production and its 'reception' by whomever, but also by the principle of equality between the artist, the local inhabitants and the visitors interested in the work of a renowned contemporary artist:

[T]he only social relationship I wanted to take responsibility for was the relationship between me, as an artist, and the inhabitants. The artwork didn't create any social relationship in itself; the artwork was just the artwork – autonomous and open to developing activities. An active artwork requires that first the artist gives of himself. The visitors and inhabitants can decide whether or not to create a social relationship beyond the artwork. This is the important point. But it's the same in the museum. (Hirschhorn 2004: 29)

Put in Rancière's words, Hirschhorn's distinction between artistic 'activity' and social responsibility is one between the specific aesthetics of politics with 'its own modes of dissensual invention and characters [. . .] which distinguish it from, and sometimes even oppose it to, the inventions of art' (2009a: 46). To be clear: Hirschhorn 'takes responsibility' only for the *social* relationship between himself as artist and the local inhabitants, but leaves the *artistic* relationship open to 'developing relationships' which are beyond the power of the artist himself. While this may sound like a revamped assertion of art's modernist autonomy, such a claim is here taken as being concomitant to the assertion of equality in intelligences and capacities between the local residents and the art cognoscenti, who usually belong to a very different kind of sociological class. In this respect, Hirschhorn's artistic declaration is closer to Rancière's sense of politics than his social responsibility: the monuments are political because their account is not in the hands or mouths of those who 'know their art' – the artist included – nor in those of who know the areas in which they are situated, but in the clash of the two or more ways of speaking, doing and being.

Schematic though the example may be, the crudeness of Hirschorn's *Monuments* and his discourse on them is instructive in highlighting the two primary vectors in Rancière's conceptualization of *how* politics predicated on the principle of equality is occasioned. Their elaboration will not only return us to Rancière's insistence on aesthetics rather than the *logos* as condition of politics but will also, for that reason, make clear the severe limitation of any substantial sense of politics proposed on this basis – including, most proximately, the claims to politics made in and by contemporary art.

First, Hirschhorn's rudimentary juxtaposition of sociologically distinct milieus in the siting of the *Monuments* as well as his juxtaposition of disposable images, philosophical texts and trade building materials within his work are modes of collage that Rancière identifies as a key strategy in critical art, notably in Brecht (2009a: 47–52). But collage is not just one technique among others of modern art for Rancière; it in fact obeys a 'more fundamental aesthetico-political logic' (2009a: 47) in that aesthetics is what '*allows* separate regimes of expression to be pooled' (1999: 57, emphasis added). As such it is the condition for the connecting and disconnecting of different areas, functions, operations, and so on, that is the 'reconfiguring of the partition of the sensible' which 'overturns legitimate situations of communication, the legitimate parceling out of worlds and languages' (1999: 55) – or, in a word, politics. This *general* political principle is demonstrated *in particular* in aesthetics-art as the realization of a 'pure encounter between heterogeneous elements' and as a demonstration of 'the hidden link' between apparently incompatible worlds or ways of being and doing (2009a: 47): the vegetables in Brecht's *Arturo Ui* serving at once as common vegetable and index of the power of commodity capital; Meckseper's vitrines positing objects in the world that are at once desirable (either as commodity or protest politics) and objectionable (the indistinction of the two); Hirschhorn's ramshackle constructions and impoverished locations as venues for prestigious reputational investments for the intellectual and transnational art milieu.

If politics is necessarily predicated on aesthetics, and aesthetics is that which identifies art in its exappropriation of the partition of the sensible then it is understandable that contemporary art looks to Rancière's 'aesthetico-political logic' to secure its claims to be effecting a politico-critical operation that succeeds where the conventional models of critical art did not. Notwithstanding his success in that milieu, Rancière in fact warns against such identifications by insisting on the singularity of aesthetics-art – predicated on its originary complexity – and distinguishing it for this reason from the 'specific aesthetics' of politics. However, even despite Rancière's caveat, if politics is aesthetic 'in principle', if *aesthetics in general* is the condition for politics, then the politics of aesthetics-art has no particularity compared to politics *in general* (and the solace sought by contemporary art in Rancière's aesthetico-political logic is not only warranted but also provided). But it is then not only the 'pragmatic criteria for isolating [art's] singularity' that is destroyed but also that singularity – its criterialess identifiability – which is destroyed with respect to politics.

The quandary here troubles Rancière's formulations of the relation between aesthetics-art and politics to the core. In schematic terms, if contemporary art is political by virtue of its manifestation of the repartition of the sensible it is no longer identifiable as such; the tension between its logics of autonomy and heteronomy tendentiously slackens in favour of its identification with politics in general. The question is whether and how art's singularity, predicated as it is on an *aesthetics in particular* – both identity and non-identity, heteronomy and autonomy – can be sustained if its politics are general. Or, put the other way, the question of how politics happens given Rancière's conceptualization of it then falls back to the question of what the general aesthetics of politics is; that is, whether or not it is distinct from the particular aesthetics of aesthetics-art. The issue here is whether the singularity of art is indeed also the singularity of its politics. That is, it is an issue of identifying what the political instance is *in fact*.

That there is more than one politics to be had within art is expressed by Hirschhorn's distinguishing between 'working politically' as opposed to 'making political work', continuing: 'I wanted to work in the height of capital and the height of the economic system I'm in. I wanted to confront the height of the art market with my work. I work *with* it but not *for* it' (2004: 21). The issue for Hirschhorn, as for Rancière in other terms, is how 'working politically' can be distinguished from 'making political work' and what the latter politics is if it readily accommodates itself to the 'height of capital and [...] the economic system'. The problem here can be elaborated by turning to the second vector in Rancière's conceptualization of how politics is realized: political subjectification. It has been seen that politics' repartitioning of the sensible is how 'those who have no right to be counted as speaking beings make themselves of some account' (1999, 36–7); that is, manifest themselves in both dimensions of the *logos*. What is political in this manifesting is the 'placing in common [of] a wrong that is nothing more than this very confrontation' (Rancière 1999: 37). Wrong is the name for the conflictual conjunction of the police order and politics. The 'transforming [of] egalitarian logic into political logic' is what Rancière calls 'the constitutive function of wrong' (1999: 35). Wrong is how equality occurs in the police order, its political appearance or, more stringently, it is the appearance of politics:

politics is the practice whereby the logic of the characteristic of equality takes the form of the processing of a wrong, in which politics becomes the argument of a basic wrong that ties in with some established dispute in the distribution of jobs, roles, and places. (Rancière 1999: 35)

Wrong is not the 'established disputes' of the police order, however iniquitous they may be, but the transformation of police order and logic. The principle of equality only has particularity and 'content' in the 'processing of a wrong' that is bound, each time specifically, to particular inequalities of that order. Rancière calls the processing of wrongs modes of subjectification: the *production* of 'a body and a capacity for enunciation not previously identifiable within a given field of experience' (1999: 35) and which, identified, thus reconfigures that field. Assuming the principle of equality, political subjectification is the undoing of the conventionalized or naturalized relation between who an individual is and what she or he is or does (role, place, activity, expectations, etc) – the opening of questions such as 'what is it to be a woman or a man?' for feminism and 'what is it to be worker?' for labour-class movements. Since subjectification is the transformation of the given roles and places of the police order into 'instances of experience of a dispute' (1999: 36), it effects not a social bond (1999: 34) but a political bond: not the assigning of places in the social order but a *dis*identification with established social categories, which is what politics is *in fact* and not just in principle for Rancière.

Subjectification reorders the relation of the two dimensions of the *logos* to one another by either asserting a new account (*logos*) of speech (*logos*) or by the opening of 'free play' between these two dimensions; hence Rancière's claim that 'the modern political animal is first a literary animal' (1999: 37). In this respect, politics is 'enabled' by aesthetics in general and Rancière calls it a 'principle of politics' (1999: 58). Most generally, political subjectification is how

specific subjects take the wrong upon themselves, give it shape, invent new forms and names for it, and conduct its processing in a specific montage of *proofs*: 'logical' arguments that are at the same time a way of reshaping the relationship between speech and its *account*. [. . .] A political subject [. . .] is an operator that connects and disconnects different areas, regions, identities, functions, and capacities existing in the configuration of a given experience. (Rancière 1999: 40)

From which it is clear that the 'fundamental aesthetico-political logic' manifest in collage is that of political subjectification. Simply identifying aesthetics-art with political subjectification on this basis would however be misguided, if not entirely without cause. Although Rancière cautions, as we have seen, against identifying political subjectification in general with 'a politics that is peculiar' to aesthetic experience and education (2009a: 33), if it is to be at all political the equality of *poiesis* and *aisthesis* in aesthetics-art must be the processing of a wrong. In fact, as the manifestation of the fundamental aesthetico-political logic of montage it is intrinsically and necessarily such a processing, and that is what is indexed by the 'singularity' of its maintenance of the Schillerian 'free play'. What is processed however is not and cannot be an established dispute *within* the police order since such disputes are consigned by the *logos*. Rather, the equality of aesthetic-art's free play reorganizes the partition of the sensible *in general*; that is, it repartitions aesthetics *qua* the police order as such, exposing its total contingency (Rancière 1999: 14–15). In other words, the wrong processed by aesthetics-art is that of the police order itself, the iniquity that the partition of the sensible is. Observing Rancière's discretion, then, the processing of a wrong by aesthetics-art is not so much a political subjectification as it is an aesthetic subjectification (not Rancière's phrase). But the distinction can be only partially sustained: since political subjectification is in any case aesthetic montage, aesthetic subjectification is no less a political subjectification. It is only that its politics are generalized since the wrong it processes is the *fact* of the police order rather than any iniquity or dispute within it.

The torsion in Rancière's aesthetico-political logic of art is that political subjectification, tied to particularities of the police order whose repartitioning it is, is enabled by aesthetics in general while what is here called the aesthetic subjectification of art is tied to politics in general and is restricted to a particular aesthetics – that of art in its singularity. Summarily put: aesthetic generality enables political particularity (Rancière's logic of politics), and political generality is enabled by aesthetic particularity (Rancière's logic of art). It is the latter generality that destroys any pragmatic criteria for isolating the singularity of art. And it is this generality that marks aesthetics-art as what Rancière calls a metapolitics (2009a: 33). In *Disagreement* Rancière remarks that metapolitics is the 'change of scene' of politics from political appearance – the processing of a wrong – to the truth of its underlying cause or reason that lies behind or below its appearance (1999: 81–3). Marxism is Rancière's local example: it transforms the 'what' of politics from the appearance of politics to otherwise subterranean forces of production that it presumes shape such appearances and on this basis posits the appearance of politics to be at best an epi-phenomenon or a lie that obscures the true dimension of the 'real movements of society'. It declares the truth of politics to be 'the gap between any political process of naming or inscribing in relation to the realities subtending them', thus hardening the gap between the two dimensions of the *logos* – speech as a putatively originary production, and the account of that speech as its 'superstructural' perversion – and even dissociating them (Rancière 1999: 82). More generally, since politics happens precisely with the intercalation of equality between the two dimensions of the *logos*, metapolitics 'achieves-eliminates' politics *qua* political subjectification of the disputes of the police order. Aesthetics-art fits this account: it posits the truth of politics to be not the wrongs processed as particular political subjectifications but the fact of the police order *qua* the partition of the sensible. It 'changes the scene' of politics from the appearance of political dissensus and dis-agreement – the encounter of police logic and egalitarian logic transforming an established dispute in the police order into politics – to the iniquity of the police order as such.

If Rancière's own theory of politics as an aesthetic montage is at risk of falling into this metapolitical account of politics in the very effort to get away from any such account, then the increasing importance of aesthetics-art to it can be understood as an important corrective to this misfortune. Political subjectification as the montage of the police order, aesthetics-art and Rancière's aesthetico-political logic itself 'changes the scene' of politics not to a truth other than that of the appearance of politics, as Marxism does for example, but rather in the particularity of its political subjectification. Politics does not happen anywhere else than in its appearance in the police order as partition of the sensible yet it also does not itself appear as a political subjectification within the police order. As such, the processing of the wrong of the fact of the police order that is the subjectification of aesthetics-art can be designated a quasi-metapolitics, or what will here be called a supra-politics.

It is as a supra-politics that contemporary art's claims to politics can be understood as being necessarily partial and generalized. It is the difference, in Hirschhorn's phrasing, between 'making political work' – a politics which has a particular subjectification as its 'cause' – and 'working politically' – an art that is political by virtue of its repartition of the sensible but which has no other determinations than that. In processing the police order as such as a wrong, aesthetics-art remains indeterminate with regard to the particularities of politics. Meckseper's photograph-installation, for instance, involves the viewer in a difficult (because self-recognizing) involvement with the *problematic* of protest as itself a 'march of [...] spectacular indignations', and it is just the repartitioning of the protests against the Iraq war in 2003 with luxury items advertising themselves through images of protest that complicates the partition of the sensible between the dimensions of protest against a state-capitalist nexus and that very nexus as represented through the commodity. While this art certainly strains any attempt to obtain a conscientiously politically pure side, the ambivalent denunciation of the police order as such – the state-capitalist nexus and the media-friendly configurations of protest – bypasses the particularity of the demands of the protests themselves. Its politics become rather the question of '[h]ow [. . .] you avoid showing a dominant culture what it already knows', as the artist Liam Gillick puts it in an interview with Meckseper (2008).

It is important to stress that in Rancière's conceptualization of politics such an indeterminacy of political particularity is not a shortcoming of art. The declaration of a wrong is an inceptive act; the 'origin' of politics is for Rancière not the principle of equality itself but its encounter with the police order since 'it has no place or objects of its own' (1999: 29). It cannot, as a matter of logic: if it did, it would have exactly the differentiation and hierarchy, be the kind of organizational principle, that it undoes. No one and no thing can claim the principle of equality in advance or assume it. This is a first sense of the necessary indeterminacy of politics. It is apparent with regard to the bringing together of community and non-community that we have seen to be one of Rancière's characterizations of politics. Writing on several of Philippe Parreno's 'collectively' made films in the decade since the mid-1990s, Maria Lind (2009) gathers evidence of a radical dissimilation of authorship from Parreno's various works, describing the nature of these collaborations as follows: 'Parreno seems to be obsessed with collectivity, community and the common' as a negotiation between how to be part of a collective and an individual at the same time (Lind 2009: 102). Taking up a Rancièrean terminology, she proposes that the issue posed by Parreno's films is '[h]ow to grant the whole and at the same time its parts equal share' suggesting that the films 'perform' this as their 'subject matter' (Lind 2009: 102). In the film *Vicinato* (1995), this proposition might be understood as the way in which a group of actors is filmed playing a group of artists having a discussion among themselves, the artists all knowing each other well. In the installation *Snow Dancing* (1995), it might be the fact of staging a confusion of actors and spectators in an exhibition opening/party situation playing, dancing, drinking. This performance of ways of working, in the privileged or heightened form organized by the artist, is the exemplar of a 'relational community':

deeply embedded in current social, political and economic situations Parreno's work needs to be considered a part of that foil. Contrary to popular belief that community is vanishing today, it can be claimed that 'coming together', 'bonding' and 'caring' are more vital than in a long time. In fact, if we resist the temptation to understand community as the foundation of the formation of society, we make possible something that is non-essential and non-absolute. Community as relational if you wish, which emerges in the wake of society rather than the other way round and which is resistant to immanent power. (Lind 2009: 102)

Despite Rancière's aversion to 'relational' art as an attempt to recuperate a social bond (2009a: 21–3, 56–7), displacing art's enactment of the political bond of dis-identifications in doing so, the ambition accurately outlined by Lind for Parreno's art is an appropriate example here because of its indeterminacy as to what the particular politics of such a community in fact are. The assertion of a common world is only that: a non-essential and non-absolute 'coming together' that is resistant to immanent power. This is not any politics in particular but a phrasing of an indeterminate politics of community as a repartition of the sensible, and this is right for the politics of aesthetics-art.

The indeterminacy of community returns us to *e-flux* but now as an organization concerned, precisely, with the repartition of the sensible as the 'assertion of a common world' which in part reorganizes the given order of the contemporary art milieu. *e-flux* stands for and supports the identification of an equality of access by free information dissemination via the web and email, a variety of format and content (ostensibly anyone can buy an announcement though the prices are prohibitive). An advertisement for an international biennale of contemporary art funded by large global conglomerations has equal status on *e-flux* to an advert for a small not-for-profit gallery in Hong Kong, and both might be the subject of an article written by a leading academic and published in the journal. Orthodox codes of restriction are structurally dissipated by contemporary art's lack of 'objective structure' and organizational criteria, a condition to which *e-flux* is supremely responsive and takes its part in formatting, and from which it yields substantial profit though the privileging of the free trade circulation upon which contemporary art builds its capacity to produce marketable heterogeneity. Along with *e-flux*'s 'special projects', such as talks series and curatorial initiatives, the journal has an intellectualizing intent, the name itself proposing that which the editors identify as the flexible, temporal or fluctuating locus of contemporary art, at least in its general ambitions and claims. As a serious contender in the reputational economy of the art system, run by a respected and seemingly close-knit set of producers and attracting highly established writers, curators and artists to contribute to its online content, *e-flux* is heavily involved in repartitioning the art-system *qua* community in terms other than those that were organized by reputed art journals, communicational systems and major public or private institutions. To that extent, and insofar as it uses the web as a vector of equalization of significance in the art system, *e-flux* exemplifies Rancière's conceptualization of politics. That it does so with the indeterminacy of the politics of aesthetics-art rather than the particular politics of aesthetics in general is clear in its reflexive editorial worry over its own slippery definition of contemporary art:

> there is some agency in the idea that [parameters] remain open: how can we also take advantage of this to develop our own criteria for browsing and historicizing recent activity in a way that affirms the possibilities of contemporary art's still-incompleteness, of its complex ability to play host to many narratives and trajectories without necessarily having to absorb them into a central logic or determined discourse – at least before it forms a historical narrative and logic of exclusion that we would much rather disavow? (Aranda et al. 2009)

If *e-flux* itself contributes to this incompleteness of contemporary art, it does so in the very formulations of its task. What is telling here is that the questions posed, which are (typical) questions of contemporary art's politics, are entirely indeterminate and formal.

Such formality is not a result of unnecessary abstraction but is consistent with the generalized politics of contemporary art's particular aesthetics. This is a second sense of the necessary indeterminacy of aesthetics-art: since the wrong that aesthetics-art processes is only that of the fact of the police order – that there is inequality, a given partition of the sensible, etc – its (supra-) politics has no particularity. It is, in other words, only a formal wrong that is processed by aesthetics-art. Formal in two senses: first, that it is the forms of wrong – space and time – that are processed by aesthetics-art; second, as discussed, that there is no particularity to that wrong in terms of specific social and other determinants. This double sense of formality – the generalized politics of art's particular aesthetics – is presented and in some ways thematized by Liam Gillick in formulations that have wide currency within contemporary art:

> art is a place where you can develop modes of refusal that are qualitatively and ideologically different from the production and negotiation of other objects and ideas in the world – in terms of intentions and results. As such art is a place to heighten contemporary discussions of the way we reconfigure relations between each other and the places that we occupy and/or are forced to operate within. However many artists take a cultural form of the Fifth Amendment or a refusal to engage. By doing this they

attempt to allow the work to sit as the location of complexity, contradiction and even beauty that might be necessary in order to create alternative visions of the world without conditions or explanations but never free of them. (2009)

Gillick captures well a common sense of contemporary art as irreducibly complex, non-particular and indeterminate, whose cogency as an aesthetico-political undertaking is given by Rancière's logic of art, which can then be understood to give an exact, precise and lucid account of contemporary art in its criterialess heterogeneity.

That contemporary art is but the manifestation of the formalism of a suprapolitics, only ever taking the fact of the police order as its point of dispute, is for Rancière no shortcoming. On the contrary, the formal generality of politics granted by its aesthetic particularity gives it a two-fold advantage with respect to the principle of equality: one is art's admission of any content whatsoever as the term of the police order it takes as its 'dispute' (indeed, *theanyspacewhatever* was the name of the major 'relational aesthetics' retrospective at New York's Guggenheim Museum in 2008). Aesthetic-art's generalized politics means that equality can be effectuated across the entirety of the police order in the sense that it can have any content at all for its politics (even colour, time, pixellation, solidity, space, and so on, as well as more evident concerns such as poverty, exclusion, social and identitarian struggles). The second advantage is that what aesthetics-art demonstrates in its manifestation of formal wrong is that the politics of an egalitarian logic is entirely contingent: it is contingent in/on its 'content' (the particular inequality that the principle of equality ties in to) and it is contingent in its manifestation since, as Rancière establishes and aesthetics-art demonstrates, political subjectification can be occasioned anywhere and with everything – even when the principle of equality does not tie into a given social ordering or 'established dispute'. If politics has any particularity or content, it is only contingently so since police and egalitarian logics do not necessarily have to meet anywhere, and any one thing may or may not enable this encounter (Rancière 1999: 32–3). Politics for Rancière is then occasional; nothing is inherently political. More emphatically, that the principle of equality has no content of its own and cannot be assumed in advance of its implementation means that it is an 'empty' notion (1999: 34). The principle of equality is without content of its own – and this contingency is the characteristic of art *qua* processing the wrong that is the police order as an otherwise indeterminate aesthetics. The contingency or occasionalism of political particularity demonstrated through the particular aesthetics of aesthetics-art is why, to return to *e-flux*'s initial question, contemporary art as manifestation of that formal (in)determinate generality of politics has no thematic, no movement, no limit.

Politics is rare in the police order, Rancière remarks, because the contingency of politics is (mis)taken in its social determinations for the contingencies of power which are concerns of the police order (1999: 16–17). The question 'who has power?' posed as a matter of course by aesthetics-art, is not answerable, for if it were it would be a denial of the fundamental repartition mobilized by art as a matter of course by aesthetic-art. Evading the trap of identifying (with) power – a technique readily identifiable in what Rancière calls 'critical art' – by virtue of its suprapolitics, structuring the originary complexity of aesthetic-art's tension between its logics of autonomy and heteronomy, contemporary art demonstrates the principle of equality that attests to politics and its inventions *as such*. The appeal of such a suprapolitics as a way of recuperating politics in form while avoiding it in fact does not escape Rancière. In the conclusion to one of the essays in *Aesthetics and Its Discontents* he notes that

> it seems as if the time of consensus, with its shrinking public space and effacing of political inventiveness, has given to artists and their mini-demonstrations, their collections of objects and traces, their *dispositifs* of interaction, their *in situ* or other provocations, a substitutive political function. Knowing whether these 'substitutions' can reshape political spaces or whether they must be content with parodying them is without doubt an important question of our present. (2009a: 60)

Parody is however not the only risk in this 'substitution': contemporary art may invent a politics at precisely the time that what Rancière identifies to be the distinct space of political dissensus seems to be shrinking (if it is), and such a politics might be understood as the instantiation of a wrong that is properly indeterminate and unpredictable; but the logic of this invention is that politics is reconfigured as a suprapolitics. That is, identifying the non-identity of aesthetics is no less the identification of politics as an aesthetic category, which is what the wrong of art processes, leaving the partition of the sensible in fact undisturbed by the principle of equality – a shadow of any political particularity, of how politics is in fact occasioned.

Notes

1. We translate Rancière's phrase '*partage de sensible*' as 'partition of the sensible' rather than the now more prevalent 'distribution of the sensible' to emphasize

that *partage* is at once a sharing – a taking part – and a separation. Though it risks suggesting an underlying unity that is divided between participants – which is exactly what Rancière's conceptualization of politics and aesthetics precludes and which is anyway no less a problem with 'distribution' – partition seems to us to better capture in English the dual commonality *and* division of the aesthetic that is central to Rancière's undertaking.

Works Cited

Aranda, Julieta, Wood, Kuan Brian and Vidokle, Anton (2009), 'What is Contemporary Art? Issue One' [online], *e-flux journal*, 11. Available at: http:// www.e-flux.com/journal/view/96.
Foster, Hal (2010), 'Contemporary Extracts' [online], *e-flux journal*, 12. Available at: http://www.e-flux.com/journal/view/98.
Gillick, Liam (2008), 'Josephine Meckseper' [online], *Interview*, (November). Available at: http://www.interviewmagazine.com/art/josephine-meckseper/.
— (2009), 'Berlin Statement' [online], *German Pavillion 2009*. Available at: http://www.deutscher-pavillon.org/pdf_gillick/berlinlectureSTATEMENT.pdf.
Hirschhorn, T. (2004), 'Interview with Alison Gingeras', in *Thomas Hirschhorn*, London: Phaidon.
Lind, M. (2009), 'The Who and the How: Thoughts on Philippe Parreno's Work', in *Philippe Parreno*, ed. C. Macel, Paris: Pompidou and JPR Ringier.
Rancière, J. (1999 [1995]), *Disagreement: Politics and Philosophy*, trans. J. Rose, Minneapolis: University of Minnesota Press.
— (2004 [2000]), *The Politics of Aesthetics*, trans. Gabriel Rockhill, London: Continuum.
— (2009a [2004]), *Aesthetics and Its Discontents*, trans. Steven Corcoran, Cambridge: Polity Press.
— (2009b [2008]), *The Emancipated Spectator*, trans. Gregory Elliot, London: Verso.

The Second Return of the Political: Democracy and the Syllogism of Equality

Oliver Marchart

I. Twisting the Political

With his theorization of politics (*la politique*), Jacques Rancière has significantly contributed to a broader debate as to the meaning of the political (*le politique*), a debate unfolding within French post-foundational political thought since the early 1980s.[1] To claim that Rancière's thought developed within a particular configuration of comparable positions, all sharing a set of conceptual and argumentative 'family resemblances', does in no way diminish the originality of his own position. Current hagiographies of thinkers associated with French post-foundational thought all too often present philosophical work as if it was born out of a singular stroke of genius. Rancière would be the first to denounce such an approach. Rather than engaging in hagiographic exercises it is much more productive to study the shifts and twists initiated by a given author within a particular configuration of thought. This implies that we must not take an author's overstatement of dissimilarities vis-à-vis other authors at face value. Even though there *are* dissimilarities between authors, there are also astonishing similarities that, for obvious reasons, tend to get played down both by authors themselves and by their respective communities of acolytes.[2]

This becomes evident as soon as we locate Rancière in the above-mentioned debate about the political. It was initiated by Jean-Luc Nancy and Philippe Lacoue-Labarthe at their *Centre for Philosophical Research on the Political* where many French philosophers were invited to give lectures and discuss what the initiators referred to as the *retreat of the political*

(Lacoue-Labarthe and Nancy 1997), among them Lyotard, Lefort, Badiou, Rogozinski, Soulez, Ferry and Balibar. On 15 February 1982, Rancière delivered a lecture on the representation of the worker in Marxist discourse, followed by a discussion with, among others, Derrida.[3] The topic of this lecture was clearly embedded in Rancière's central theoretical preoccupation at that time which led to the publication of *Le philosophe et ses pauvres* a year later (English edition 2003). Yet when Rancière, partly inspired by the work at the *Centre*, started to engage in a more direct theorization of politics and democracy in the second half of the 1980s, he would silently take up the earlier debates, refashioning them in a peculiar way. While for many others, starting with Nancy and Lacoue-Labarthe, it was the notion of *the political* which had to be rethought and differentiated from politics in the ordinary sense (as particular social sphere or particular form of action), Rancière – together with Badiou, whose own talks at the *Centre* developed into the small volume *Peut-on penser la politique?* (Badiou 1985) – insisted on *politics* to be retained as an emphatically emancipatory term. The political, on the other hand, was largely discarded or relegated to a more marginal function as it was identified, by both Badiou and Rancière, as a central term of political philosophy whereby the latter, it was claimed, had to be rejected either as an outright liberal endeavour or as unwittingly bolstering liberalism.[4] When today Rancière (2010: 206) explains his conceptual intervention in terms of a critical response to the return of liberal political philosophy in the 1980s, one may think of a liberal philosopher like Luc Ferry, who would later become a minister in the conservative Rafarrin government. But a closer look at the lecture series of the *Centre* reveals that immediately preceding Rancière's presentation, Claude Lefort, on January 18, had delivered the most succinct account of his own position, a true mission statement. Under the title *La question de la démocratie* (English in Lefort 1988: 9–20) he not only proposed a notion of the political as the mode by which society is instituted through a set of form-giving principles, he also begins his lecture with the words: 'My purpose here is to encourage and to contribute to a revival of political philosophy' (1988: 9). What in Lefort's eyes had to be taken up again was the question that lies at the very core of political philosophy: 'what is the nature of the difference between forms of society?' (11)

Rancière's lecture can be read as a counter-point, the first sign of a theoretical *dissensus* to be developed later, but to depict Lefort as an antipode to Rancière would be to overstate their dissimilarities. First, and on the most basic plane, because both of them belong, as I said, to a larger configuration of thought which is most aptly described as post-foundational.[5] This term refers to a theoretical position which denies the existence of an ultimate foundation of the social without, and this makes it post- rather than anti-foundational, disputing the necessity of contingent groundings. For Rancière, social or political order cannot be instituted on a firm, quasi-natural ground, yet no nihilistic consequences follow from this, as the absence of ground is what makes politics possible in the first place. It is in this sense that we have to understand such claims as the following:

The foundation of politics is not in fact more a matter of convention than of nature: it is the lack of foundation, the sheer contingency of any social order. Politics exists simply because no social order is based on nature, no divine law regulates human society. (Rancière 1999: 16)

Most post-foundational thinkers, including Nancy, Lacoue-Labarthe, Lefort, Badiou and Laclau and Mouffe would concur. Second, a striking similarity among the theorists mentioned consists in their habit to differentiate conceptually between politics and the political. While this difference is retained throughout the post-foundational configuration, it is inflected in varying ways. As is well known to readers of Rancière, he gives a double twist to the political difference: not only is the emphasis shifted from the political to politics, in order to avoid the alleged dangers of political philosophy, also a new term is introduced to mark the other side of the political difference: *police*. Police is defined as the order by which places, parts (shares), tasks and roles are allocated. Politics, conversely, is enacted by a 'part of those who have no part' which breaks with the order of police. It emerges in the emancipatory moment in which, based on the axiomatic assumption of general equality, such 'part of no part' (the poor in antiquity, the proletariat of the nineteenth century, etc.) dissensually claims to be the whole. The political then, so dear a concept to many other theorists, becomes a residual category for Rancière, naming merely the terrain on which politics and police meet or collide.

Rancière's differentiation between politics and the police has created some confusion, and in a recent statement Rancière conceded that he may have contributed to this (2010: 206). The difference is sometimes presented by Rancière as a Manichean division between spontaneous revolt and oppressing order, even though Rancière occasionally hints at the possibility of a 'good' police order, and more recently insists that politics/police can only be found in reality in form of mélange.[6] By agreeing with this revised (or clarified) version of the politics/police difference however we will be left with some unexpected consequences, including a surprising comeback of the concept of *the political*. The reason is simple: If politics and police only surface in mixed form, then it is only logical to conclude that the political – defined precisely as the meeting ground between politics and police – is the only way in which we are confronted with politics. But then, why do we learn next to nothing about the political? Why, as a category, does it remain marginalized within the Rancièrean lexicon? Matters are getting even more complicated if we consider more recent definitions, elaborated in his work on aesthetics, of what Rancière calls the *distribution of the sensible*. It has been remarked (Rockhill 2009: 199) that at times this concept seems to be a mere synonym for the concept of police order, while on other occasions he alludes to the possibility of a dissensual, that is, political distribution of the sensible. Rancière's conceptual apparatus is riven by a couple of ambiguities and indecisions. Does the so-called distribution of the sensible always belong to the order of police? Or is there both a police way and a politics way of distributing the sensible, and if yes, in which relation do they stand to each other? Or, given that the political is defined as their meeting ground, is the distribution of the sensible simply another term for the political?

Unsurprisingly, the political, given that it is treated by Rancière as a poor cousin of politics, has not received much attention in the literature on Rancière. Now it seems that its status has to be reconsidered. If Rancière reacted to the 'return of the political' in the 1980s with a renewed interest in the concept of politics, then a *second return of the political* announces itself today within the spaces opened by these ambiguities and indecisions. A silent return, certainly unaccounted for by Rancière himself, which in my view points to a series of problems that the Rancièrean twist produced but could not handle. Because much emphasis is given to the moment of *disruption* of a given regime, the moment of *politics*, the other side of such disruptive moment, that is, the form and status of a given regime's *institution*, remains a constant problem. A series of attempts are set in motion to come to grips with the other side of politics. The most prominent attempt consists in Rancière giving increasing importance to the concept of a distribution of the sensible – without however fully clarifying the latter's status with respect to the political and the institutional dimension of politics. This is because Rancière, as a consequence of his decision to discard political philosophy, is not willing to locate the dimension of form-giving institution – identified by Lefort as the core of political philosophy – on the same ontological level as the disruptive moment of politics. To relocate the twist given to the notion of the political by Rancière within the configuration of alternative moves may cast some light onto the status and role of some of his categories.

II. The Syllogism of Equality (On Rancière's *emancipatory apriorism*)

Let us relate our initial observations to what might well be Rancière's most succinct presentation of the logics of politics: the 'syllogism of equality' as explained in his *On the Shores of Politics*. It encapsulates in a highly structured form arguments that elsewhere in Rancière's oeuvre tend to be presented in a more narrative, hence more ambiguous way. By the notion of a syllogism of equality, or an emancipatory syllogism, he seeks to account for the necessary connection between universal claims and their particular enactment. The 'syllogism of equality', supposedly underlying every emancipatory claim, consists of two premises or categorical statements (a universal and a particular one) and a conclusion. In the case of the preamble of the Charter promulgated in 1830 in France for example, the syllogism's major premise is constituted by the universal claim that all French people are equal before the law, while the minor premise formulates a particular violation of the first premise. If employers, for instance, organize themselves but deny their employees the same right to organize, such a case would enter the second premise as a particular *wrong* with regard to the major premise. In such case the workers may draw the conclusion that either the minor premise or the major premise must be changed. If they opt for the second case, the idea of universal equality as a major premise will be abandoned. But if even the bosses share the universal idea of equality before the law, and if it is decided to uphold the major premise, then equality must be *verified*.

How to verify words? Rancière's remarkable answer is: 'Essentially, through one's actions' (1995: 47). Not in an adventurist, voluntarist or decisionist sense of action, to be sure. Political actions 'must be organised like a proof, a system of reason'. If, for instance, verification takes place by transforming the words of universal equality into the practice of a strike, then the strike takes on the form of a logical proof, and it does so by transforming 'an alignment of forces into a logical confrontation. This did not simply mean substituting words for actions; rather, it meant transforming a power relationship by means of a practice of logical demonstration' (Rancière 1995: 47). The strike turns into a visible and audible set of arguments.[7] This leads Rancière to conclude that the universal claim (the universal value of equality) that serves as the syllogism's major premise is far from being an empty illusion. In fact, it is a logical operator. It operates through 'the discursive and practical construction of polemical verification, a case, a demonstration' (Rancière 1992: 60). If this operator is employed within the syllogism of equality, a conclusion is called for: a third categorical statement or action. The question imposes itself: '*What follows?*' If all men are equal, but one is able to demonstrate that some are 'less equal' than others, then *what follows*? As Rancière (1992: 60) sums up the 'logical schema of social protest': 'Do we or do we not belong to the category of men or citizens or human beings, and what follows from this? The universality is not enclosed in *citizen* or *human being*; it is involved in the "what follows", in its discursive and practical enactment'.

Politics resides in the 'what follows': the enactment of universal equality, the practical proof of the major premise. To frame political action in this way is original indeed, not least because a specific rationality of action is unclosed and decisionism avoided.[8] The syllogism of equality, however, confronts us with a serious problem concerning the status of the major premise. If the major premise is upheld, a *petitio principii* appears hidden in the 'what follows', because the conclusion forces us to simply restate the major premise: what is supposed to be verified is the universality of equality, but it is this first premise which served as the starting point of the whole argument. (Hence, the *petitio principii* reads like this: What follows from upholding equality? It follows that equality is upheld.) The problem is not that things shift between a logical, a practical and a 'poetological' employment of the syllogism of equality, the problem is that it remains unclear as to how we originally arrived at the major premise (save through our very conclusion).

Rancière's solutions to this problem are not fully convincing. Somehow sensing, I suppose, the *petitio principii* on which his syllogism rests, Rancière sets out to search for a *non-political* notion of equality as necessary precondition (a 'major premise') for politics. If he succeeded in showing that equality is always already there in a non-political form, he would be able to break the circle between conclusion and major premise. Yet success comes at a price. By turning equality into a non-political maxim, he transforms a fighting word well-known from political struggle into a transcendental, a-historical condition. One may even speak about a secret – though explicitly disavowed – Rousseauism in Rancière as any social order is supposed to rest on a hypothetical state of originary equality.⁹ This is because to understand a commandment and one's duty to obey 'you must already be the equal of the person who is ordering you' (1999: 16). For the same reason equality is not only the necessary precondition of political action, it is also the precondition of its opposite, the order of police. So Rancière concludes: 'In the final analysis, inequality is only possible through equality' (1999: 17). To illustrate this point with one of Rancière's favourite examples, Menenius Agrippa's attempt to explain to the Roman plebs their organic place in the city had to implicitly assume, Rancière believes, their equality within the domain of everyone's capacity to speak and listen: 'But to teach the plebs their place this way he must assume they understand what he is saying. He must presume the equality of speaking beings, which contradicts the police distribution of bodies who are put in their place and assigned their role' (1999: 33). Such 'equality of intelligence' is therefore assumed to be 'the absolute condition of all communication and any social order' (1999: 34). It appears that, through an operation curiously reminiscent of Habermas, the condition of equality is anchored in the very structure of communication. Where Habermas draws rationality from the hat of communication, Rancière presents to us the white rabbit of equality.

So far, this argument is not compelling. A case could easily be made for the opposite assumption that all communication – not only political *mésentente* – is *a priori* structured in an asynchronous, asymmetrical and unequal way (a primordial misunderstanding), as communication does not occur simply between a sender and a receiver, both understood as equal speaking individuals, but is precisely what stands between them as an unsurpassable barrier and recurring stumbling block, as what Lacan calls 'the wall' of language, leaving no common measure to equate the status of sender with the status of receiver.¹⁰ Rancière reserves the status of such fundamental 'disagreement' to politics, where a dissensus is staged over the existence of 'two worlds in one', but even here disagreement is ultimately subordinated to what can be called his *emancipatory apriorism*: the idea of politics being egalitarian *eo ipso*. Politics, for Rancière (and Badiou for that matter), is either egalitarian, *or it is not politics*. Without doubt, to resort to the principle of equality in order to stage disagreement might be *one* possibility for political action. But I see no reason why politics should be emancipatory in principle whereby all non-egalitarian forms of politics are nominalistically defined out of the picture. Neither on a theoretical nor on a practical plane is this assumption convincing – and certainly not from a perspective more inclined to the Machiavellian-Gramscian trajectory of political thought. One may simply imagine the less than hypothetical case of a bunch of disenfranchised Neo-Nazis, a part of no part claiming to be the whole. In some countries, and in violation of any 'universal premise' of equality, they are legally stripped of this possibility for very good reasons – simply because the universal principle of equality can be used for other than emancipatory purposes. In such a case we may reasonably respond to the syllogism's injunction *'what follows?'* by deliberately upholding a given *wrong*, a given violation of the major premise.

To reserve the term politics for emancipatory action appears implausible when confronted with the realities of our political world. But to empty equality from its political nature and turn it into a non-political condition appears equally implausible against the background of a post-foundational approach to politics. For, in the last instance, equality (as a non-political condition of both politics and police) is used by Rancière as a theoretical figure of contingency. It is thus extracted from the mere fact that an ultimate ground of political and social order is not available. Equality is assumed to be a necessary implication of society's groundless nature. If this were the case, the major premise would simply follow from, or be grounded in, a post-foundational view of society. As a figure of contingency, equality is 'simply the equality of anyone at all with anyone else: in other words, in the final analysis, the absence of *arkhê*, the sheer contingency of any social order' (1999: 15). Thus Rancière defends without doubt an 'ontological' form of *an-archism*.[11] Anyone is equal to anyone else, so the argument goes, because 'of the ultimate *anarchy* on which any hierarchy rests' (1999: 16) – that is, because of the absence of a fundamental principle.

This claim can easily be identified as an extension of Rancière's argument as to the necessary egalitarian nature of communication which now is located right on the ontological level of the ground/abyss of order *eo ipso*. But again, to frame equality in such way is not recommendable. First, for political reasons: to avoid wishful thinking and leftish self-complacency, one shouldn't give in to the temptation to ontologically ennoble egalitarian politics by rooting it in the very ontological, *an-archic* condition of every order. Egalitarian politics must do without any ontological privilege over non-egalitarian, non-emancipatory politics – it must confront its enemies on the ontic plane without ultimate guarantee in the ontological. Second, for theoretical reasons (which again may have political implications): for a common confusion should be avoided on the modal level between the contingent and the arbitrary – that is, the accidental. Something is contingent because it could be different (or not at all), or put differently: because its essence does not entail its existence. Yet to claim that something could be different or not at all is not the same as claiming that it is arbitrarily so, that is, that everything else could be *equally* possible. (We will return to Rancière's confusion of the contingent with the accidental in our discussion of his theory of democracy).

Let us illustrate this point with a political example: To say that the rule of a governing party is contingent is not the same as saying it is accidental. In the first case it is simply stated that a *different* party could be in power so that any claim for a non-contingent rule is ultimately unfounded (a given order's essence does not entail its existence) and, as one may conclude, can therefore be challenged. To say it is accidental would mean, however, that a party stays in power by pure chance or good luck and *any other* party, provided it is lucky enough, could equally be in power. While the first position is defendable from a post-foundational perspective, the second smacks of an outmoded 'anything goes' version of postmodernism or anti-foundationalism. What makes the latter untenable is the simple fact that no one operates in a vacuum. The terrain on which we act is always already deformed by relations of power and subordination, by institutional fortifications, and by a multiplicity of competing political projects. In other words, the social world, although ungroundable in principle, is always *partially* grounded in reality. We will never be able to reach a point where the absence of foundation presents itself to us in form of pure accidentally – or, which is the same, in form of a primordial equality. Social order is structured contingently, not arbitrarily. And political action, contingent as it is, is not accidental either.[12]

I hope to have demonstrated that the absence of an ultimate ground does not necessarily imply the equality of 'anyone at all with anyone else' as even on the most fundamental level our social reality, although ultimately ungroundable, will always already be partially grounded. To institute the signifier 'equality' on the level of ground, as Rancière proposes, does amount to nothing more than just another attempt at partially grounding what remains ungroundable. For this reason, equality cannot be the non-political condition of politics because it will have to be politically instituted in the first place. As regards our question of where the major premise of universal equality comes from, we are thus confronted with the horns of a dilemma. On the one hand, the major premise cannot be derived from the very structure of communication or the mere level of 'ground'. On the other hand, it appears that it has to be instituted as ground by egalitarian political action – but then we are back to our *petitio principii* (egalitarian politics has to ground what it relies on as its own ground). Is there a way to avoid this dilemma? A critical engagement with Rancière's theorization of democracy may provide the clue for escaping this dilemma.

III. Democracy: Interruption vs Regime

Demos, in Rancière's definition, is a figure of 'at once everybody and anyone at all' (2010: 53) which comes to supplement the process of politics. A *demos* appears on the scene via the dissensual process of politics as soon as subjects challenge the police distribution of the sensible and 'restage the anarchic foundation of the political' (Rancière 2010: 54). For this reason there is a disruptive quality to a *demos*. Rancière's notion of democracy is supposed to capture this quality. Democracy consists in the interrupting force of political action premised upon the axiom of equality (of anyone with anyone else). In this case, however, a question immediately arises: how is democracy different from egalitarian politics per se? Isn't Rancière using two terms for roughly the same thing, thereby repeating with his arguments about democracy what has already been said about equality and politics? Statements like the following point in this direction: 'Every politics is democratic in this precise sense: not in the sense of institutions, but in the sense of forms of expression that confront the logic of equality with the logic of the police order' (Rancière 1999: 101). Are we not encountering here the same emancipatory apriorism dressed up as *democratic apriorism*? Politics is democratic – the subject that is produced as a supplement to political action is necessarily a *demos* – or it is not politics. One should not be surprised then to discover the same ambiguities and problems that were discussed in the above section on equality. Only that the accidental (under the mistaken name of the contingent) now reappears as a central category of democracy.

In his critical evaluation of Plato, Rancière sets out to defend what for Plato constitutes the ultimate scandal of democracy: 'the choice of the god of chance, the drawing of lots, that is, the democratic procedure by which a people of equals decides the distribution of places' (2006: 40). A procedure by which public offices are allocated via the drawing of lots runs counter to the right of birth and wealth. If the places of the police order are re-distributed by chance – Rancière speaks about the *law of chance* – anyone is considered to be equally qualified to hold public office, and order as such is de-naturalized. This might well be the case, but again we encounter an ambiguity in Rancière: it is quite telling that the drawing of lots is defended against Plato and the whole tradition of democratic thought which, according to Rancière, tended to forget this procedure (2006: 42), yet the very same procedure is not included in the list of recommendations for democratic renewal given at the end of *Hatred of Democracy*. Did Rancière himself 'forget' to include it? What he seeks to achieve with these recommendations is not to abolish representation but rather to democratize it in order to prevent it from producing fixed and foreseeable outcomes in accordance with 'vested interests' (so he proposes short and non-renewable mandates, the reduction of campaign costs to a minimum, etc.). Not even the appointment of jurors from the population 'by lot', which is a common procedure in the judicial system of many countries, is mentioned. So while Rancière accuses the whole tradition of political thought of having obliterated the law of chance, it appears that he himself does not see a way to integrate it into today's democracies. And there are good reasons for this.

Let us imagine what would happen if we were to implement the fundamental or ontological level of groundlessness – that is, in Rancière, the an-archic arbitrariness of rule – in an immediate way, that is through procedures that would turn the 'law of chance' into a central feature of democracy. Of course, representational mediation would be abolished, but the scandal would not be that everyone and anyone may now assume a role in government without being qualified. The scandalous outcome would be precisely the *end of democracy* because we would have managed, ironically, to rid democracy of all *politics* in the strict Rancièrean sense: any dimension of dissensus and disagreement would ultimately disappear, no part without a part would enter in a syllogistic play with a universal premise of equality by way of staging a fundamental disagreement. Any individual would be able to incarnate the universal in a direct and unmediated way provided she or he is lucky enough to be selected by lot – no conflict and no collective subjectification needed. A world in which the law of chance reigns is a world without politics. This it has in common with a world governed by the rule of *fate*. In fact, chance and fate are exactly the same thing: it is simply a matter of perspective whether I think it is fate or luck to be elected by lot.

Such an outcome can be avoided as soon as we stop mistaking the contingent for the arbitrary.[13] Of course, Rancière is to be fully endorsed from a post-foundational perspective when he speaks about the paradox of democracy (2010: 50) whereby the absence of ground is turned into the very ground of government (a position shared by Lefort, Mouffe, Laclau, the early Žižek and others). Democracy is 'the institution of politics as such' to the extent 'that the very ground for the power of ruling is that there is no ground at all' (2010: 50). This is true with only a small yet important qualification: there is never 'no ground at all', nor is there a possibility to institute 'politics as such'. A dissensually and democratically revolting subject is never 'anyone', it is always a *particular* subject, and for the same reason it is not automatically a *demos* either. Fundamental contingency means exactly this: that it could be a *different* subject (not just any subject) with a *different* political project (not just any project).[14] What was said above about the impossibility of a non-political notion of equality being extracted right from the unfounded nature of every social order must now be repeated with respect to democracy. The latter cannot simply be identical with the absence of an ultimate ground because contingency, the modal *terminus technicus* for this absence, implies that there might always be different, perhaps entirely undemocratic forms of politics. And if democracy is not simply pregiven together with contingency, it will have to be instituted against competing political projects – which implies that it will have to assume modes of permanence: *institutions*.

If this is agreed upon, all questions regarding political institution assume an entirely different valence. It becomes impossible to describe democratic institution in terms of 'fleeting' inscriptions (Rancière 1999: 40). Nor can it be plausibly claimed, as Rancière repeatedly does, that (necessarily democratic) politics 'in its specificity, is rare', that it 'is always local and occasional' (1999: 139), and 'doesn't always happen – it actually happens very little or rarely' (1999: 17). The major premise of equality, if we relate it to democracy, has to be instituted in a more permanent sense if it is to function as legitimatory background and political reference point. And indeed, examples given by Rancière himself point in the opposite direction, for instance a worker's strike bringing together 'the equality proclaimed by the Declaration of the Rights of Man and some obscure question concerning hours of work or workshop regulation' (1999: 40). The Declaration of the Rights of Man, the major premise of this strike, is not just a fleeting inscription but, rather, a *major political institution*.[15] Unfortunately, Rancière is not prepared to account for this institutional dimension of democracy as he fiercely disputes the idea of democracy being a *regime* of equality. As he states again and again: democracy is not a regime or a form of government, nor is it a social way of life (1999: 101). On the contrary: 'Equality turns into the opposite the moment it aspires to a place in the social or state organization' (1999: 34).

Rancière thereby strips himself of any possibility to plausibly explain the universal valence of equality. As long as we refuse to conceptualize democracy as the *regime* of equality which has to be politically instituted and kept alive, we will not be able to explain how the major premise of the egalitarian syllogism has assumed its universal status in the first place.[16] If it is not pregiven in an aprioristic fashion, it has to be anchored both in institutions and in a given 'way of life'. And this does not occur by chance, it is the outcome of, in Antonio Gramsci's terms, a long and protracted hegemonic 'war of position' at the end of which we encounter, exactly, a *regime* of universal suffrage, of the Rights of Man, etc. This regime might be internally disputed, externally endangered or even on the verge of shifting into a state of 'post-democracy' – it is nevertheless a regime.

To explain the shape and function of this regime we will have to turn towards alternative options within the configuration of post-foundational political thought. And if democracy has been analyzed by Claude Lefort precisely as a regime,[17] it was not because his aim was to obfuscate the post-foundational nature of society – the ontological fact that that no order is based on an ultimate ground – but because he wanted to show how the ultimate absence of ground is inscribed, in an entirely mediated fashion, into democratic procedures and institutions. While, for Lefort, every regime is unfounded and unfoundable, it is only with the democratic regime that the groundless nature of society is symbolically accepted and institutionalized. To speak, as Lefort famously does, about an empty space (of power) in the 'centre' of the social then is nothing more than a shortcut, an abbreviation for all the institutional means by which social groundlessness is indicated within the symbolic structures of democratic society: the periodic evacuation of the place of power through elections; the separation of the spheres of power, law and knowledge; the separation of a civil society from the state and the emergence of a public sphere within the gap resulting from this separation. Accordingly, the decapitation of the King – by which the place of power is emptied in the first place – should be read as a moment of symbolic condensation, a metaphor for the widespread and institutionally regulated acceptance, within democracy, of the ungroundable nature of the social.[18] For this reason Lefort's claim that the place of power is kept empty under democratic conditions can by no means be reduced to the historical event of the execution of Louis XVI. The king is beheaded time and again whenever society's non-identity with itself, the *self-alienation of the social* as I propose to call it, is marked symbolically through democratic institutions. And what is more, markers of uncertainty and self-alienation have to be inscribed into what Lefort refers to, in Merleau-Pontyan terminology, as the 'flesh of the social'.

A *regime* in this widest sense includes both the institutional framework of democracy and a democratic 'way of life' (in the same way in which, as Lefort reminds us, the term 'ancien régime' is understood to refer not only to the institutions of monarchy but also to a specific way of life) – precisely what Rancière rejects as potential dimensions of democracy. I'm not claiming that Lefort is right and Rancière is wrong on that point. The question comes down to matters of plausibility and of conceptual economy. It is implausible, on the basis of a more realist view of our political world, to reduce politics aprioristically to emancipatory and democratic actions only. And it is questionable why one should introduce a second term, democracy, which just redoubles the features of politics rather than adding a further dimension – especially if this new dimension would allow for conceptually grasping the difference between a police style division of the sensible and a division of the sensible by which the ungrounded nature of the social is recognized.

It is not without reason that I refer to Rancière's notion of a 'distribution of the sensible' at the end of this chapter, because it is with this concept that a potential point of convergence could be expected. When Rancière assumes that 'police' is not just any division of the sensible but a particular one 'that claims to recognize only real parties to the exclusion of all empty spaces and supplements' (2003: 226), he leaves open the possibility of a division of the sensible in which the existence of empty spaces and of the *demos* as supplement *is* recognized. But wouldn't such particular form of a division of the sensible meet precisely the post-foundational definition of democracy as a *regime* in the Lefortian sense of the term, a regime in which society's self-alienation, the absence of an ultimate foundation and the non-self-identity of the sovereign people is accepted politically, culturally and institutionally? Rancière's notion of the 'distribution of the sensible' could very well be pushed in this direction. In this case, however, Rancière would have to relinquish one of his claims and consent to the conclusion that democracy *is* a regime.

IV. The Second Return of *the Political*

So far we have arrived at the following conclusion: If equality does not jump out of the hat of communication like the proverbial rabbit, and if it is not simply given with our ontological condition either, *it must be instituted* in order to become a 'major premise'. And if it is instituted, it will be the result of an ultimately political act. But this does not yet resolve our initial problem of a *petitio principii* – it rather seems to re-instate it. In order to institute a major premise of universal equality egalitarian politics has to presuppose as a premise what it is about to institute or verify. The very precondition of democratic politics – the legitimating horizon of equality – appears to be the result of democratic politics. How can we insist, contra Rancière, on the political nature of the major premise of equality and at the same time avoid this *petitio principii*? There is only one possibility: we have to split our notion of politics from within. As a matter of fact, it is not the same form of politics which is involved in a major premise (the horizon of what is taken for granted or accepted as legitimate) and in the political action of verifying it. Our discussion of democracy as a regime has provided us with the key to this solution. As a regime the term democracy refers to the horizon of a more or less established 'way of life' and a set of democratic institutions: a 'symbolic *dispositif*', a set of principles by which a given society is symbolically staged, given form and furnished with sense. This is what in Lefort's lexicon is termed *the political* – and which we have to differentiate from *politics* whereby by the latter may well be understood as an enactment or 'practical verification' of the political.

Without any doubt Rancière deserves praise for developing theoretically an active concept of equality: we must not take equality as something given, even if it is inscribed institutionally into the democratic horizon. It has to be enacted in practice time and again, which amounts to saying that politics is as much an instituting as it is a disrupting force. (But the same must be said, I would add, about all political projects and articulations, egalitarian or not – they all have to be re-instituted time and again to remain effective.) By over-stressing the disruptive dimension of politics, and by denying democracy the status of a regime, Rancière strips himself of the means to explain how the legitimating principle of equality has assumed some degree of permanence and stability as a reference point for emancipatory action today. This price is paid because the very dimension of institutional organization of a given symbolic *dispositif* or apparatus remains untheorized. Rancière is in need of an elaborated theory of *the political*, the meeting ground of politics and police.[19] Our observations have come to converge in a single point: what imposes itself today is a second return of the political.

Notes

1. I have presented the main lines of this debate in Marchart (2007).
2. Of course, there can be an overstatement of similarities as well, for instance when Badiou reacted to the publication of *La Mésentente* (1995) [tr. *Disagreement* (1999)] with a thinly veiled allegation of plagiarism (Badiou 1998).
3. The lecture together with a synopsis of the discussion can be found in Lacoue-Labarthe et al. (1983: 89–111).
4. On a more general note, political philosophy is denounced as 'the set of reflective operations whereby philosophy tries to rid itself of politics' (Rancière 1999: xii), in particular via the 'specific masking' of the distinction between politics and police (xiii). From a post-foundational perspective, political philosophy can therefore be described as a foundational enterprise which aims at founding politics on a more elementary principle: 'And political philosophy, by its desire to give to the community a single foundation, is fated to have to re-identify politics and police, to cancel out politics through the gesture of founding it' (Rancière 2010: 41).
5. The term post-structuralist would be too narrow, as Lefort – as a direct pupil of Merleau-Ponty's – is more a phenomenologist than a post-structuralist.
6. This revised version moves Rancière's political difference closer to a more Heideggerian understanding of difference as difference: the constant chiasmatic movement between both sides of a difference which have to be somehow distinguished and yet are always intertwined and inseparable – a reading with which Rancière himself, being a staunch anti-Heideggerian, would certainly disagree.

7. In *Disagreement*, Rancière (1999: 40) speaks about politics as a 'montage of "proofs"'.
8. On political rationality, see also Rancière (1999: 43ff). For a more extensive discussion of Rancière's syllogism, see Marchart (1997).
9. This secret Rousseauism of originary equality is particularly evident in Rancière's *The Ignorant Schoolmaster*.
10. This assumption might well be a *non sequitur* too, but at least it is a *non sequitur* in line with a more realistic account of our political world.
11. Not necessarily a political one. From the post-foundational assumption of the 'an-archic' ultimate groundlessness of any order it does *not* follow that anarchism as a political ideology or movement would be more (or less) adapted to our ontological condition (this would simply amount to an *anarchist apriorism*). There is no unmediated passage from an ontological condition to a particular political project.
12. This is not to deny that accidental events happen, in politics as much as everywhere else. It is to deny that the accidental can be made into a ground (albeit paradoxical) of politics.
13. If both a society built on the principle of fate and a society built on the principle of chance exclude political dissensus and articulation, it is because politics only opens up when there is contingency, not the rule of either fate or chance.
14. The point relates critically to Rancière's aprioristic formalism. For Rancière, to relate – through a process of political verification – to the universal maxim of equality is enough for politics to be called emancipatory. In this case however, the particular 'content', the programme, the ideology and all the particular discursive articulations of a political project become irrelevant as long as only the major premise is verified.
15. The same can be said of most examples given by Rancière. The case of Jeanne Deroin, for instance, who presented herself as a candidate for legislative elections in 1849, thereby demonstrating 'the contradiction within a universal suffrage that excludes her sex from any such universality'. Such operation exploits the internal inconsistency, as Rancière himself concedes, of 'a regime founded on a declaration of equality that does not recognize any difference between the sexes' (1999: 41) – yet this is only possible, of course, if such regime has been instituted in the first place.
16. It is evident that a historical dimension has to be introduced in order to explain the universal status of the major premise, which explains – *ex negativo* – why only modern examples and examples from Greek and Roman antiquity are given by Rancière. In his model he has to rely on historical conjunctures in which a certain sense of equality (of a relatively significant number of citizens) was already instituted politically. It would be hard to draw examples from

feudalist societies. Certainly, some egalitarian signifiers with a Christian inflection were floating around, yet rarely were they articulated into an egalitarian political project. Political articulation, as in the case of peasants' rebellions or corporate uprisings, were premised not on universal equality but on traditionally granted rights of a particular group. It was the goal of such politics to re-institute a major premise of *particularity* rather than universality.

17. I'm leaving aside, for reasons of space, the similar cases of Laclau and Mouffe's (1985) theory of democracy and of the Lacanian assumption of an ethics of democracy (Stavrakakis 1999).

18. There is no sacrificial logic, no theatre of sacrifice involved in this Lefortian point, as Rancière (2010: 34) claims. Lefort's description is closer to the way in which the terror of the French revolution is laconically described by Hegel, in the *Phenomenology*, in terms of cleaving a cabbage head or swallowing a gulp of water. The significance of the execution of Louis XVI does not consist in any grandiose theatre of sacrifice (or, vice versa, in the royalist drama of victimization), but in the minimal displacement in the real – not much more than a gulp of water – which provides for a maximum symbolic condensation in the symbolic. Saint-Just, in his eventually successful tautological argument for the execution of the king, was well aware that the king is fundamentally metaphor: he has to die not because of his particular crimes (because he betrayed his country to the foreign enemy), that is to say, not as an individual, but because he was the king, because his earthly body acted as a metaphor for monarchy's transcendent principle of legitimation. Nobody will ever be able again to proclaim 'the king is dead, long live the king'. As soon as the link to the transcendent ground is symbolically severed, it becomes publicly evident that no sovereign – neither the king nor the people – is identical to himself. Which is also why Rancière's alternative claim that not the king but the people is internally divided does not present an alternative to Lefort, as it is Lefort himself who claims that the people, as a sovereign subject, does not exist in democracy but is only available in a fragmented, non-self-identical form.

19. Of course, if Rancière's concept of a distribution of the sensible is understood in a sense analogous to 'the political', a Machiavellian-Gramscian reading of a given distribution of the sensible would require a much more concrete, and less metaphorical, analysis of the shifts and continuities within hegemonic formations. I submit that such analysis would neither qualify as 'historical' in the sense of the science of history nor in Rancière's alternative definition of a poetology of history writing, but rather as a specific form of political analysis on the diachronic axis: an analysis, in the last instance, of social struggles unfolding over time. One may call this historical materialism.

Works Cited

Badiou, Alain (1985), *Peut-on penser la politique?*, Paris: Seuil.
— (1998), *Abrégé de Métapolitique*, Paris: Seuil.
Laclau Ernesto, Chantal Mouffe (1985), *Hegemony and Socialist Strategy*, London and New York: Verso.
Lacoue-Labarthe, Philippe and Nancy, Jean-Luc (1997), *Retreating the Political*, ed. Simon Sparks, London and New York: Routledge.
Lacoue-Labarthe, Philippe et al. (1983), *Le retrait du politique*, Paris: Galilée.
Lefort, Claude (1988), *Democracy and Political Theory*, Minneapolis: University of Minnesota Press.
Marchart, Oliver (1997), 'Nasilni silogizmi. Rancière, Blanqui in neformalna logika akcije', in *Acta Philosophica* XVIII 3/1997, 151–62.
— (2007), *Post-foundational Political Thought. Political Difference in Nancy, Lefort, Badiou and Laclau*, Edinburgh: Edinburgh University Press.
Rancière, Jacques (1992), 'Politics, Identification, and Subjectivization', *October* 61, 'The Identity in Question' (Summer): 58–64.
— (1995), *On the Shores of Politics*, London and New York: Verso.
— (1999), *Disagreement. Politics and Philosophy*, Minneapolis: University of Minnesota Press.
— (2003), *The Philosopher and His Poor*, Durham and London: Duke University Press.
— (2006), *Hatred of Democracy*, London and New York: Verso.
— (2010), *Dissensus. On Politics and the Aesthetics*, London and New York: Continuum.
Rockhill, Gabriel (2009), 'The Politics of Aesthetics: Political History and the Hermeneutics of Art', in *Jacques Rancière. History, Politics, Aesthetics*, eds Gabriel Rockhill and Philipp Watts, Durham and London: Duke University Press, 195–215.
Stavrakakis, Yannis (1999), *Lacan and the Political*, London and New York: Routledge.

Police Reinforcement: The Anti-Politics of Organizational Life

Linsey McGoey

In 2004, David Ross, a former medical officer at the Food and Drug Administration, watched news coverage of one of the highest-profile pharmaceutical controversies in recent years: Merck's withdrawal of Vioxx, its bestselling painkiller drug, from the global marketplace. At the time, David Ross railed to his wife about the actions of David Graham, an associate director of drug safety at the FDA who drew international attention for testifying before the U.S. Senate about the FDA's handling of Vioxx. Graham said his supervisors ignored warnings that Vioxx could lead to cardiac arrest, and asked him to change his conclusions on an internal report about Vioxx's risks.

Today, David Graham is still at the FDA. David Ross is not. But something both have in common is a concern that FDA has not amended policies much in the wake of the Vioxx controversy, and may be, in some ways, seeking to police internal criticism more strictly.

I met for an interview with Ross in Washington DC in November 2010. He told me that when he first witnessed David Graham publicly criticizing the agency in 2004, he said to his wife, 'How dare he!', with the implication being, how dare he publicize concerns better handled internally.

Two years later, Ross revised his own perceptions of Graham's actions after struggling himself to convince supervisors about the risks of Ketek, an antibiotic drug linked to kidney failure. Ross's efforts to flag Ketek's risks embroiled him in a bureaucratic battle that threatened his own impartiality and credibility the more his concerns proved correct, impugning his authority and undermining his professional position the more influential his warnings turned out to be.

In this chapter, drawing on interviews with current and former FDA staff, I look at this paradox, exploring an obvious and yet underappreciated truism of organizational life: the way that individuals who call attention to regulatory errors are often vilified more than those who quietly perpetuate them. Within large bureaucracies, and within democratic politics more generally, an emphasis on the moral authority of objectivity limits opportunities for effective dissent by constraining the pool of legitimate dissenters to those who can convey a lack of personal commitment or interest in the stakes at hand, thereby enrolling themselves in a form of politics which succeeds most when actions are perceived as having as little effect as possible, when an action cannot be traced to a single instigator.

It is a politics that tends to succeed best at its own expense; a politics that reaches its pinnacle, to paraphrase an insight from Jacques Rancière, as its possibilities are diffused; a politics that reaches fulfilment only at its end (Rancière 2007). The problem is not that individuals are barred from voicing dissent, but the sheer act of doing so impugns their impartiality, rendering their arguments proportionately *more* dismissible the louder and more persistently they are voiced.

One of Rancière's key arguments is the distinction he draws between the police and politics, suggesting politics is a mode of action which 'perturbs the forms of perception' established by police, by instituting a 'contradictory theatre of its "appearances" [...] [politics] is the production, within the determined, sensible world, of a given that is heterogeneous to it' (Rancière 2004a: 226). Stressing the insightfulness of Rancière's distinction, this chapter explores cases where attempts to disturb divisions of the sensible have the unintended result of strengthening, rather than challenging, the authority and dominance of the police. In the case of drug controversies, the necessity to speak in a language comprehensible to the 'police' requires an adoption of the police's language – a concession that undermines the effort to establish an act 'heterogeneous' to the perceptual field one wishes to disturb.

This point helps to address a paradox common to contemporary politics, which is how political acts that are most successful in attaining legitimacy tend to have the simultaneous effect of effacing or diffusing their own efficacy. Politics defeats politics. The self-effacing nature of politics, while neither absolute nor inescapable, is more pervasive than most, including Rancière, tend to acknowledge.[1]

I. The Scarcity of Politics

Against popular conceptions of 'the political' as an arena where, through reaching consensus over conflicts about authority, communication, engagement and governance, local, national and international governmental bodies engage in the art and science of administration, Rancière posits politics as, in essence, the antithesis of how the political is typically perceived. To Rancière, politics is the ground over which assertions of equality challenge established orders of classification, contesting configurations of the 'police', his term for the constellation of organizations and actors with the authority to determine distributions of the sensible in political and daily life. The police are those with the mandate to establish parameters between the sayable and unsayable, the visible and the invisible, the audible and inaudible; while 'politics' is the aesthetics which breaches such parameters: 'it makes visible what has been excluded from a perceptual field, in that it makes audible what used to be inaudible' (see Dillon 2005; Rancière 2004a: 226; 2004b).

There are useful parallels between Rancière's conception of politics and recent work from the field of science studies which suggests that, in contrast to popular and sociological perceptions of the ubiquity of politics, the belief that politics can be found everywhere – in the everyday, in local life, in the bedrooms and boardrooms of nations – politics is actually, as Andrew Barry suggests, 'a rather specialist activity', contingent not on a diverse and plural range of actors, but to an ever-narrowing field of experts and advisors capable of arbitrating on technical and instrumental matters (Barry 2002: 268).

Barry proposes a distinction between 'politics', which he terms a 'set of technical practices, forms of knowledge and institutions', and the 'political', which he views as a barometer, or an index, of the space available for disagreement and contestation (Barry 2002: 270). In this light, an action can be viewed as political to the extent that it creates room and openings for the possibility for disagreement. Technical discussions, scientific deliberations, the minutia of debates over quantifiable measurements – phenomena which are regularly drawn on in political debates, can be seen as *antipolitical*, in that they close the space for disagreement to those who have the expertise and scientific capital to involve themselves in technical decisions. Calculations and measurements 'redraw the boundaries between politics and objectivity by purporting to act as automatic technical mechanisms for making judgements, prioritizing problems and allocating scarce resources' (Porter 1995; Rose 1999a: 198).

At the same time, the very anti-political nature of measurements, the widespread assumption that calculations are untainted by political impurities or tampering, often creates unintended effects precisely *through* the appearance of being irreducible to politics or partisan policies. Through 'disrupting the frame of politics, and creating a conduit for the cross-contamination of the economic and the political' seemingly anti-political phenomena often create avenues and opportunities for disruption where they are least expected (Barry 2002: 268).

Barry offers the example of a rail crash at Hatfield, a station north of London, in October 2000. Investigations following the accident revealed that it had been caused by a broken rail, itself the result of 'metal fatigue', or deterioration of the rail track. Railtrack Plc, the owner of the track, had been informed of the problem in January 2000, months before the accident, but had chosen not to act, exposing the company as potentially liable for the accident. The measurements of metal fatigue had tangible *political* effects, inculpating Railtrack as an accomplice in an incident otherwise dismissible as an untraceable act of technical failure. Although such calculations were obviously 'political demonstrations of a kind', Barry writes, 'they were not ones that could be associated with any identifiable political actors. As a result, they were much more difficult to police than demonstrations conducted in the street' (Barry 2002: 278; 2010). Through their sheer anonymity and irreducibility to any particular political camp, seemingly apolitical calculations fostered a form of politics that managed to escape its own constraints, to escape being identifiable with partisan positions or traceable to any sole player or group of players.

The political and anti-political effects of tools of measurement are often contingent on their location and tangibility within what Michelle Murphy calls 'regimes of imperceptibility': historically and socially constituted terrains of visibility and invisibility which render certain risks or benefits more perceivable, preventable or challengeable than others. A paradigmatic example is the tacit pervasiveness of white privilege in the United States in the later half of the twentieth century, in the era after desegregation rendered explicit forms of racism more illicit. In contrast to the early twentieth century, Murphy writes, when those both capitalizing from and subject to white privilege frequently named and invoked it, the post-segregation refashioning of 'race' as a social category, and the explicit disavowal of institutionalized racism 'encouraged U.S. citizens to suspend their awareness of persistent racialized distributions of privilege and to look only for expressions of racialized disadvantage. White privilege operated through this regularized suspension of perception – in other words, through a regime of imperceptions [. . .] white privilege was generated, like white noise, precisely by "seeming not to be anything in particular"' (Murphy 2004: 268).

Legal desegregation had the unintended effect of shifting partitions of the sensible in ways that rendered ongoing systematic racism and white advantage less obvious than in previous decades. The parameters of what constituted racism or prejudice had been altered; the very explicitness of newfound awareness of the ways non-white individuals had been systematically disadvantaged under segregation made it harder to perceive or articulate the way continued forms of white privilege persisted and flourished in the post-segregation era, nourished by the very illusion of their absence. To challenge or disturb partitions of the sensible today, a political act would have to convince a dominant strata of society that their 'whiteness' was not the unraced identity they had deemed it, and that, not only had their hopes for a meritocratic, 'colour-blind' society not come to pass, its establishment had been forestalled by their assumptions of its imminent arrival through the banishment of segregation. An act of politics today has *more* layers of the unsayable and the unperceivable to breach than in the past when racism was more blatant.

Murphy and Barry's work highlights the anti-political consequences of seemingly political acts, the way that passing new laws – even welcome ones – can forestall or preclude disagreement and contestation by rendering injustices less obvious, thereby leaving 'people shorn of a vocabulary of protest' (Thrift 2007). Their work helps illustrate some of the mechanisms through which individuals are stripped of a language for disturbing the sensible; the mechanisms through which individuals are left 'on the shores of the politics', displaced and diffused as threats to the imperturbability of police life (see Labelle 2001; Rancière 2007; Rancière and Panagia 2000). 'By resigning positions and the passions that target them, by altering the perception of those positions and the emotions attending that perception, politics presides over its own erosion', Rancière writes. 'Depolicization is the oldest task of politics, the one which achieves its fulfilment at the brinks of its end'(Rancière 2007: 18–19). This is a sentiment that has received recent criticism. Jodi Dean, for example, suggests the argument that 'politics has been foreclosed, excluded, prevented from emerging, is childishly petulant'. She insists that it is particularly inapplicable to the United States in the post-9/11 environment, where, if anything, there has been an explosion of engagement in the form of new political movements over climate change or evolution, where:

> polls taken daily, even hourly, during the long U.S. presidential campaign of 2008 *differ* from each other; consumers of political news ingest numbers that *differ* from each other, call each other into doubt, rendering the very categories of polling unstable. Indeed, the gap between polls and electoral outcomes, the failure of exit polls accurately to predict the votes tallied (an issue in both the 2000 and the 2004 elections), and the politicization of this gap as corruption, crime, theft, and racist disenfranchisement of African-American voters express a politics [that is irreducible, she argues, to what she sees as Rancière's vision of a post-political] triumph of consensus. (Dean 2009: 23–4)

Dean misses the point. Rancière's argument is not that *attempts* to disturb the sensible are rare, or that evidence of political engagement is absent in contemporary democracies. His point is how rarely they *succeed* in perturbing 'the determined, sensible world', partly because the forms of political expression listed above – opinion polls, electoral voting – are part of the constellation of actions sanctioned and encouraged by the police themselves. To insist, as Dean does, that the mere appearance of public engagement is evidence of *politics*, that shifting opinion polls provide proof of a vibrant public, is to remain rooted in the banal slogans of a regrettable sociological fallacy, a sociology where politics are naively and optimistically assumed to be everywhere.

As Kristin Ross suggests, politics, for Rancière, is not a matter of illusion or disillusion, nor of a dialectic between governors and the governed, nor of movements deemed 'conservative' or 'progressive'. It is an interlocutory event, one that reconfigures the parameters of what *counts* as a political act, one that is 'still exceptional or scarce' and one that often occurs beyond the arenas where politics are typically assumed to be found (Ross 2009: 28). Rancière stresses this point in a recent article, asserting that for him

> 'disagreement' and 'dissensus' do not imply that politics is a struggle between camps; they imply that it is a struggle about what politics is, a struggle that is waged about such original issues as: 'where are we?', 'who are we?', 'what makes us a we?' ... where the question 'how is this thinkable at all?' points to the question 'who is qualified for thinking at all?' (Rancière 2009: 116)

Politics is the act which reconfigures assumptions of who has the credibility to define and articulate visions of what politics could be, or ought to be. Examples may be scarce, but they can be found. One example is the explosion of activity in the mid-1980s onward surrounding the development of new treatments for HIV/AIDS. As the sociologist Steven Epstein writes, a striking aspect of the conduct of AIDS research in the United States is the diversity of players with the credibility to influence how clinical trials are carried out and which political and financial mechanisms are useful in expediting new treatments to the public. Within literature on drug regulation, AIDS activists are often upheld as an example of how a politicized patient group, united around a shared cause, can affect regulatory processes. They are typically credited, for example, as being one of the largest influences on the FDA's 1992 decision to introduce user fees, making the FDA less reliant on federal funds and more reliant on direct financing by the pharmaceutical industry in exchange for drug licensing. Whatever the eventual costs of this shift – and many suggest the effect has been quite pernicious, making the U.S. regulator overly beholden to the industry it is meant to be regulating – it is indisputable patient activism played a decisive role (see Daemmrich 2004; Epstein 1995; Greene 2007).

Epstein suggests the novelty of AIDS activists is not merely that they influenced regulatory policies, but that they radicalized notions of what counts as scientific credibility and which groups have the legitimacy to contribute to the production of scientific facts:

> My point in stressing the breadth of participation in claims making is not simply to say that AIDS research is heavily politicized or that it has a public face. More profoundly, this case demonstrates that activist movements, through amassing different forms of credibility, can in certain circumstances become genuine participants in the construction of scientific knowledge – that they can (within definite limits) effect changes in both the epistemic practices of biomedical research and in the therapeutic technique of medical care [. . .] AIDS activists did not achieve influence simply by amassing political muscle of the conventional sort (although that did prove necessary at points along the way). In addition, they found ways of presenting themselves as credible *within* the area of credentialed expertise. At the same time, these activists succeeded in changing the rules of the game, transforming the very definition of what *counts* as credibility in scientific research such that their particular assets would prove efficacious. (Epstein 1995: 409)

Sufferers proclaimed their right to be heard as equals, not through insisting their expertise was on par with scientists, but through reconfiguring notions of what constituted expertise itself. In the face of a crisis shrouded in unknowns, magnified by the sheer mystery surrounding the scale and aetiology of the disease, activists harnessed the uncertainty surrounding potential treatments to their advantage. Their status as 'treatment activists' in medical experiments testing novel therapies enabled them to wield unprecedented influence over the design and interpretation of clinical trial methodologies, effectively challenging FDA policies over who had the right to enrol in trials with unknowable medical risks (Epstein 1995: 416).

'There is no hierarchy in ignorance', Ranciere once wrote, and the strategies of AIDS activists seem to reflect this aphorism (Rancière 1991: 32). Pointing out how *little* experts knew about the origin and treatability of AIDS helped them to challenge the epistemological privileging of scientific over 'lay' expertise. They mobilized ignorance itself in order to defend their status as equal pioneers in the discovery of new therapies. This strategy, however, had its limits. One of the key tactics for amassing credibility was to become as literate as possible about the science of HIV treatment. Many activists, even while asserting the importance of 'non-scientific' imperatives – the cultural effort to challenge the stigmatization of AIDS as a 'gay' problem, for example – 'nonetheless assumed that the capacity to speak the language of the journal article and the conference hall is a sine qua non of their effective participation' (Epstein 1995: 417). So, over time, as activists themselves became more knowledgeable about the science of AIDS, many of them came to place increasing faith in the cultural frames of mainstream biomedicine, some developing a more 'fastidious' perspective on the superiority of clinical trials over other forms of evidence, partly because of the need to acquire 'hard data' that could be of use politically. The need to speak in a language persuasive to scientists and other authorities, to point to hard facts in order to lobby for more R&D funding, has had the unintended effect of discrediting the tactics of an earlier wave of activists, those who harnessed the fragility and vulnerability of scientific knowledge in order to assert their equal footing in devising new research hypotheses and trial methodologies (Epstein 1995: 424).

This problem is similar to debates over climate change, where to be persuasive, both sceptics and adherents of the need to tackle global warming often frame their political arguments in technical terms, something that typically earns scientific credibility at the expense of precluding or foreclosing discussions of the social impact of environmental degradation. 'Too often', as David Demeritt writes, 'policy decisions are legitimated in purely technical terms, leaving opponents with only scientific grounds for contesting policies that they oppose for other reasons' (Demeritt 2006: 473). The problem also emerges in drug regulation, as the recent controversy over the safety of Ketek illustrates.

II. The Ketek Case

Ketek is an antibiotic drug manufactured by Sanofi-Aventis for the treatment of upper respiratory tract infections such as sinusitis and bronchitis. In 2000, when Aventis first sought an FDA licence for the drug, a number of FDA reviewers grew concerned when a patient treated with Ketek developed severe liver damage. In April 2001, an FDA advisory committee stipulated that the company should conduct a large clinical trial to help determine Ketek's safety before a licence could be granted. The trial, known as study 3014, involved dozens of research sites and thousands of participants across the United States. Early on during the trial, a routine FDA safety investigation uncovered grave violations of good clinical practice at the lead research site where the study was being carried out, such as the fact that most of the participant consent forms appeared to have been forged. Despite knowing that data from the trial was compromised by these violations, the FDA presented results to an FDA advisory committee without mentioning that data had been distorted by trial investigators. Unaware of the unreliability of data, the advisory group recommended approval of Ketek (Hundley 2007; Ross 2007).

The FDA awarded a licence for Ketek in 2004. Between 2004 and 2006, more than five million prescriptions were written for the drug in the United States. During those years, 14 adult patients suffered liver failure after taking Ketek, at least four of whom died. Dozens of others suffered serious liver injury – most of them otherwise healthy individuals (see Harris 2006; Ross 2007). In 2007, the FDA implemented label changes for the drug, banning its use for two of its three previously approved indications, acute sinusitis and chronic bronchitis, and insisting on a black box warning for its third: community-acquired pneumonia. The FDA has stated there was no intention to 'deceive the advisory committee or the public regarding our review of study 3014', and that it had chosen not to reveal concerns over the integrity of study 3014 in order to avoid compromising an investigation into possible fraud. The agency defended its earlier decision to license Ketek in 2004, and suggested that as soon as reports of serious liver toxicity emerged, the agency moved swiftly to impose a bolder safety warning on the drug (Soreth et al. 2007: 1675).

David Ross, now working at the U.S. Department of Veterans Affairs, disputes the FDA's insistence that the agency acted swiftly, pointing out that the FDA did not move to relabel Ketek until 16 months after the first case of severe liver toxicity emerged. Throughout 2005 and 2006, as reports of liver toxicity increased, Ross pleaded with supervisors to take action. In June 2006, a number of FDA reviewers, including Ross, were summoned to a meeting with the FDA Commissioner at the time, Andrew von Eschenbach. During the meeting, von Eschenbach compared the FDA to a football team and told staff that if they publicly discussed problems with Ketek outside the agency, they would be 'traded from the team'.[2]

Ross is not the first FDA officer to face internal threats for raising concerns about a drug's risks. As the *New York Times* reports, since 2003, at least four FDA safety reviewers have been punished or discouraged for uncovering previously undetected risks, including Andrew Mosholder, a safety officer barred from presenting data to an FDA advisory committee which suggested antidepressants lead to suicidal reactions in children, and Rosemary Johann-Liang, who left the agency after raising concerns over the safety of drugs such as Ketek and Avandia, a diabetes drug linked to heart failure (Harris 2007).

Their experiences suggest a pattern. Typically those who have been most vocal in flagging risks have been the same individuals *most* discredited or resented by peers or employees reluctant to revise earlier positions on a drug's safety. The resentment of 'whistleblowers' who publicize a drug's risks is often palpable regardless of whether concerns prove correct. In fact, quite ironically, particularly in scientific arenas, where, as Nikolas Rose writes, 'impersonality rather than status, wisdom or experiences' (Rose 1999b: 208) provides the measure of truth, the more persistently and relentlessly someone seeks to call attention to flawed policies or practices, the more they erode perceptions of their own impartiality – therefore sacrificing their own credibility the *more* influential their warnings turn out to be. Had David Ross been *wrong* about Ketek, his concerns might have elicited less resistance from supervisors concerned with maintaining public trust in the agency. The gravest risk in voicing dissent is typically not being wrong but being right.

III. Anti-politics at the FDA

Why would the FDA be slow at detecting side effects, and slow to disclose risks once they are apparent? The reasons are numerous and interrelated.

One stems from the 1992 decision to introduce user fees from industry for drug licensing. Although seen as a welcome move by many, drug manufacturers stipulated certain conditions. They refused to let their money be spent on post-market safety studies, and insisted drug reviews be completed within six months, leading critics to suggest the agency has come to value speed over safety (Harris 2007). Another factor is reputational concerns, where regulators have seemed reluctant to act swiftly on risks for fear of drawing attention to earlier regulatory lapses in licensing the drug in the first place (see Abraham and Sheppard 1999; Carpenter 2006; McGoey 2007; McGoey and Jackson 2009). A third reason is less explicitly self-interested. In fact, it emerges from the opposite impulse, from the effort to minimize partisan or commercial biases on drug licensing. Historically, clinical trials have been valued precisely because, through the use of control groups, they can guard against biased results, determining whether the drug itself, or an external variable, has produced a particular effect. Clinical trials, like other tools of measurement, are valued for their seeming imperviousness to political bias or manipulation (see Greene 2007; Marks 1997).

Even though it is widely known that many clinical trials are too short in duration and have too few participants to demonstrate adverse risks that might appear during post-market epidemiological studies, faith in the superiority of clinical trials over observational or anecdotal evidence has led to a situation where, as one FDA staff member said to me, agency staff:

will only believe – this has been said to me more than once by people from the Office of New Drugs, very high level people – they will only believe that an adverse effect is real when a controlled clinical trial has been done that shows an effect with a p value of less than 0.05.

At first glance, the reliance on clinical trials seems to foreclose avenues for regulatory disagreement by narrowing the scope for challenge to those who can draw on clinical trial data to support their arguments, a problem when a drug's risks are not apparent on the trials used to test it. But, just as, as Barry's work illustrates, assumptions of a technology's imperviousness to political tampering can have deeply political effects through appearing free of partisan influence, harnessing perceptions of the superiority of clinical trials can be useful even to those who wish to challenge the dominance of these methodological tools. By calling attention, for example, to the fraudulent factors that undermined the reliability of study 3014, Ross and others were able to bolster support for their detection of post-market adverse effects, effects that might have otherwise been dismissible because they did not appear on clinical trials. A similar example appears with antidepressant drugs such as Prozac, where suggestions of a suicidal risk were first scoffed at, and then confirmed when a series of re-analyses of company-held clinical trial data revealed statistically significant risks between antidepressants and suicidal reactions, risks that had been dismissed during earlier regulatory inquiries because they were not detected on available trial evidence (see Lenzer 2006).

Ross and other FDA insiders succeeded in exposing the fragility of what Barry calls 'metrological regimes', systems where the standardization of measurements enables a cross-fertilization of political deliberations and market transactions in ways that often diffuse the potential for political confrontation. The reliance on clinical trials within drug regulation offers an example of a metrological regime. Drugs reach the market through a complex process linking clinical trial participants, drug manufacturers and regulators together through a process that thrives through the illusion of the inability of individual actors to unduly bias trial results. Precisely because metrological regimes derive credibility through appearing free of bias, they are always vulnerable to the very elements that lend them strength. By exposing the 'weaknesses of measurement and the uncertainties of economic and scientific calculation', individuals can pierce the impenetrability of regimes which depend on the perception of being above or beyond politics (Barry 2002: 276).

Drawing attention to the fragility of measurements has its pitfalls. The mere act of *exposing* uncertainties often erodes perceptions of an individual's disinterestedness or impartiality, diffusing the value of the criticisms the moment they are voiced. As the case of Ketek suggests, political actions often incriminate their own efficacy through the sheer act of being articulated. Politics defeats itself just as often, if not more often, than it manages to escape its own limitations. Most of the FDA staff who raised concerns about Ketek have since left the agency. The ones I spoke with called attention to an inescapable bind. Either they could stay at the agency, vocalize concerns with current licensing procedures, and sacrifice opportunities for career advancement, or they could leave the agency and lose the credibility to draw attention to regulatory shortcomings at their former place of work. As one former officer said to me, 'we're painted as disgruntled former employees and nothing we say matters'.

In some ways, of course, the pacification of opinion – the way that one's authority is eroded through the sheer act of drawing on it publicly – is hardly a new story. As Rancière notes, Alexis de Tocqueville was one of the first to identify how the emergence of a new sociality within modern democracies, a sociality insistent on an equality of condition among all citizens, managed to mitigate the political effectiveness of individual opinion by encouraging all citizens to believe in their ability to make their views known. As a direct result of faith in their own freedoms – of speech, assembly, of the press – individuals within democracies forge their own constraints. Their assurance of their capacity to speak out publicly both weakens the imperative to do so and indicts the credibility of the few who do. The authority allocated to each citizen by her peers decreases in proportion to the freedom to express opinions. Dissent is *stifled* through the assumption of one's equal right to be heard (see de Tocqueville 1848: 184; McGoey draft; Rancière 2007: 20).

Paying more attention to the politics of testimonial credibility in political and organizational life could help to examine a paradox: the question of why calling attention to regulatory errors is often treated as more of an aberration of correct procedure than quietly perpetuating them. The cynical view is that all forms of regulation – and all partitions of the sensible, for that matter – are necessarily dependent on the deliberate, pernicious suppression of any criticism that might impede the efficiency or impugn the reputation of an organization. Another perspective, the one favoured in this chapter, is the less cynical, but also far more intractable possibility that dissenting opinions are persistently ignored because of the assumption that they *should* be: because of the subtle distaste for the voicing of opinion in arenas where tools of quantification are revered for the democratic ability to decide without appearing to decide.

Notes

1. Versions of this chapter were presented at a workshop on Experimental Subjects, Lancaster University, January 2010, and a seminar at the Institute for Cultural and Social Anthropology, Oxford University, February 2010.
2. The meeting with von Eschenbach is described by Ross during testimony before the U.S. House of Representatives' Committee on Energy and Commerce, which launched a series of hearings in 2007 and 2008 to determine whether a range of parties, from the FDA to Aventis, knew about the adverse risks of Ketek and chose to ignore or conceal them.

Works Cited

Abraham, J. and Sheppard, J. (1999), 'Complacent and Conflicting Scientific Expertise in British and American Drug Regulation: Clinical Risk Assessment of Triazolam', *Social Studies of Science*, 29: 803–43.

Barry, A. (2002), 'The Anti-Political Economy', *Economy and Society*, 31: 268–84.

— (2010), 'Materialist Politics: Metallurgy', in *Political Matter: Technoscience, Democracy and Public Life*, ed. B. Braun and S. Whatmore, Minneapolis: University of Minnesota Press.

Carpenter, D. (2006), 'Reputation, Gatekeeping and the Politics of Post-marketing Drug Regulation', *Virtual Mentor: Ethics Journal of the American Medical Association*, 8 (6): 403–6.

Daemmrich, A. (2004), *Pharmacopolitics: Drug Regulation in the United States and Germany*, Chapel Hill: University of North Carolina Press.

de Tocqueville, A. (1848), 'Democracy in America', in *Democracy in America (reprinted 1969)*, ed. J. P. Mayer, New York: Perennial Classics.

Dean, J. (2009), 'Politics without Politics', *Parallax*, 15: 20–36.

Demeritt, D. (2006), Science Studies, Climate Change, and the Prospects for Constructivist Critique. *Economy and Society*, 35: 453–79.

Dillon, M. (2005), 'A Passion for the (Im)possible: Jacques Rancière, Equality, Pedagogy and the Messianic', *European Journal of Political Theory*, 4: 429–52.

Epstein, S. (1995), 'The Construction of Lay Expertise: Aids Activism and the Forging of Credibility in the Reform of Clinical Trials', *Science, Technology and Human Values*, 20: 408–37.

Greene, J. (2007), *Prescribing by Numbers: Drugs and the Definition of Disease*, Baltimore: John Hopkins University Press.

Harris, G. (2006), 'Approval of Antibiotic Worried Safety Officials', *New York Times*, July 18.

— (2007), 'Potentially Incompatible Goals at FDA', *New York Times*, June 11.

Hundley, K. (2007), 'Drug's Chilling Path to Market: How a Broken FDA Approved a Cold Antibiotic Despite a Wide Trail of Alarms', *St. Petersburg Times*, May 27.

Labelle, G. (2001), 'Two Refoundation Projects of Democracy in Contemporary French Philosophy: Cornelius Castoriadis and Jacques Rancière', *Philosophy and Social Criticism*, 27: 75–103.

Lenzer, J. (2006), 'Manufacturer Admits Increase in Suicidal Behaviour in Patients Taking Paroxetine', *BMJ*, 332 (7751): 1175.

Marks, H. M. (1997), *'The Progress of Experiment'*, Cambridge: Cambridge University Press.

McGoey, L. (2007), 'On the Will to Ignorance in Bureaucracy', *Economy and Society*, 36: 212–35.

— 'Bad Faith and the Economy of Ignorance', unpublished manuscript.

McGoey, L. and Jackson, E. (2009), 'Seroxat and the Suppression of Clinical Trial Data: Regulatory Failure and the Uses of Legal Ambiguity', *Journal of Medical Ethics*, 36: 107–12.

Murphy, M. (2004), 'Uncertain Exposure and the Privilege of Imperception: Activist Scientists and Race at the US. Environmental Agency', *Osiris*, 19: 266–82.

Porter, T. (1995), *Trust in Numbers: The Pursuit of Objectivity in Science and Public Life*, Princeton: Princeton University Press.

Rancière, J. (1991), *The Ignorant Schoolmaster: Five Lessons in Intellectual Emancipation*, Stanford: Stanford University Press.

— (2004a), *The Philosopher and His Poor*, Durham: Duke University Press.

— (2004b), *The Politics of Aesthetics: The Distribution of the Sensible*, Trans. Gabriel Rockhill, Basingstoke: Continuum.

— (2007), *On the Shores of Politics*, London and New York: Verso.

— (2009), 'A Few Remarks on the Method of Jacques Rancière', *Parallax*, 15: 114–23.

Rancière, J. and Panagia, D. (2000), 'Dissenting Words: A Conversation with Jacques Rancière', *Diacritics*, Summer.

Rose, N. (1999a), *Governing the Soul: The Shaping of the Private Self*, London: Free Association Books.

— (1999b), *Powers of Freedom: Reframing Political Thought*, Cambridge: Cambridge University Press.

Ross, D. B. (2007), 'The FDA and the Case of Ketek', *New England Journal of Medicine*, 356: 1601–4.

Ross, K. (2009), 'Historicizing Untimeliness', in *Jacques Rancière: History, Politics, Aesthetics*, ed. G Rockhill, P Watts, Durham and London: Duke University Press.

Soreth, J., Cox, E., Kweder, S., Jenkins, J., and Galson, S. (2007), 'Ketek – The FDA Perspective (correspondence)', *New England Journal of Medicine*, 356: 1675–6.

Thrift, N. (2007), *Non-Representational Theory: Space; Politics; Affect*, London: Routledge.

Paul de Man and Art History I: Modernity, Aesthetics and Community in Jacques Rancière

Martin McQuillan

'How "aesthetic" is to be understood here is not self-evident'
(de Man 1986: 63)

I. Another Jacques

This essay is a response to a challenge and a commission to read Jacques Rancière on art. Having worked my way through Rancière's texts on what he calls 'aesthetics' I must confess to a sense of disappointment and to feeling a little awkward in assembling my thoughts to respond to Paul Bowman and Richard Stamp's friendly solicitation. I feel a bit like someone who sees everyone around them laughing but who fails to get the joke himself. The experience of reading Rancière has been akin to wading through a theory soup of everyone I have ever been suspicious of (a little semiology here, a grating of Foucault there, a large pinch of Althusser, a smidgen of psychoanalysis, a dusting of Deleuze, all with a strong flavour of an un-reconstructed, un-deconstructed French philosophical discourse on canonical art (the national and institutional philosophical variety rather than the exported 'theoretical' kind). In contrast say to the complexity and innovation of a thinker such as Derrida, I am compelled to wonder out loud: what is all the fuss about? On the one hand, there is a rather obvious and easily dismissed answer to this question, namely, that of academic fashion. Rancière is someone whose work has been with us for a while (since the collective text, *Lire le Capital*, with Althusser, Balibar, Macherey and Establet [1965]) but now in the growing absence of senior Parisian figures his time has come. With the assistance of friendly review, anglophone allies and publication with novelty-hungry presses he has emerged along with the likes of Alan Badiou as the next big thing in French Theory. However, it seems self-evident that his writing is not 'the next big thing' but rather something quite interestingly 'retro'. The fashion for Rancière will need to be accounted for because after all, as Paul de Man (someone who was once in fashion himself but no longer) suggests fashion itself is an aesthetic and historical category (de Man 1986: 65). I am by disposition immediately suspicious of the notion of that the future of theory depends upon the uncovering of fresh 'big names' from the Grandes Écoles. There is no good reason why this model of translation and importation, that fed the theoretical opening in the anglophone humanities for three decades, should continue unchecked (as we shall see I am equally by disposition suspicious of the model of the model itself). The search for the latest greyhaired authority from Paris is a repetition of a nostalgia that denies the very dissemination that, what we might now be obliged to call, 'the theoretical tradition' put in play. Much time and treasure has been spent in American graduate schools and in British research centres constructing the reputations of new grand figures of the French scene at the expense perhaps of local talent or the next generation who might not be that turned on by this imitation of this historical model. Equally, it may be this generation that is responsible for seeking out their own French idols in repetition of a schema they have inherited from the theoretical past. However, comments such as these could be quite rightly dismissed as either in some way theoretically sectarian or anecdotally unrigorous, and there is no reason to be satisfied by them even though they might tell us something about the pathologies of the academy.

There are other reasons why I confess to being under-whelmed by my encounter with the text of Rancière that I will attempt to outline before expanding my discontent into a wider argument concerning the challenge of critical thought to art history and practice. First, and I think most significantly he is someone who is reluctant to read (all Rancière's issues stem from this). Rancière's philosophical enterprise is set up around the demarcation of what is translated as three 'regimes of the art' (the ethical, the representational and the aesthetic) and from this he seeks a certain clarity of definition around the idea of the aesthetic as a 'distribution of the sensible' which then has consequences for the material realm of politics in the Modern period. Accordingly, Rancière needs this dialectical system to work at a level of descriptive and predictive generality. The consequence of this in his writing is that he tends to gesture towards broad brush and universalizing descriptions of artistic epochs rather than the detailed consideration of textual examples that might suggest, explain or challenge a more general theory (for example see Rancière 2007: 14, 20, 103). It is not that 'reading' is entirely absent from the text of Rancière, one will occasionally find an instance of literary quotation or a description of an art object (for example, Rancière 2007: 80ff; or Rancière 2009: 27) but that these 'readings' are never particularly close. They rarely operate at the level of the signifier, brush stroke or pixel, they tend to be gestures towards what a reading might look like rather than reading itself. Rancière is not someone who goes in for unnecessary textual explication. This is equally true of his commentary on the philosophical which also tends to operate on the level of a general synthesis and frequently at the level of pointed condemnation of the abstract such as 'postmodernism' or 'Critical Thought' (see Rancière 2009: 25 ff, or 45; or Rancière 2007: 45) without identifying the authors of their ignominy. 'Postmodernism' is a particular sinner responsible in Rancière's view for all manner of errors but which in his writing speaks with a homogeneous voice, effecting unfeasible epochal change despite its clear wrong-headedness. Whenever Rancière offers us a philosophical villain (Barthes on the image or Lyotard on the sublime, for example) his account of them is at the level of his own singular summary rather than a matter of quotation and analysis. Equally, his literary and artistic objects seem to be drawn from a fairly narrow range with a number of notable favourites (such as *Madame Bovary*, Plato's commentary on theatre and Godard's *Histoires du Cinéma*, for example) being put to use again and again to demonstrate the truth of his philosophical discourse. All this is a problem because it produces a discourse on art in the absence of the challenge of art. The theoretical statements and philosophical system are not sufficiently tested against the singularity of art objects that might otherwise disturb the thetics and axiomatics of that system. Rancière goes to some length for conceptual clarity and is keen to pin down art but does not sufficiently risk his own discourse by offering art the opportunity to get up and walk away with the pin. What we have instead is a series of references rather than readings and these references might just as well be otherwise since they are never fully actualized as readings. The references support a discourse that works at a level of considerable generality that then becomes wholly detached from the objects it purports to describe, rendering it of limited value in the interpretation or explanation of those objects. The discourse seems to exist on its own terms and to refer to nothing but its own status as a discourse on art or as a philosophical system.

Second, and consequently, there is nothing undialectical about Rancière's dialectic. The ethical, representational and aesthetic regimes of the art in Rancière work, for good or ill, according to a familiar formulation of historical development that we might find in Hegel's dialectic of the classical, symbolic and romantic. On the one hand, there is nothing wrong with an attraction to the hopeless allure of the dialectic (I have commented on this elsewhere (McQuillan 2008: 132)). However, when it comes to something as complex as art or literature, or indeed politics, it is necessary to ask in what way the art object might resist dialecticalization. In accounting for art, literature or politics it is not a question of opposing the dialectic (for that would be the most dialectical of gestures). Rather it is necessary to think in terms of 'a dialecticity of dialectics that is itself fundamentally not dialectic', as Derrida puts it in one of the interviews with Maurizio Ferraris (Derrida 2001: 32). Within any dialectical situation there remains an element, which does not allow itself to be integrated into the systematicity of the dialectic, but which presents non-oppositional difference that exceeds the dialectic, which is itself always oppositional. This is what Derrida calls the supplement (among other things) which does not allow itself to be dialectized and which not being dialectical is necessarily then recuperated by the dialectic that it relaunches. 'Thus the dialectic consists', says Derrida, 'precisely in dialectizing the non-dialectizable' (2001: 32). This scenario is not recognizable as the dialectic in any easy sense of synthesis, totalization, identification and transcendence. Rather this non-dialectical dialecticity of the dialectic is a form of synthesis without synthesis, what Derrida frequently terms 'ex-appropriation', which is both an essentially anti-dialectical concept and the necessary condition of dialectics as such. The point here is not that, as Rancière says, a new regime of art does not necessarily abolish the previously dominant one (2004: 50), thus rendering Rancière's schema different from the classical dialectic. Rather, it is that when we read Hegel, for example, closely (see McQuillan 2010), this situation is exactly what happens in Hegel all the time, particularly when he risks his dialectic against the singularity of art objects; and that this sort of epochal contamination and co-existence is endemic to the dialectic as such. Whenever Hegel's dialectic comes into contact with the art object we are always left the non-dialectizable residue that problematizes the dialectical approach and renders the text of Hegel only ever an allegory of the dialectic. The point would be that given that philosophy since Heidegger has taken this disarticulation of the dialectic really quite far, especially in relation to art, it is something that a philosopher of the theoretical tradition writing today might hope to treat as something to be gone through rather than ignored entirely. Given that the non-dialecticity of the dialectic is probably just about the most difficult thing to think about in relation to philosophy, this absence might explain the current popularity of Rancière.

Third, and related to this, all of Rancière's terms, without exception, are metaphysical. I do not think this is just a question of whether one ascribes to a deconstructive principle or not. The difficulty is Rancière's certainty that entities like 'art' and 'aesthetics' exist and that their categorization, while not straightforward, is only a matter of conceptual clarity. On the one hand, this drive for precision only leads to confusion as the determination of the exactitude of his definitions leads him towards the creation of a set of supplementary categories whenever his fixed criteria shows up its lack when confronted by the facts of art history (the difference between 'Modernity' and what he calls 'modernatism' would be a good example of this (Rancière 2004: 27)). The care to be taken when approaching the categories of the metaphysical tradition is not that of avoiding inherited terms, this is impossible and one is never more clearly part of the history of a category such as the aesthetic as whenever one conspicuously attempts to ignore it. Rather, one should be careful not to assume the stability of the term as a fully formed, self-identical concept. Any notion of a regime of art presupposes the idea of art as well as so much else suggested by the word regime. On this point Rancière is poorly served by the translation into English of '*régime*' as the English word 'regime'. In French the word is considerably more elastic and while referring to a political order it also can be used to mean a 'settlement' ['*régime matrionial*'], grouping (or in the case of bananas 'un régime' is a bunch), diet/regimen or in the case of rivers and engines flow, rate, rhythm or speed, all of which might suggest a more porous concept of aesthetic distribution. Equally, '*partage*' as in Rancière's phrase '*le partage du sensible*' can mean 'distribution' but more accurately 'sharing out' with the emphasis on responsibly allotted portion. However, translation is not really the issue here (nor are the difficulties of translation a particular thematic for Rancière). Rather what is at stake is the idea that critical leverage can be brought to bear either on art, aesthetics or politics by continuing to use these archaic Western categories with impunity. It is not possible for Rancière to use these terms without becoming contaminated by the inheritance he wishes to oppose. Instead the confident use of his inflated vocabulary wants to suggest that there is such a thing as the category of 'art' or the 'aesthetic' that we can all agree upon as an understood thing (even if he has to redefine it for us by way of re-education) and about which we could say something new in the very place where art and the aesthetic might escape any systematization or measurement. Rather, when we speak of art let us say, 'art, if there is any' in order that art and thinking about art might have a future. Equally, philosophy cannot be held accountable to art or the aesthetic (i.e. be used in a utilitarian way to explain art) because both 'art' and 'aesthetics' are philosophical concepts. Therefore, it is a curiously circular task for philosophy to seek an autopsy on a body of its own making, revisiting its own failure by smuggling back into a philosophical discourse as an object of study something produced by philosophy in the first place. Let's not imagine that Rancière can use these terms without being reclaimed by the tradition he attempts to countermand. Ultimately, what is dissatisfying about reading Rancière is that his writing on art is merely philosophy (i.e. it repeats all the old universalizing gestures and all the secure terminology of philosophy) at a moment after philosophy has opened itself to living on as more than philosophy in the recognition of the inadequacy of these gestures and the waning of the security of these terms, even if what they have held in store might allow for another future of philosophy.

Fourth, and finally for now, what is one to make today of Rancière's use of a term like the 'sensible'? While one does not need to deprive oneself of the metaphysical inheritance and its vocabulary (it is after all the only resource open to philosophy), Rancière's privileging of art as a category has in common with all aesthetics the foundational assumption of a division between the sensible and the intelligible. It is the very cornerstone of his writing. However, as with all aesthetics as philosophy his writing works towards a reduction of that distinction in favour of the intelligible (Rancière might deny this but we shall shortly demonstrate this). It thus effaces the art it privileges by positing it as secondary from the beginning: it is not by accident that the art object is seldom allowed to speak for itself in his discourse. Any attempt to reduce the distinction in the opposite direction, as Rancière frequently does (for example Rancière 2010: 12) continues to rely on the same structure of transcendental contraband that is constitutively unable to disarticulate the predicament it has entangled itself within and the tropes upon which it relies. On this question of the inheritance of philosophical terms, it will be necessary to put into question the transcendental terms of Rancière's discourse: art, aesthetics, politics and history. This can only be done (given all that has been said above, which will no doubt have sufficiently tried the reader's patience) via a close reading of an exemplary text by Rancière. However, before I take that particular turn I would like to consider what Paul de Man has to say concerning the general problematic that Rancière has chosen to confront, what Rancière calls '*le partage du sensible*' and what de Man calls 'aesthetic ideology'. In so doing, I would like to posit by way of counter-example the sorts of questions that Rancière's writing might have chosen to address through reading rather than synthesis. Accordingly, we might find that Rancière despite himself might be engaged in a considerable philosophical struggle, the stakes of which run beyond the currently fashionable or generational misprisions.

II. Demanding Histories

Of all of the troubling and challenging things that Paul de Man has to say some of the most troubling and most challenging concern history. The implications of de Man's writing for the idea of history and historically determined disciplines such as the History of Art or Cultural History has never been fully elaborated; the challenge of de Man's later writing having been swept away by the sound and fury that accompanied the posthumous discovery of his wartime journalism. However, in the light of the current interest in the historical determination of the aesthetic proposed by Jacques Rancière, it may be beneficial to return to those texts. First, against stereotype, de Man states in the text transcribed from the Messenger Lecture series as 'Kant and Schiller' that the topic that has emerged most forcefully from his reading of figurative language in literary texts is 'the question of reversibility, linked to the question of historicity ... [it is] more interesting than any other to me' (de Man 1996: 132). De Man has in truth been a frequent commentator on history up until this point, including for example the provocative closing line of his reading of 'The Social Contract' (the manuscript of de Man's text was written as early as 1972 (see de Man 2010)). Now, there is a piece of work to be done ('Paul de Man and Art History II') that would deal exclusively with the implications of the

Aesthetic Ideology book for the discipline of Art History. I do not propose to undertake a full elaboration of this here. Rather, I would like to consider what de Man says about history and aesthetics in this text on Kant and Schiller and in several essays that precede it in the de Manian corpus. The first of these is the relatively early essay, 'Literary History and Literary Modernity'. Here de Man outlines the institutional difficulty of putting history itself in question. He suggests:

> The vested interest that academics have in the value of history makes it difficult to put the term seriously into question. Only an exceptionally talented and perhaps eccentric member of the profession could undertake this task with sufficient energy to make it effective, and even then it is likely to be accompanied by the violence that surrounds passion and rebellion. (de Man 1983: 145)

From here he goes on to offer an account of Nietzsche's '*Vom Nutzen und Nachteil der Histoire für das Leben*' ['Of the Use and Misuse of History for Life'] as an example of one such talented eccentric. What the talented, if not institutionally eccentric (he only ever taught in elite IVY League universities) de Man draws out of Nietzsche is the idea that not only might literature and modernity be incompatible concepts but that 'history and modernity may well be even more incompatible' (de Man 1983: 142). This is an important stake in the context of a discussion of Rancière since he equates the 'aesthetic regime of art' with Modernity itself (Rancière 2004: 24). De Man's reading goes something like this: there is nothing specifically modern about modernity (1983: 144) – the term has its roots in Late Latin, *modo* meaning 'just now' giving *modernus* in Middle English. Modernity is then a problematic term in literary history because it names an epoch in which writers become aware of the impossibility of being modern. This is merely indicative of a more general difficulty, 'the problematic structure of a concept that, like all concepts that are in essence temporal, acquires a particularly rich complexity when it is made to refer to events that are in essence linguistic' (de Man 1983: 144). De Man's reading is then drawn not towards an account of his own modernity but the challenge to the methods of literary history that this conceptual difficulty implies. For example, Modernity (as conceived by literary history and avant-garde writers as their own time keepers) invests in the power of the present as an origin only to discover that 'in severing itself from the past, it has at the same time severed itself from the present' (de Man 1983: 149). In this way, Modernity and history are in some curious way incompatible terms and not, as literary history has it, a sub-set of one another. Literature itself, says de Man, has an impulse towards immediacy and in this sense is always a question of a modern consciousness. Accordingly, literature is the most modern of things and so is equally incompatible with a straightforward notion of its own historicity. However, following Nietzsche, de Man suggests that the diremption of history-oriented educational practices and the impulse of the modern spirit in art towards the making of a 'new time' must be understood in historical terms. The modernity of literature, says de Man, before his encounter with the vocabulary of deconstruction, presents 'an unsolvable paradox' (1983: 151) that both denies and affirms its own specificity as an attitude towards immediacy. Now, all of this, insofar as it is valid, could equally be said of art in general, which sits ambivalently between the categorization of the art historian and the artist's own modernity. In fact, the example that de Man goes on to take up is that of Baudelaire's essay of Constantin Guys as the 'painter of modern life' and 'emblem of the poetic mind' (de Man 1983: 157) who is both a modern man of action and a record keeper. De Man's commentary at this point concerns both Baudelaire and Guys in an interchangeable way, literature and art having no clear distinction at this point as both are equally concerned with negotiating the problematic of the collapsing walls between the conceptualization of history and modernity. De Man draws out of his encounter with Baudelaire the suggestion that despite their impulse towards the modern, literary (i.e. artistic) texts know themselves to be fictional and allegorical 'repetitions [...] forever unable to participate in the spontaneity of action or modernity' (1983: 161). Accordingly, as soon as art or literature replaces a singular moment of invention with its repetition as a textual and successive movement that involves more than one distinct moment, it 'enters into a world that assumes the depths and complications of an articulated time, an interdependence between past and future that prevents any present from ever coming into being' (de Man 1983: 161). Hence, literature or art itself as signifying practices may not be compatible with the idea of their own modernity; just as the falling away of this present moment gives literature and art a duration and historical existence. De Man goes on in this essay, first published in 1971, to wonder 'whether a history of an entity as self-contradictory as literature is conceivable' (1983: 162). Certainly to think of literature in terms of a positivistic literary history, as the collection and classification of empirical data, is to assemble a history of something other than literature. This disciplinary practice, says de Man, might open the way to, if it doesn't get in the way of, what he calls 'actual literary study' (1983: 163). Equally, any formalist study of literature that claimed to be a-historical would merely be presupposing this same idea of history that its own methodology was unable to account for (such is the nature of the oppositional gesture that reaffirms that which it opposes).

However, it is towards the end of this essay that de Man's theoretical rigour becomes ever more challenging to the authority of literary history. De Man is not saying that there is no history or that history is a fiction. Rather, the narratives of literary history can only ever be metaphors for the fluctuation that this essay describes and 'history is not a fiction' (de Man 1983: 163). Positivistic histories of literature transcend the literary text as text by viewing literature as something it is not, an empirical fact, even if we are thrown back on history as a mode of studying literature because, as the Formalists and the Structuralists discovered, there is no adequate science of literature given its instability and fluctuations. 'Could we conceive of a literary history', asks de Man in conclusion,

that would be able to maintain the literary aporia throughout, account at the same time for the truth and the falsehood of the knowledge literature conveys about itself, distinguish rigorously between metaphorical and historical language, and account for literary modernity as well as for its historicity? (1983: 164)

This task would seem to present an enormous challenge to literary study, one that would involve a revision of both our understanding of temporality (already contaminated by a historical hierarchy between past, present and future) and a reconsideration of the idea of history as a succession of generative moments in which the ancestral past begets its succession as a moment of unmediated presence, which in turn is capable of repeating the same generative process. This would have obvious implications not only for the study of art history or cultural history but all history in general. However, de Man suggests that the task may be less considerable than we might assume because in fact during the act of reading we do indeed take for granted these literary aporias, making good reading the actual production of literary history.

The point of returning to this 1971 text by de Man, in the context of a discussion of theoretical approaches with some currency in 2010, is to remind ourselves of the structural inadequacy of attempting to construct a history of art, and a dialectical history of art at that, which is unable to read. That is, to understand the art object or literary text in terms of what it is (something that solicits a reading and only exists in that reading) rather than what it is not (empirical data in a history of human subjectivication). It would be difficult to imagine what a 'Rancièrean' reading of an art object or literary text would look like (he is reluctant to fully elaborate one) because he does not approach art or literature in this way (i.e. on their own terms). Instead art and literature for Rancière are always just 'data' that prove the truth of a dialectical philosophy and its sub-categories. This is difficult because, on the one hand, the privileging of art and literature in Rancière turns out to be just another submission of them to philosophy, and on the other hand, in silencing the art object we find ourselves once more in the presence of the teacher and his historically oriented educational practices. De Man ends the essay with one of his characteristic concentrated and hitherto (in the essay) undeveloped affirmations: 'If we extend this notion beyond literature, it merely confirms that the bases for historical knowledge are not empirical facts but written texts, even if these texts masquerade in the guise of wars or revolutions' (1983: 165). Here de Man opens the door to what Rancière calls 'the politics of aesthetics', but not because good readers can interpret the events of history but because the temporal concept that we call history has its place in the linguistic moment when we give a name, category and narrative to the material (such as the War on Terror or the French Revolution) that replaces a singular moment of action with its repetition as a textual and successive movement that involves more than one distinct moment. History as a practice and idea is textual because it approaches the material as an articulation of an idea of time in which an interdependence between past and future prevents any present from ever coming into being; at once preceding the material and transcending it simultaneously through a narrativization that could just as well be otherwise (no doubt there are many French Revolutions). History can only ever be the metaphor of its own historicity, something like an allegory of history.

Given that History and all the historical disciplines such as 'the History of Art' then depend upon a consideration of textuality that extends well beyond a certain archival, palaeographic or antiquarian competence, de Man wonders in the 1982 essay 'Reading and History' why hermeneutic subtlety 'is rarely demanded from historians, among historians, least of all from literary historians' (de Man 1986: 59). Now, certain art historians and literary historians (I'm thinking of the likes of Fred Orton and Mark Currie) might be in a position today to say with some justification that they have taken on board the lesson of de Man here. However, this is by no means universally true, with connoisseurial art history remaining the dominant discourse of our universities, galleries and research councils. One could add here for good measure, with our new philosophical idols as well. There is almost nothing in Rancière's historical categorizations that one could point to as hermeneutically intricate. We continue to live in an unchallenged culture of the historian and this epoch needs to be understood historically; equally the idea of the epoch itself also needs to be understood historically. The figure of the historian may well be one of the defining motifs of what we continue to call Modernity, co-terminus with the idea of the author and the figure of the critic, indicative perhaps of the literary origins of disciplinary history as a modern phenomenon. As such, history itself would be a modern category; not in the sense of its temporal location in, say, the eighteenth or nineteenth century (Michelet, Gibbon, Jaurès, etc.) but in its literary, poetic or artistic attitude to its own *modus* as its point of departure and consciousness (Herodotus, Thucydides, Pliny). History, unlike literature, does not recognize itself as fictional or allegorical, any more than philosophy does. Instead, the writing of history, like the writing of philosophy, involves a system of synthesis that conveys an impression of methodological mastery that simultaneously effaces its own written status and the linguistic factors that would interfere with the synthesizing power of historical discourse, by claiming special referential exceptionalism with respect to its object of study (the material facts of history) as if bullets on a stage and bullets in the street were not also a case of assiduously distinguishing between reference and referent. In this sense, the writing of history is also an aesthetic category whether one is a historian of the Annales school or a dialectical philosopher of the new school. History and practices of historization must also be part of the aesthetic regime of the sensible even if they come to dominate the discursive construction of that regime in a way that can neither be avoided nor understood by that discourse. This is significant because it calls into question the attempt at conceptual mastery around the category of the aesthetic in Rancière. Rather than identifying the aesthetic as a form of provisional cognition (as Hegel does), Rancière, like so many others before him, imagines the aesthetic as holding the promise of totalization making, as de Man says of Jauss' *Rezeptions-ästhetik*, a symptom 'into a remedy for the disorder that it signals' (de Man 1986: 64). At this point I will break from these two de Man essays to return to the text of Rancière in order to put into play some of the implications of de Man's challenge to the historization of art around a recent collection by Rancière, *The Emancipated Spectator* (2009).

III. A Model Education

The Rancière text is the result of a solicitation from the Swedish performer and choreographer Mårten Spånberg to open the fifth International Sommerakademie with a reflection on the artist and the spectator in relation to ideas first proposed in *The Ignorant Schoolmaster* (1991 [1987]). This is then, from the beginning, a book that is tied very closely to the possibility of an aesthetic education. As we shall see, such a proposition is not without historical precedents and these precedents are not without consequence for Rancière. The idea of the ignorant schoolmaster, following the singular Foucauldian case of Joseph Jacotot, is a pedagogical scene in which the teacher does not set out to transmit knowledge to the pupil but rather a renunciation of explication as an educational strategy in favour of the equal intellect of the student being assisted to learn something that neither master nor pupil had known before. Now, as a commentary on education, Rancière's 1987 text is at pains to suggest an educational scene without hierarchy and resulting in intellectual emancipation rather than popular instruction (see Rancière 1991). However, this is not the same thing as an education without model. Rather, while Rancière–Jacotot's pedagogical paradigm makes a different assumption regarding the idiom of educational delivery, it still assumes the repeatability of a set of relations as an educational structure. All education ultimately assumes equality between pupil and master as its telos, and so the intelligence of the pupil and the potentiality of equality is assumed throughout the traditional pedagogic scene; Rancière–Jacotot merely short circuit the relationship without displacing the idea of the educational model as such. Autodidactism is still a model. The repeatability of the model of ignorance is assumed in the solicitation Rancière accepts in *The Emancipated Spectator*, that is, that this model can be applied to the spectator with regard to the work of art. Further to this, as with all of Rancière's writing on art, he begins from the position of assuming the category of the aesthetic and the need to work this category within the strict limits of his own definition of it. In fact, 'aesthetics' (along with 'art' and 'culture') might just be one of the vaguest terms in the philosophical lexicon precisely because it attempts to name a fluctuation that challenges meaning itself. None the less, Rancière will hold to this most archaic of terms and hope that by the power of his political good intentions his discourse will be immune to the metaphysical virus it brings with it. This is a bit like attempting to hold back the plague with a sprinkling of holy water. As soon as we are in the realms of an aesthetic education, even an ignorant one, we are participating in the history of aesthetics as a series of footnotes to Schiller's creative misprision of Kant. Rancière is aware of this and will lean on his own version of Schiller as the book proceeds.

The opening, eponymous essay in Rancière's book offers a model for an emancipated spectator of performance (the theatre and in particular the theatre as discussed by Plato is one of Rancière's favourite leitmotifs). For Rancière, there is no theatre without a spectator, who in the traditional manner of theatre is held in passivity and ignorance by the action on the stage before being led to knowledge of the reality concealed and revealed by the action. In contrast, the emancipated spectator would be one who became an actor 'dispossessed of this illusory mastery, drawn into the magic circle of theatrical action where she will exchange the privilege of rational observer for that of being in possession of all her vital energies' (Rancière 2009: 4). So far, so the Barthes of *S/Z* and 'The Death of the Author'. However, Rancière goes on to deal with the question of the theatre as an exemplary communal form. As an embodiment of 'the living community', the emancipation of theatre will, says Rancière, involve an opposition to 'the illusion of mimesis' and a 'critique of the spectacle' (2009: 6). Citing the proper name of Artaud (as opposed to reading any of his texts) Rancière suggests that drama, the true essence of theatre, when 'presented as a mediation striving for its own abolition' might be the basis for a reformulation of the logic of theatre and lead us to a description of intellectual emancipation. The analogy here is then between the autodidactic student and the active spectator: Jacotot's model is translated, but in principle repeatable, in another set of relations and at this point in his essay Rancière embarks upon a lengthy summation of his previous work on Jacotot. If Rancière is offering a model for an aesthetic education it would be one based not on the explication of a set of exemplary texts as touchstones for good taste but on a drawing out of the spectator from a passive attitude to be transformed into an active participant in a world shared by the artists, actors and spectators. In this situation, just as the pupil learns from the ignorant schoolmaster something he does not know himself, so the performance in the theatre in this new relation would not be a transmission from actor to audience but 'a third thing that is owned by no one, but which subsists between them' (Rancière 2009: 15). Accordingly, Rancière is offering us a form of communion without mediation, which he calls 'the affirmation of a communitarian essence of theatre as such' (Rancière 2009: 16). The assumption of the communitarian nature of theatre is fundamental for Rancière and the emancipation of the spectator is not at the expense of the community. The shared experience of anonymous individuals marked by 'irreducible distances' produces 'an unpredictable interplay of associations and disassociations' (Rancière 2009: 17) that disrupt the otherwise given distribution of the sensible (i.e. their role as passive spectator) leaving the newly active spectator with 'no time to spend on the forms and insignia of individuality. That is what the word "emancipation" means: the blurring of the boundary between those who act and those who look: between individuals and members of the collective body' (Rancière 2009: 19). This is a slightly curious idea of what the word 'emancipation' means: in its normative usage it refers to freedom from slavery from the Latin verb *emancipare*, meaning to be transferred as property. Here it would seem to mean the freeing of the individual from their previous atomized role in order to embrace the commune. In Rancière's political schema this escape from the policed role of the passive spectator to an embrace of an active communism constitutes the emancipation of the spectator. In fact, in this essay, Rancière's ultimate concern is with the 'emancipated community' as a community of narrators and translators who have actively appropriated their own stories (2009: 22). Although not translators who have worried about the impossibility of translation.

This is stirring stuff and I hope not an inaccurate account of what Rancière has to say in this essay. On the one hand, much will depend here upon one's disposition towards the commune, the *comme une*. However, leaving that aside for the moment I would like to question some of the emancipatory claims made in and for this text. First, we have the issue of the model. The model offered by Rancière is no doubt progressive, even 'radical' in its own way: who would not wish to be an active constructor of meaning and teller of their own tale? However, what Rancière presents here for the opening of the Sommerakademie and the opening of his book is a model of emancipation for the spectator of art that is based on a description of the spectator of theatre, the one being analogous to the other, who in turn is analogous to Jacotot's Flemish pupil who wants to learn how to speak French. However, the spectator of art is not reducible to the theatrical spectator because art (pictorial art, sculpture, even so-called performance art) is not a communal experience in the same way that theatre might be, if Rancière's a priori assumptions concerning theatre are correct. The co-option of the spectator of art for the living community by the sleight of hand that substitutes one experience into another masks a violent appropriation that will need to be accounted for, as will the difficulty of a model for art in which art itself is entirely absent. Second, the blueprint for the emancipated spectator is a model for an aesthetic education based upon Jacotot-Rancière's alternative pedagogic scene and as such would not seem to disrupt Schiller's own model of aesthetic education. The model that Schiller offers, one in which the ignorant pupil is introduced to a range of paradigmatic texts in order to cultivate knowledge of aesthetic taste, would seem at first glance to be a repeat of the very Platonic model that Rancière wishes to oppose (it would take too long a diversion to demonstrate that in fact such a model is nowhere to be found in Plato, so let's leave that for a later date). At this point we might also raise the issue of Rancière's own explication of the model that is nowhere reproduced by his actively participating audience at the Sommerakademie but is presented to them by the invited and privileged professor. However, what Rancière and Schiller both share is the model of the model itself. Schiller's aesthetic education involves the resemblance of the pupil to another, the work of art that they are invited to imitate. In this way Schiller's pupil from the beginning is only ever copying a reproduction or representation. However, the work of art is only exemplary of, and a displacement for, the authority of judgement derived from the teacher who prescribes the educational programme. Rancière would be at pains to distance himself from such a scenario, but readers of *The Emancipated Spectator* are at several calls away from Jacotot's francophone. On the one hand, there is the slightly comic scene of the professor at the Sommerakademie, like Brian addressing the masses, earnestly telling his rapt audience that they are all different. He encourages them to tell their own story before offering them the universal paradigm of someone else's story (Jacotot's students) and exhorting them to collectivization. A certain ventriloquism has taken place here in which the thematic of Jacotot's story stands in place of an actual dismantling of the boundaries of the pedagogical scene, which remain firmly in place between Rancière and his readers. A scene in which we are still left with the specular model of the text as imitation and an aesthetic education that depends upon the authority of proscribed judgement. It might be the case that an aesthetic education is not possible without the idea of mimesis, even if the aesthetic regime of the arts was supposed to displace the representational regime for Rancière (Rancière 2007: 73–6). Rancière's appropriation of the spectator of art for the living commune is just as violent a gesture as Schiller's co-option of the pupil of aesthetic taste as a citizen of the state. What is absent in both Schiller and Rancière, and which makes the appropriation violent, is critical reading. In the case of Schiller 'reading' takes the form of imitation of the artwork, in Rancière his own reluctance to read offers us no model for critical reading other than the synthesis of the exemplary. Jacotot's pupils may become active readers of French but Rancière's readers are offered an imitation that conceals the idealization it performs. In this sense, Rancière's 'emancipated spectator' is just another product of a system devised by Schiller that as de Man suggests in his own reading of the aesthetic letters, 'succeeds all too well, to the point of hiding the violence that it makes possible' (de Man 1984: 289).

One could also take Rancière to task over the notion that the teller of a tale is ever in any way master of her own story but at that point one would really be in the position of reminding ourselves of things that should never be forgotten. Rather, by way of drawing this discussion to a close I would like to press on a little further into Rancière's text to pick a little more at this question of the emancipated community (another classical term that Rancière wishes to use with impunity). Towards the end of the second chapter in *The Emancipated Spectator*, 'The Misadventures of Critical Thought' (which names a series of seeming theoretical errors without naming, or quoting, anyone responsible for them), Rancière states that the 'collective understanding of emancipation is not the comprehension of a total process of subjection. It is the collectivization of capacities invested in scenes of dissensus' (2010: 49). A few lines earlier he has glossed the scene of dissensus for us:

what 'dissensus' means is an organization of the sensible where there is neither a reality concealed behind appearances nor a single regime of presentation and interpretation of the given imposing its obviousness on all. It means that every situation can be cracked open from the inside, reconfigured in a different regime of perception and signification. (Rancière 2009: 48–9)

The definition of 'dissensus' goes on but we are once more back in the familiar territory of the teller who is master of her own tale, a political agent independent of the disruptive, mediating effects of signification and unencumbered by the interference of the wholly other. In the next chapter, 'Aesthetic Separation, Aesthetic Community', Rancière goes on to define 'an aesthetic community' which he explicitly calls 'a community of sense, or a *sensus communis*' (2009: 57). Having positioned himself in the orbit of Kant he loops back to define the *sensus communis* in terms of figures of dissensus, suggesting 'to the extent that it is a dissensual community, an aesthetic community is a community structured by disconnection' (Rancière 2010: 59). To go too quickly here, but to get to the point, Rancière correctly surmises that the figural and ruptured nature of the aesthetic is a problematic basis for building a community and suggests 'the ontology of the dissensual is actually a fictional ontology, a play of "aesthetic ideas"' (2009: 67), placing his own collectivization of dissensus on a much less firm footing than it might otherwise appear. This one might think would knock the declarative confidence out of the self-knowledge of emancipation, but Rancière salvages his project through a pass by Schiller suggesting that because what he is calling 'aesthetic separation' implies 'there is no longer any boundary separating what belongs to the realm of art from what belongs to the realm of everyday life', then this is why 'the "aesthetic education" conceptualized by Schiller after reading Kant's third Critique cannot identify with the happy dream of a community united and civilized by the contemplation of eternal beauty' (Rancière 2009: 69). It would seem that Rancière's understanding of Schiller is very different from that of de Man in his essay on Kleist's *Über das Marionettentheater*. In truth, neither de Man nor Rancière ever quote Schiller at any length and both use him as the model of a model they wish to either oppose or support. However, while we might provisionally accept from Rancière that in Schiller there is no love of a 'community united and civilized by the contemplation of eternal beauty', there is still a community that reproduces itself through education as the state. Rancière's own aesthetic community is also a political community but one characterized by separation and dissensus that constructs political relations according to aesthetic effect, which for Rancière means an originary 'suspension of any direct relationship between cause and effect' (2009: 73). He calls this diremption of reference and referent 'dis-identification'; and following the logic of the ignorant schoolmaster he reads the 'emancipated proletarian [as] a dis-identified worker' who eludes the rhetorical persuasion of the artist in a multiplicity of connections and disconnections that constitutes a 'community of dis-identified proletarian subjects' (Rancière 2009: 73).

Now, Rancière is not one for what he calls 'postmodern politics' but this aesthetic community of emancipated, dis-identified subjects is beginning to look a lot like the product of a theory that wants to have its postmodern cake and it. However, what remains undisturbed here is the very idea of community itself and the long historical bond from Schiller that ties that community to the aesthetic. The aesthetic remains an exemplary and unifying category and model for education, even if this education is said to be taking place according to a different typography. As with the philosophical tradition since Schiller, in which Rancière's text is firmly rooted, there remains an a priori valorization of art as a model for human experience, even if it is frequently only the idea of art rather than specific works of art in Rancière. At the same time art is subordinated to the telos of Rancière's ambition, the emancipated collective in which political relations (the collectivization of the dis-identified proletarians) matters more than the 'fictional ontology' of aesthetic relations that binds them together. In Rancière we will not find any 'and therefore' moments in which the emancipated community collapses or fails as a consequence of its aesthetic provenance. Rather, the aesthetic community in Rancière seems able to hold itself up on nothing but the gaps produced by dissensus and separation. This might be true enough but it suggests that Rancière's proletarian community is just another ideological ruse resulting from a linguistic illusion. At this point, the latterly introduced autodidactic proletarian is in danger of seeming like a principle of closure not open to the same critical discourse that Rancière directs towards the bourgeois artist; and the construction of the emancipated collective is really only a displaced version of collectivization of the idea of art as culture in Schiller, which leads in both Rancière and Schiller to the political order of the state (different as this might be for Rancière and Schiller). Rancière states elsewhere that 'artistic practices are not "exceptions" to other practices' (2004: 45), meaning that artistic practices are also subject to the inequalities of the distribution of labour. However, as we saw with de Man's idea of reading as the production of literary history, this is actually not true and that artistic practices are exceptions, perhaps the only exceptions, because they contain within themselves as their own haeccity the self-contradiction of falsehood and knowledge, metaphor and history, active reader and orphaned text, in which the distribution of labour and the distribution of the sensible do not run according to pre-determined tram lines.

A couple of things concern me at this point. Firstly, as in Schiller, philosophy itself seems to have dropped out of the educational picture for Rancière. His *sensus communis* is an aesthetic community, not a community of thought (philosophy is not taught in Schiller's aesthetic education). While, as suggested above, Rancière's own writing does not follow the model of 'the ignorant philosopher' (perhaps philosophy is an exception to this model), his notion of emancipation as aesthetic effect at once relegates art to a popularization and metaphorization of philosophy and hands the aesthetic to the masses. That is to say, the collective have culture but not philosophy; and in this sense Rancière is a much more Schillerian thinker than a Kantian one. The very acceptance of the supposed separation of art from philosophy, with which the opening solicitation of *The Emancipated Spectator* begins, is a fall into an aesthetic trap that we might find indicative of Schiller rather than Kant, who always inscribes art within the philosophical enterprise as a philosophical problem to be understood as such rather than an object that philosophy has to be brought towards in order to arrive at another destination, that of politics. Finally, if I might return to Paul de Man's challenge to art history, the other business that has fallen out of Rancière's *sensus communis* is its historical nature. I am not referring to the epoch-making proletarians who resist the police regime of the sensible but rather the passage from cognition to performance of a community of the dis-identified. As de Man states in the text on Kant and Schiller, history is 'not a temporal notion, it has nothing to do with temporality, but is the emergence of a language of power out of a language of cognition' (de Man 1996: 133). For de Man this emergence is not dialectical, nor a continuum, nor is it reversible. It is a one-way street that does not allow for the reinscription of history back into cognition. Any regression that would imagine a return of the 'materiality of the inscribed signifier' as history to cognition would no longer be historical because it would take place according to a temporal mode that would no longer be history as such (de Man 1996: 134). Rancière's aesthetic community by contrast creates history not by means of its own choosing but by dissensus and the potentiality of separation, which at once assumes an idea of history as a temporal continuum without being able to approach this idea critically as the effect of the aesthetic gestures that also produce the community's notion of its own materiality. In Rancière's schema, the claim to equality is the a priori condition of possibility for politics not as an ontological principle but as a condition that must be put into action in order for politics to be thought (Rancière 2004: 52). This action would then be the motor of history in an aesthetic community of dissensus. However, inequality itself is not an action, it is a relation and an economic relation at that (let us understand 'economic' in its fullest sense here) and is therefore itself irreducibly conceptual. The worry here would be that 'inequality' and the community of dissensus is transforming a language of cognition into its own language of power and repeating the same aesthetic distribution of the sensible it is seeking to rearrange.

Perhaps this somewhat polemical response to Bowman and Stamp overstates the case against Rancière in order to better hit the target of the current theoretical scene in which the texts of Rancière circulate. And without doubt Rancière is one of the more sophisticated and democratic-minded thinkers on that scene. However, the emancipated reader of today might begin to contribute more effectively to the debates engendered by Rancière's intelligent texts by resisting the self-idealizations of theoretical declarations in favour of a practice of critical reading that can distinguish between politics in the street and politics in prescription.

Works Cited

De Man, Paul (1983), 'Literary History and Literary Modernity', in *Blindness and Insight: Essays in the Rhetoric of Contemporary Criticism*, 2nd edition, Minneapolis: University of Minnesota Press: 142–65.

— (1984), 'Aesthetic Formalization: Kleist's *Über das Marionettentheater*', in *The Rhetoric of Romanticism*, New York: Columbia University Press.

— (1986), 'Reading and History', in *The Resistance to Theory*, Minneapolis: University of Minnesota Press.

— (1996), 'Kant and Schiller', in *Aesthetic Ideology*, ed. Andrzej Warminski, Minneapolis: University of Minnesota Press.

— (2010), *Textual Allegories* [online], ed. Martin McQuillan, *http://ucispace.lib.uci.edu/handle/10575/1091*.

Derrida, Jacques (2001), *A Taste for the Secret*, Cambridge: Polity.

McQuillan, Martin (2008), *Deconstruction after 9/11*, New York: Routledge.

— (2010), 'Aesthetic Allegory: Reading Hegel after Bernal', in *The Origins of Deconstruction*, eds Martin McQuillan and Ika Willis, Basingstoke: Palgrave Macmillan.

Rancière, Jacques (1991), *The Ignorant Schoolmaster*, trans. Kirstin Ross, Stanford: Stanford University Press.
— (2004), *The Politics of Aesthetics*, trans. Gabriel Rockhill, London: Continuum.
— (2007), *The Future of the Image*, trans. Gregory Elliott, London: Verso.
— (2009), *The Emancipated Spectator*, trans. Gregory Elliott, London: Verso.

Film, Fall, Fable: Rancière, Rossellini, Flaubert, Haneke

Mark Robson

I. The Obscene Question

In a particularly striking passage from *Short Voyages to the Land of the People*, Jacques Rancière makes the following comment in relation to a film by Roberto Rossellini:

> 'What did he say?' Not: 'Why did he kill himself?' The latter is the obscene question, the question posed by the politicians who know in advance why the child killed himself: because there is war, poverty, and the disturbances of the time and of consciences. It is the question posed by people who make knowledge out of what others do not know, and for whom, as a consequence, what happens or what happened is of no interest. Death is enough to set explanation going. There is never a lack of deaths or explanations. (2003: 111)

Death is enough to set explanation going, but the explanation that answers one question may itself be a way of avoiding the posing of another, more disturbing question. The obscene question disappears from the scene. Or rather, it is disappeared in the act of explanation, and this is attributable to 'the politicians'. So, then, there is a politics of the question, a politics of explanation and, of course, a politics of death, especially of suicide. To explain a suicide – to explain it away – is a political act or the act of a politician. In particular, the explanations that are all too readily to hand – the usual thanatological suspects – are rounded up with such ease that they fail to explain anything, and are merely further evidence of the poverty of thinking that accompanies and responds to suicide. It is not that these explanations are straightforwardly wrong, but rather that their insufficiency is all too apparent, their generality marking an erasure of the singularity of the event. Insufficient answers to the wrong questions, then. And this is not an accident or a simple incapacity.

The scene that prompts such questioning is both a moment in a cinematic narrative and also one that calls for consideration of the status of the film itself. In staging the death of a child who steps out into the void, falling simultaneously into and out of a bombed out cityscape, *Germany Year Zero* (*Germania anno zero*, 1948)

> places itself not under the sign of trauma but under the sign of the event, under the sign of the intolerable: *a child kills himself*. What makes this intolerable is not the repetition of an impotence, but rather the apprenticeship of the unique power that goes forth to meet the event. (Rancière 2003: 109)

As Rancière goes on to say: 'The event relates to nothingness, to the radical lack of any cause or good cause that would reattach it to the rationality of the profits and losses of a collective trauma' (2003: 111). The event is – in this sense at least – aneconomic, beyond calculation, an interruption of the economy of explanation by those who know. Such an interruption offers a moment of potential equality by disrupting an economy to which inequality is inherent.

This idea of equality is linked to the insistence in Rossellini's *Germany Year Zero* and *Europa '51* (1952) on the difference between making *sense* and *making* sense, between that which allows itself to be explained and that process that offers something up for explanation:

> The moment arrives when the call of the void has an effect but no longer makes sense. The time to connect, explain, and heal has passed. Now something else is at stake: to repeat the event, go look somewhere else, see for oneself. This is how one falls into the unrepresentable, into a universe that is no longer the society sociologists and politicians talk about. For there are a finite number of possible statements, of credible ways of putting together a discourse or a set of images about society. And the moment arrives when the border is crossed and one enters into what makes there be sense, which for that very reason does not itself make sense, so that one must continue to walk under the sign of interruption, at the risk of losing the way. (Rancière 2003: 117)

To lose one's way is to lose sense, and in French *sens* also means direction. The one who risks being lost most obviously appears in Rossellini's films in the figure of the foreigner. It is the foreign figure whose presence poses the questions that puncture political and sociological accounting. And once these questions are posed they also evoke an uncanny sense of foreignness among those apparently 'at home'. What Rancière identifies in this interruption is what he will call Rossellini's 'equality of respect':

This aesthetic and ethical practice of equality, this practice of egalitarian foreignness puts into peril everything that is inscribed in the repertories of society and politics, everything that represents society, which can only be represented under the sign of inequality, under the minimal presupposition that there are people who don't know what they do and whose ignorance imposes on others the task of unveiling. (2003: 123)

The point is to construct a point of view of foreignness that allows for or forces a perspectival shift: 'It is the foreigner's gaze that puts us in touch with the truth of a world' (Rancière 2003: 125). Truth may be perceived through a form of indirection that is not strictly a revelation. The anamorphotic possibilities of the figure of the foreigner in *Europa '51* are thus tied to the possibilities of Rossellini's version of realism, transforming and translating the expected relations of materiality to art: 'the material inscription of what has no place in the system of reality, the rigorously material dispensation of the immaterial that, in art as in religion, is called grace' (Rancière 2003: 129).

II. Unbelievable

A child steps out into space, into the whiteness of a void. Another child throws himself down a stairwell in order to set his mother off on a quest. A doctor's wife poisons herself. A whole family decide to remove themselves and all of their possessions from the world. A man cuts his throat in a Paris suburb. No explanation could account for all of these occurrences in their singularity. No explanation could assert their absolute separateness. Each of these 'suicides' – and in a moment we shall need to rethink the appropriateness of this description – each of these suicides demands interpretation, yet each is already overloaded with interpretation.

In the first, Roberto Rossellini's *Germany Year Zero*, the boy Edmund has seemingly been led by the promptings of a Nazi ideologue to kill his father. In the second, Rossellini's *Europa '51*, Michele, like Edmund, has been deeply affected by the horrors of war. Emma Bovary, the third, inspired by her reading of romances, has been led into adultery, debt and fraud. The family in Michael Haneke's *The Seventh Continent* (*Die siebente Kontinent*, 1989) lead lives of numbing repetition and there have been deaths in the family that lead the parents into a terminal depression. In Haneke's *Hidden*

(*Caché*, 2005), the last instance, Majid is an immigrant whose childhood was seemingly destroyed by the jealous fantasies and lies of Georges, and whose death is the culmination of a campaign of vengeful terror many years later.

The only problem with such explanations – with what we might call the dominant self-readings of these texts, those all-too-obvious explanations that 'make sense' – is that they are insufficient. And crucially, their insufficiency takes place at the levels of both form and content. There is always something potentially 'unbelievable' about suicide, but there is also a sense in which the explanations offered in these cases cannot account for the effect that these texts produce.

III. Realism and Reality

Since Bazin, it has been conventional to speak of Rossellini's films in terms of a certain conception of realism.[1] Bazin says in his brief discussion of *Germany Year Zero* that Rossellini's realism is 'not a realism of the subject but of the style'. He ends that essay by suggesting: 'Isn't there a solid definition of realism in art there: to oblige the mind [*esprit*] to take a side without playing around or being dishonest with [*tricher avec*] beings and things?' (2002: 206). This is a realism that is not content to point moral lessons in a didactic fashion: 'It works not by demonstrating [*démontrer*] but by showing [*de montrer*]' (Bazin 2002: 360). For Bazin, realist cinema is best understood in relation to the novel rather than to other art forms:

> As in the novel, the aesthetic implicit in the cinema reveals itself in its narrative technique. A film is always presented as a succession of fragments of imaged reality [*fragments de réalité dans l'image*] on a rectangular surface of given proportions, the ordering of the images and their duration on the screen determining its import ['*sens*']. (2005: 30–1)[2]

(In this way, Bazin suggests, Rossellini can come to the same kind of effects produced by Welles in *Citizen Kane* (1941), even though Rossellini does not use the same technique, namely, the deep focus that allows Welles to change the grammar of cinema by allowing everything that is in shot to be in focus. Haneke will use deep focus in a similar refusal to offer the viewer a hierarchized frame, as in the famous opening and closing shots of *Hidden*.) The aesthetic of Rossellini, Bazin claims, is simply the equivalent to the American novel, by which he is thinking of Faulkner, Dos Passos and

Hemingway. This aesthetic does not operate according to the principle of the traditional realist author – his example is Zola – who

> analyzes reality into parts which he then reassembles in a synthesis conforming to his moral conception of the world, whereas the consciousness of the neorealist director *filters* reality. Undoubtedly, his consciousness, like that of everyone else, does not admit reality as a whole, but the selection that does occur is neither logical nor is it psychological; it is ontological, in the sense that the image of reality it restores to us is still a whole [*l'image de la réalité qu'on nous restitue demeure globale*]'. (Bazin 2005: 98)

Ultimately, for Bazin, 'Rossellini directs [*met en scène*] only facts. [. . .] Gesture, change, physical movement constitute for Rossellini the essence of human reality itself [*l'essence même du réel humain*]' (2005: 100, translation modified).

At a pivotal moment in *Film Fables*, Jacques Rancière distances himself from Bazin's conception of realism, or at least, from Bazin's mode of reading realism. As Rancière puts it, Bazin identifies cinematic realism with the ability to 'reveal the hidden meanings in people and things without disturbing the unity natural to them' (2006: 107). A few pages later, Rancière notes 'Bazin's image of Rossellini's cinema as a patient search for the secret of beings and things', seeing this reading as an error parallel to that which he finds in Deleuze (2006: 126). For Rancière, Rossellini's films are a trap into which both interpreters have hurled themselves. Rancière's objection lies in the quasi-theological, quasi-platonic structuring motif of the latent versus the manifest, the hidden versus the revealed, depth versus surface, and so on. Distancing himself once more from Althusserianism, he comments in an interview in the English edition of *The Politics of Aesthetics*:

> I by no means think, for my part, that there is no science but of the hidden. I always try to think in terms of horizontal distributions, combinations between systems of possibilities, not in terms of surface and substratum. Where one searches for the hidden beneath the apparent, a position of mastery is established. I have tried to conceive of a topography that does not presuppose this position of mastery. (Rancière 2004: 49)[3]

So, despite the apparent similarity of some of the claims made by Bazin and Rancière concerning the relation of film to literature – particularly in their shared assertion of realist cinema's proximity to the novel – their respective modes of reading differ considerably. Perhaps it is telling here that Rancière chooses a rather different form of literary realism in thinking about cinema, as he does elsewhere when considering the politics of literature. In both cases, his most frequent reference is not to Zola but to Flaubert, and more specifically to *Madame Bovary*.[4]

IV. Passivity and Possibility

One clue to the nature of the topography that Rancière invokes is his reference to 'systems of possibilities'. This must be understood in terms of the 'distribution of the sensible', that sharing and sharing out of the perceptible that

> is a delimitation of spaces and times, of the visible and the invisible, of speech and noise, that simultaneously determines the place and the stakes of politics as a form of experience. Politics revolves around what is seen and what can be said about it, around who has the ability to see and the talent to speak, around the properties of space and the possibilities of time. (Rancière 2004: 13)

Cinema and literature are equally caught up in this distribution since '[t]he question of fiction is first a question regarding the distribution of places' (Rancière 2004: 13). Later in the same book he will say: 'Politics and art, like forms of knowledge, construct "fictions", that is to say *material rearrangements of signs and images, relationships between what is seen and what is said, between what is done and what can be done*' (2004: 39, emphasis original). It is this argument concerning systems of possibilities that will guide his reading of Flaubert.

Cinema is like Flaubert's prose in the impassivity of a gaze, in the reasonless exposition of everyday actions, in its alignment with the presupposition characteristic of the aesthetic regime that anything and everything in the world is available to art (Rancière 2006: 9). Such, at least, is one fable of film. But Rancière contrasts this passivity with another, doubling and displacing the mechanicity of the camera's gaze to thwart that fable: the cinema is at least as capable of reviving classical and representative forms of art as it is of pursuing the ambitions of the aesthetic regime. Where novelists have to create a passivity as an act of style, the camera can never be anything but passive. In this thwarting of the fable, Rancière also uncouples the link between cinema as a technical form and cinema as an art. As such, film is aligned more closely with regimes of art and the distribution of the sensible than with narratives of technological determinism.

V. The Trajectory of Liberty

In his readings of the films of Roberto Rossellini, Rancière makes clear his rejection of Bazin's surface/depth model: 'A Rossellini film is a surface of inscriptions that does not tolerate the least trace of dissimulation, the presence of something that must remain latent, a truth hidden behind the appearance, or a scandal concealed behind the smooth surface of things' (2006: 135). His discussions of *Germany Year Zero* and *Europa '51* match that of *Rome, Open City* (*Roma, città aperta*, 1945). In each case, Rancière follows Rossellini in giving privilege to a specific moment that acts as an emblem of and justification for the whole film:

> In *Rome, Open City*, Pina tears herself free from a line of soldiers who clearly should have been able to restrain her and dashes after the truck driving away her fiancé. Originating in the mode of the burlesque movement only to end in a mortal fall, Pina's dash after the truck at once exceeds the visible of the narrative situation and of the expression of love. Similarly, the jump into the void that brings Edmund's wanderings to a close in *Germany Year Zero* exceeds every (non)reaction to Germany's material and moral ruin in 1945. These movements are not oriented towards a fictional end, nor have they been disoriented by an intolerable situation: they've been deflected by the imposition of another movement. Rossellini has transferred a dramaturgy of the call from the religious to the artistic level. This is what drives his characters from one mode of movement and gravitation to another mode, where they cannot but free-fall. (2006: 13)[5]

Just as he resists the theological underpinning of Bazin's criticism, he finds in Rossellini a movement from the theological to the aesthetic so that grace becomes an aesthetic term that displaces its religious resonance. Crucial to this is the recognition of a call, of a demand or a command, but in a deliberately loaded inversion this is a call that *demands* a fall.

> Rossellini's *mise-en-scène* presupposes the exact identification of spiritual and material, political and artistic, so that we would do better, in his case, to formulate the problem [of knowing how to live or die well] in terms of falling well or badly. [. . .] There are two ways of falling, and they are separated by a bare nothing that in art can only be called the soul: not a part of the representation, but an almost imperceptible difference in the light that shines on it. The exact measure of Rossellini's 'realism' is in the precision with which he traces the gesture that sums up the trajectory of liberty, in his determined identification of the believer's spiritualism and the artist's materialism: the so-called soaring soul perfectly circumscribed by the curve of the falling body. (Rancière 2006: 129)

VI. A Trace of the True

In *The Politics of Aesthetics*, Rancière suggests that

> When *Madame Bovary* was published, or *Sentimental Education*, these works were immediately perceived as 'democracy in literature' despite Flaubert's aristocratic situation and political conformism. His very refusal to entrust literature with any message whatsoever was considered to be evidence of democratic equality. (2004: 14)

It is their very indifference to political position-taking that gives Flaubert's works their political position. The death of a farmer's daughter and wife of a doctor in a small country town becomes equal in significance – or insignificance – with tales of kings or gods. There is no longer any necessary relation between the subject matter and the form deemed 'appropriate' to it, and this is reinforced by a doubled form of anonymity; the written word in the form of the novel can pass from anyone to anyone, that is, it can be written by any person who can write and read by any person with the ability to read. Like Rossellini, Flaubert depicts and portrays without instructing. One of the crucial connections that Rancière makes between cinema and literature rests on a further sense of anonymity. For Rancière, the 'aesthetic revolution' can in part be characterized by the fact that the life of the anonymous becomes recognizable as a subject matter, and this takes place in literature and painting before it is taken up by photography and film: 'the ordinary becomes beautiful as a trace of the true' (2004: 34).

Rancière's readings of *Madame Bovary* hinge on the sensorial possibilities that this work brings forth in and as itself. But this has nothing to do with the 'commitment' of its author:

The literary equality is independent from any political stance in favor of democracy. But it is dependent on a wider redistribution of the sensible, which has it that there is no difference of nature between two humanities, between the men dedicated to noble actions and women dedicated to 'practical life'. The blurring of borders and the levelling of differences that define this new artistic power also define new possibilities of life for anybody. (Rancière 2008: 238)

One of the possibilities is that which is often seen to be the main charge to be laid against the novel's central character: Emma Bovary confuses art and life, she wants her life to be like the romances that she reads as a child, that is, she wants her books to have the materiality of life itself. But it is this equivalence between Art and non-art that is her mistake, she wishes to concretize the sensations and images of Art, to give them the status of objects in the world. The name for this, Rancière notes, is 'the aestheticization of everyday life', and it is this that Flaubert must resist by undermining and ultimately killing Emma (2008: 239). As Rancière wryly puts it, 'Flaubert needs for his own sake to construct Emma's wrong or disease as the confusion between literature and furniture' (2008: 240). Flaubert's way to avoid becoming the bad artist that Emma represents is through style. Style is 'an absolute manner of seeing things', which Rancière glosses as a form of impersonality, as the manner of seeing things 'when they are released from all the ties that make them useful or desirable objects. It is the manner of enjoying sensations as pure sensations, disconnected from the sensorium of ordinary experience' (2008: 241).

The consequences for reading *Germany Year Zero* are clear. Rossellini is the one who kills Edmund because *Germany Year Zero* must end with the death of a child. The deceptively simple move that Rancière makes here – tying together narrative structure, content and resonance or effect, in other words, tying aesthetics to politics – is the same that he makes in the essay on Flaubert. The political reading of suicide fails in these instances because it is incapable of accounting for the suspension or interruption of the referential function that these 'realist' aesthetics entail.

VII. Affect and Essence

Robert Bresson's influence on Michael Haneke is particularly marked in his frequent use of shots which show only the part of a body directly involved in the action. It is tempting to see this as a highly filmic exploitation of the possibilities of tight focus and cropping of the frame. But thinking of the emphasis on hands and their movement in *Au hasard, Balthazar* (1966) and *Pickpocket* (1959) leads Rancière towards a connection between cinema and literature rather than to any assertion of something essentially cinematic.[6] Of the opening shots of *Au hasard, Balthazar*, he says:

> the camera's fixing on the hand that pours the water and the hand that holds the candle is no more peculiar to cinema than the fixing of Doctor Bovary's gaze on Mademoiselle Emma's nails, or of Madame Bovary's gaze on those of the notary's clerk, is peculiar to literature. [. . .] By separating the hands from the facial expression, it reduces the action to its essence: a baptism consists in words and hands pouring water over a head. By compressing the action into a sequence of perceptions and movements, and short-circuiting any explanation of the reasons, Bresson's cinema does not realize a peculiar essence of the cinema. It forms part of the novelistic tradition begun by Flaubert: an ambivalence in which the same procedures create and retract meaning, ensure and undo the link between perceptions, actions and affects. (Rancière 2007: 5)

Just as Bresson's realism insists on framing the mechanical and ritual nature of physical movement, so Flaubert refusal to observe the hierarchies that dictate appropriate subject matter for a particular literary form; neither brings us closer to the essence of cinema or the novel, but both participate in a novelistic tradition.

Michael Haneke's first film, *The Seventh Continent* (1989), pushes Bresson's technique to an extreme in its opening and closing sequences. In a filmed interview, Haneke explains his structural decision regarding the shape of a film's narrative. *The Seventh Continent* began as an attempt to show the story of a suicide through flashback, but it didn't work in this form because each moment of flashback effectively said 'he did this because of this': 'Each flashback immediately became an explanation. An explanation gives the spectator a sense of security' ['*Chaque flashback immediatement devenait une explication. Une explication donne une securité au spectateur*'] (Bernard 2004, my translation). Haneke thus chose a structure in which three days are shown, each a year apart, without explaining why the protagonist (for want of a better word) commits suicide. Nevertheless, there are 'signs and traces' in the earlier sections which might inform an understanding of the third, but which each spectator can interpret in her or his own fashion.

As Haneke explains in his interview with Bernard, the worst aspect of *The Seventh Continent* is the monotony with which the family destroys itself. Echoing the shots from the first third of the film ('1987') in which mechanical actions are repeatedly shown as movements of body parts rather than of 'characters', the extraordinary final sequence of destruction and death is unsettling precisely because it always runs the risk of becoming boring. The monotony of the images is underscored by the soundtrack and by the family's own use of television to entertain themselves. It is as if the family members themselves find their suicides too dull to be carried out without the banal images and sounds that accompany everyday life. Haneke's use of pop music to contrast his own images with a glossy but vacuous manufactured sentiment – pointedly including Jennifer Rush's 'The Power of Love' – goes beyond a facile irony to reinforce the sense that the sleeping tablets that the family overdose on are analogous to the televisual anaesthetic that blares in the background as they die.

VIII. Shock and Interpretation

It is precisely Haneke's aesthetic sense that has led some to question *Caché*'s political resonance. Paul Gilroy offers a particularly forceful reading of the film by arguing for a complicity between, rather than critique of, the audience's relation to the main characters and to its political frame. Concerned by the lack of depth in the characterization, particularly of Majid, Gilroy is also suspicious of the genre and of Haneke's aesthetic more generally:

> In view of *Caché*'s obvious strengths, I was particularly troubled by what could be interpreted as Haneke's collusion with the comforting idea that the colonial native can be made to disappear in an instant through the auto-combustive agency of their own violence. If this reading of Majid's suicide sounds rather too literal, I am prepared immediately to concede that his death represents a step forward from older modernist explorations of the psychological and philosophical ambiguities involved in murdering Arabs, but his eventual sacrifice belongs on ground from which all varieties of political reflection are doomed to disappear. (2007: 234)

Rather than seeing the references to the massacre of Algerian protestors at an FLN march in Paris on 17 October 1961 – in which Majid's parents are thought to have died, leaving him an orphan – as a positive attempt to question the relation of current French or Europeans to a largely unacknowledged colonial history, Gilroy sees Majid's suicide as aligned with what is either a disturbing or comforting fantasy. Majid's suicide becomes not a sign of violence in which Georges is implicated through his role in the betrayal of Majid in childhood, but instead a moment of disappearance which solves rather than creates problems. Indeed, Gilroy extrapolates from this moment in the film to the political context of its supposed audience:

> Getting the Arabs to do away with themselves is a timely fantasy in the context of today's pervasive Islamophobia. In that light Majid's suicide becomes in effect an exclusively aesthetic event, devoid of all meaning apart from what it communicates about Georges. Haneke's unsettled audience can even derive a deep if guilty pleasure from it precisely because that horrible death can represent a flowering of their own investments in the idea that Europe's immigrants should be induced to disappear by any means possible. (2007: 234)

The proposal that the suicide of Majid can be 'an exclusively aesthetic event' is intriguing, since it depends upon a particular separation of the aesthetic and political. The notion of 'guilty pleasure' is also worthy of note in the context of discussing a film that is generally seen (not least by Haneke himself) to be primarily 'about' guilt. Gilroy seems to suppose that he has found a point from which to mount a critique of Haneke, and it is certainly true that the interpretation of this moment in the film is likely to be emblematic of any interpretation of *Caché* as a whole. But need we necessarily think that Gilroy has spotted something of which Haneke was unaware? In other words, might Majid's suicide act as a point of departure from which we might read the film in terms of its aesthetic qualities that refuses to see the aesthetic in a truncated and apolitical manner?

Just as Jacques Rancière posits a relation between literary and cinematic realism and a politics that cannot be identified with what passes for political explanation, I want to point towards a political reflection on *Caché* that begins from the question of 'Why does Majid have to be killed?' rather than 'Why does he kill himself?' There is only space here to sketch out a sense of what this reading might look like, but it will quickly become apparent where my sense of the aesthetic differs from that of Gilroy.

What is there to see in the scene of Majid's suicide? Are we seeing the event 'directly' or is this a tape that someone (who?) is viewing at a later point in time? The opening scene of the film – set on the Rue des Iris – notoriously confuses any sense of spectatorial position by beginning with video images of the outside of a house only to reveal that this is a tape being shown on a TV screen inside the house. The suicide scene is shown from a perspective that appears to be the same as that of a tape of an earlier visit by Georges to Majid's apartment which is later sent to the Laurents and to Georges's boss at the TV station. If it is a tape, then who has made it? Majid kills himself having denied any knowledge of the tapes and drawings. At their first meeting, Majid claims only to have seen Georges on television since their childhood, and to have had nothing to do with the family's 'persecution'. Majid's son, who at points in the film seems to be the obvious suspect, also denies having anything to do with the tapes. Are they to be believed? To pose the questions in this form – separating out 'what has happened?' from 'what have we seen happening?' – is already to recognize the possibility that these two questions may have different answers. But ultimately it is not the answers to these questions that matter, since they will not explain the central event of the suicide. As Mark Cousins puts it, in discussing why the film provoked so much discussion when it first appeared: '*Caché* did not compel us to work out the implications of the answer, but the implications of the question' (2007: 226).

In fact, in *Caché* Haneke accentuates the ambiguity and inadequacy of suicide's explanations partly through his refusal to provide an explanatory framework and partly through his directorial choices with respect to narrative structure and visual style. Most notable in *Caché* are the shots that put the viewer on the wrong side of the street. What we are 'supposed' to be watching happens at a remove, traffic comes between us and the 'significant' part of the frame, the frame is busy, filled with objects and people we are not supposed to be interested in, so much so that the characters we are 'meant' to be seeing are obscured or lost for at least part of the time, or we fail to see them at all. The effect is both a disorientation, since the focal point of the shot becomes increasingly difficult to locate, and a reorientation, since it becomes necessary to make sense of what we do actually see. In the case of Georges's visit to the cinema after the death of Majid – which might appear to be an odd reaction to witnessing a suicide and which Georges feels the need to lie about when he later tells Anne about the events of the day – it is hard to notice him at all. Even when he appears exiting the cinema (and it would be easy to miss him), this only prompts further questions to which we receive no answers (why go to a cinema? what film did he watch? what was his reaction to it? was he alone? why lie about it to his wife? what relation does this act of watching have to all the other such acts in *Caché*? and so on).[7] This inset of cinema within the film, rather than serving a traditional intertextual or self-reflexive function of illuminating some aspect of the main text through similitude, and so on, acts rather like Hamlet's book: when he is asked what he is reading, Hamlet replies 'Words, words, words'. Georges's trip to the cinema works primarily to produce a space within *Caché* – a hidden space or crypt, the space of a secret that cannot simply be revealed – full of yet more images that cannot be properly 'seen'. In other words, this is a depthless space that remains on the same plane as the surface.

The last scene of the film has become a classic example of this technique, and was immediately and remains one of the most discussed aspects of the film. This non-ending – in that it resolves nothing, and definitively explains nothing of what has preceded it – opens up further narrative possibilities through its ambiguity. Indeed, Haneke relates in an interview that there is some debate as to what the audience sees at all in this scene. There are those who see only the collective group of kids outside a school. A friend to whom Haneke showed the film apparently talked at great length about how wonderful the scene was because it showed how the social problems that the film touches on are passed to the next generation. For this viewer, the scene is successful because it offers a general image of youth and of a non-specific future that counterpoints the main narrative but nonetheless falls under the shadow of past events. But other spectators saw something that this man like many others apparently failed to see altogether, which is the meeting that takes place between Pierrot and Majid's son. As in the cinema scene, it is easy to miss because of the distance, the crowded frame and the interruption of the point of view. What are they talking about? Haneke claims that he did write dialogue for this scene, but that he won't tell anyone what it is. Did they know each other prior to this moment? Is there a sinister threat posed to Pierrot in which Majid's death will be avenged? Were the two sons accomplices from the very beginning? Might Pierrot be the one who has made the video tapes and drawings? Is there some hope in the smiling way in which they part?[8] And so on.

Ultimately, there is no explanation for the decisions that 'Family S' make in *The Seventh Continent*, and there is no secure rationale for Majid's death in *Caché*. There are gaps in the narrative of both films that we might expect to be filled, and these gaps are almost always causal, avoiding the 'therefore' that characterizes more conventional film-making, especially thrillers. Haneke's realism – inspired by both Rossellini and Bresson – depends on a refusal of explanatory frameworks, especially those which are too readily supplied by politicians and sociologists: from its title onwards, *Caché* represents a trap to those viewers and critics who would seek to go beneath its surface. Haneke seems to be seeking to liberate the gaze from the two fundamental techniques of society that Rancière finds described in Rossellini's *Europa '51*: shock and interpretation (Rancière 2003: 125). Like Rancière, like Rossellini and like Bresson, he seems to want to find this in a gesture that grants to cinematic realism something that could only be called grace.

Notes

1. See 'An aesthetic of reality: Neorealism (cinematic realism and the Italian school of Liberation)', in Bazin (2005, vol. 2: 16–40); and 'In defense of Rossellini', in Bazin (2005, vol. 2: 93–101). Relevant essays not translated for these volumes include 'Allemagne Année Zéro' and 'Europa 51', in Bazin (2002: 203–6 and 359–61). All translations are my own.
2. The word '*sens*' is in inverted commas in the French text (274), and while it does mean import, as Gray translates it, it also carries senses of meaning, sense or direction.
3. See also Robson (2009).
4. Rancière explicitly rejects Zola – Bazin's example – as a model for thinking and writing a democratic history, suggesting that Virginia Woolf provides a better way into a thinking of dissensus through literary structures. See Rancière (2004: 65).
5. As Rancière comments in *Film Fables*: 'To unravel the arabesque of Pina's falling Rossellini turns it into the plot of another film, *Germany Year Zero*' (130).

6. He reads these two films in Rancière (2006: 119–22).
7. Ezra and Sillars (2007) identify the films as *Ma mère, Deux frères, La mauvaise éducation* and *Mariages*. Noting the resonances of these titles for the narrative of *Caché*, and the generic possibilities that Haneke's film deliberately avoids, they avoid speculating on which of these films Georges may have seen.
8. On this 'positive' reading of the next generation collaborating to solve historical problems, see Silverman (2007: 249) and Gilroy (2007: 235).

Works Cited

Bazin, André (2002), *Qu'est-ce que le cinéma?*, 'Septième Art', 14th ed., Paris: Cerf.
— (2005), 'An Aesthetic of Reality: Neorealism (cinematic realism and the Italian school of liberation)', in *What is Cinema?*, trans. Hugh Gray, 2 vols, Berkeley: University of California Press.
Bernard, Jean-Jacques (2004), *Le pari de Haneke*, dir. Jean-Jacques Bernard, France.
Cousins, Mark (2007), 'After the End: Word of Mouth and *Caché*', *Screen*, 48 (2): 223–6.
Ezra, Elizabeth, and Sillars, Jane (2007), '*Hidden* in Plain Sight: Bringing Terror Home', *Screen*, 48 (2): 215–21.
Gilroy, Paul (2007), 'Shooting Crabs in a Barrel', *Screen*, 48 (2): 233–5.
Rancière, Jacques (2003), *Short Voyages to the Land of the People*, trans. James B. Swenson, Stanford: Stanford University Press.
— (2004), *The Politics of Aesthetics: The Distribution of the Sensible*, trans. and intro. Gabriel Rockhill, London and New York: Continuum.
— (2006) *Film Fables*, trans. Emiliano Battista, Oxford and New York: Berg.
— (2007), *The Future of the Image*, trans. Gregory Elliott, London and New York: Verso.
— (2008), 'Why Emma Bovary Had to Be Killed', *Critical Inquiry*, 34: 233–48.
Robson, Mark (2009), '"A Literary Animal": Rancière, Derrida and the Literature of Democracy', *Parallax*, 52, 15 (3): 88–100.
Silverman, Max (2007), 'The Empire Looks Back', *Screen*, 48 (2): 245–9.

On the Shores of History

Alex Thomson

'[A]ny mode of thinking that is the least bit singular reveals itself in always saying basically the same thing, which it cannot but hazard every time in the colorful prism of circumstances' (Rancière 2004: xxviii). I propose in this chapter to take Rancière at his word. His writings are essayistic in two senses: they combine close attention to literary presentation with the restlessness of the experimental thinker. The consequence is that their styles are nearly as various as their topics; and that if certain phrases, themes or examples recur, there is no underlying attempt to form a system, to elaborate a theory or to defend a new philosophy or methodology. But for all their variety, from the time of the break with Althusser, through his archival work and involvement with *Les Révoltes Logiques* to his most recent writings on politics, art and literature, the unfolding of a single project can be clearly discerned. The consistency of Rancière's work is that of the repeated thrust of a single point, the challenge of equality, posed as a polemical intervention into two counter-posed domains, those of philosophy and history.

The challenge of equality is summed up in the scene of reading at the heart of *The Ignorant Schoolmaster*: 'The book – *Télémaque* or any other – placed between two minds sums up the ideal community inscribed in the materiality of things. The book *is* the equality of intelligence' (1991: 38). Two minds meet in the presence of a third object. It need not be a masterpiece, or a classic, although in this case it happens to be the latter. It need not even be a book: it could be any product of human agency. Each mind judges the other equally able to understand the third. Each can challenge the other on their understanding, and through doing so verify not only the other's understanding but also the presence of an intelligence: 'the book seals the new relation between two ignorant people who recognize each other from that point on as intelligent people' (1991: 38). 'Society as such', *The Ignorant Schoolmaster* tells us, 'will never be reasonable, but it could experience the miracle of reasonable moments arising not in the coincidence of intelligences – that would be stultification – but in the reciprocal recognition of reasonable wills' (1991: 96). The possibility of such miracles, of moments of equality in practice, is the central presupposition of Rancière's authorship. In *On the Shores of Politics* he describes this as setting a heading based on trust, rather than suspicion: 'starting from the point of view of equality, asserting equality, assuming equality as a given, working out from equality, trying to see how productive it can be and thus maximising all possible liberty and equality' (1995: 51–2).

In accordance with this principle, Rancière's work seeks again and again to illuminate the meaning of equality in principle and show its practical survival in the modern era. The critical defence of the intelligence of people in general, of artisans and spectators, of imitation and aspiration, of artisans who wish to think, of workers who wish to drink and dance rather than plot a revolution, of slumming bohemians and aspiring poets, against the practitioners of intellectual distinction is itself an affirmation of the equality of anyone with anyone. There is no despair in Rancière's writing, despite a persistent bemusement at the inegalitarian traps into which the self-assigned path of the intellectual seems so recurrently to lead. If *Hatred of Democracy* (2006) is caustic about the failures of democratic thinking in the current situation, this analysis remains underpinned by a cautious affirmation of what in *The Ignorant Schoolmaster* he names 'the democracy of the book' (1991: 38), the defence of a modern world in which mass literacy and the circulation of print culture signal not the 'hydrophobia' (1994: 20) feared by Hobbes, in which the opinions of the multitude threaten the progress of truth and the stability of authority, but new possibilities for the revolt of intelligence against inequality.

Rancière's caution with regard to philosophy is exemplary. In the closing pages of *The Philosopher and His Poor* he makes what with hindsight may seem a surprising proposition, given what is often taken to be his unrelenting hostility towards the very idea of philosophy. Looking back over the argument of his book, and situating his work in the context of the apparent triumph of 'sociocracy', he wonders whether 'certain questions of philosophy could recover some of their vigor'. 'It remains important today', Rancière suggests, 'to be able to judge if what our institutions, our images, and our discourses imitate is democratic hope or its mourning'. This is a project in which 'philosophy can find itself implicated without pretending to give lessons about it', but the cost would be of putting at risk its own self-definition, which has up until now always consisted in 'linking its purity with the vigilant guarding of its borders'. This would be a philosophy 'detached equally from the melancholies of the origin and an eagerness to eclipse modernity. The stake for this is not "totally ahistorical"' (2004: 216–7).

The quotation marks around the phrase 'totally ahistorical' refer us back to a passage Rancière cites from Bourdieu, who has sought to distinguish sociology from philosophy on the grounds that the latter is 'totally ahistorical, like all philosophical thought that is worthy of the name' (2004: 197). In doing so they ought to remind us of the extent to which a text by Rancière is rarely a statement or manifesto but is always the exploration of a particular historical conjunction of intellectual forces, an attempt to inhabit and make a home in the ravaged terrain over which opposing positions contend. So rather than attempt to outline the elements of Rancière's thinking which do recall the contemporary revival of practical philosophy, hermeneutics or deconstruction, we should remember that what is at stake here is not a defence of philosophy as such, but rather a counter-attack on the sociological claim to have overcome philosophy, a claim shown by Rancière to rest not only on a naïve repetition of positions already to be found in Plato, but in a radicalization of these positions. The instituting requirement for philosophy that it pose the question of its own distinction from opinion has hardened in Bourdieu's work into the claim that every opinion may be traced back to its social ground. The strategy of reversal by which Rancière shows Bourdieu to be a latent Platonist exposes the parallel overstatement which since 'the technological passion that seized the philosopher in the modern age' (2004: 165) pairs the philosopher's claim to be exempt from history with the sociological claim to have mastered it.

What the modern philosopher and his sociological opponent overlook is not the self-delimitation by which philosophy distinguishes itself from other forms of knowledge, but the limits which philosophy draws in regards to its possible knowledge of its objects. Philosophy draws up in front of history because it acknowledges that the realm of action is not governed by causal necessity, but is instead marked by fate and accident, just as politics is essentially a sphere of power, opinion and persuasion rather than of truth. Can philosophy do justice to the realm of praxis? That this is an open question does not mean that we need reject philosophy, but rather that we carry a properly philosophical hesitation into the disciplines to which our knowledge of the sublunary world has been entrusted. This exploration into the possibility of a properly historical philosophy in part determines Rancière's return to the ancients: 'I refer to Plato and Aristotle because they are in fact the most modern theorists of the political. In terms of the political, they are the basic thinkers, and they are therefore the most modern thinkers' (1997: 30). 'Properly historical' turns out to mean suitably anachronistic.

Responses to his work by both historians and philosophers underscore the extent to which Rancière frustrates and challenges the categories of both philosophy and history. His works seem to offer us histories of politics, of literature, of modern art; but in his interviews and methodological reflections he stresses both the strategic, polemical and occasional nature of his writing, and the apparently trans-historical or universal ideal of equality to which his whole enterprise is devoted. The verification of the possibility of equality must be sought in the world of history, of practice: but there can be no history of equality, which breaks with the time and strategies of historical narration. Although select historical references remain an important tactical weapon in his writing, they are deployed critically, as much to undercut the authority of his own voice as to challenge his opponents through his display of historical erudition.

So for all that his work plays history off against philosophy, Rancière remains on the shores of the historical discipline, as Kristin Ross has argued. For Ross (2009), Rancière's orientation towards temporality is a powerful antidote to the spatial turn in cultural studies, but is inspired by a persistent emphasis on the surprise of an event which mainstream historiography tends to efface. Indeed, Ross's study of *May '68 and Its Afterlives* (2002) inherits the original programme of *Les Révoltes Logiques*, seeking to show the ways in which subsequent accounts of the events by intellectuals and historians have tended to subject them to powerful revisionist strategies which close down the event as an experience of new possibility. The task of the historian, they had argued, was 'to recognize the moment of a choice, of the unforeseeable, to draw from history neither lessons nor, exactly, explanations, but the principle of a vigilance toward what there is singular in each call to order and in each confrontation' (cited Ross 2002: 128). But if he has been an inspiration for Ross, as for Arlette Farge (1997a; 1997b) and others, Rancière is not exactly a historian himself: his work is more strategic, transdisciplinary, problematic. Ross notes that although '[h]is concern is, first and foremost, with what specific historical actors have said and written in contingent situations' he will 'use history against philosophy', treating history more like fiction in order to reframe the arguments of his opponents (2009: 25).

Philosophers such as Jean-Luc Nancy and Alain Badiou have had equal trouble accommodating his work. For Nancy, Rancière remains a philosopher despite everything – the desire to exit from metaphysics being a familiar strategy of the metaphysician – courting but unable to answer the necessarily speculative question about the eruption into history of the political division whose principle he celebrates (2009: 85; 87–8). Badiou comments on Rancière's historical virtuosity – 'he is capable of erudite scholarship and is a keen archivist' – but seems to hint that he is hiding there: 'In this regard, Rancière is an heir to Foucault [. . .] whose approach consists in a rebellious apprehension of discursive positivities' (2006: 107). He notes too the 'sharply anti-philosophical tone' of his work, but although Badiou sees this as 'a subtle variation on the anti-Platonism of the twentieth century', we might equally remark that Rancière has regularly noted a disconcerting proximity between the positions he explores and those already made by Plato. Like Nancy, Badiou suggests that the violence of Rancière's polemical opposition to philosophy is a form of blindness to philosophical presuppositions, which limits his work's power of engagement with political philosophy.

It seems that Rancière's parallel challenges to philosophy and history sets up something like an interference pattern, particularly dense at the point where the two domains converge: at which we ask what kind of knowledge is possible of politics. We should note too that the polemical context of Rancière's political writing over the last 20 years has forced him to wage war on two fronts at once. On the one hand, by identifying politics with democracy, he seeks to defend democracy against its enemies, who would suppress it in the name of politics. Against those who have argued for a return of political philosophy, of the necessity of accommodation to political reality, or of a revival of properly political virtues, Rancière has argued that a politics without democracy would be the abolition of politics itself. On the other hand, by identifying democracy with politics, he seeks to defend democracy from its professed friends, for whom democracy entails the suppression of politics. The identification of democracy with dissensus is aimed not just against those for whom democracy means rational agreement, an ideal of civic or ethnic community, but also those pluralists for whom democracy entails the managed conflict between competing interests and values.

These political aims require Rancière to argue on the one hand against the revival of political philosophy in France, largely under the guise of political history, and on the other against the revival of metaphysics, under the guise of new materialist ontologies. This results in a double gesture: to play history, as the realm of contingency, off against ontology, which can only be thought in terms of necessity; but at the same time to outflank historical responses to political thought, which share the sociological tendency to distribute appropriate modes of political activity.

The tension involved in this double movement is reflected in Rancière's interest in anachronism. As Rancière told an interviewer:

it is imperative to revoke the authoritative principle derived from the succession of historical events. And it is the implications derived from this second transgressive imperative that I understand to be critical to an idea of contemporaneity. To conceptualize the contemporaneity of thought requires the reliance on a certain anachronism or untimeliness. (2000: 121)

There is a longstanding tension within the discipline of history between the relevance of our understanding of the past for the present, and the critical displacement by which the past is constructed as an object of knowledge that authenticates the objectivity and authority of the historian herself. So Rancière's apparent distrust of historicism might equally be seen as a critical fold within the historical discipline, rather than as a polemic addressed to it from without. What I will argue in the rest of this chapter is that the pursuit of the challenge of equality requires Rancière to step outside the disciplinary identification of the historian, and towards that of the philosopher, in exploring something like the conditions of possibility, not only of historical writing, but of history itself. Or as he puts it in *The Names of History*: 'There is history – an experience and a matter of history – because there is speech in excess, words that cut into life, wars of writing' (1994: 88). However this project remains short of any attempt to open up questions of an ontological or phenomenological type concerning the 'historicity' or temporalization of experience itself.

The Names of History is a characteristically dense and at times polemical intervention into debates about the status of history as a discipline. At one level it poses a fairly straightforward analytical question: what is the specificity of history as a modern discipline? But at a more radical level, it asks about the ways in which the constitution of history as a discipline functions politically. The result is the presentation by Rancière of an aporetic relationship between the work of the historian and the regime of 'historicity' which underlies it: '[g]iving the republican age the means of thinking and writing its own prehistory, the contract prohibited it, in the same gesture, from conceiving its own history and the forms of its writing' (1994: 95). Rancière's own experience of archival work in the 1970s had led him to question the possibility of a social history that could do justice to the variety and plurality of the voices of the workers (cf. 1986). But what had in earlier writings (cf. Rancière 1981) been seen as an empirical failure of the French historical profession to adequately respond to the demands of social history is, in *The Names of History*, traced back to the constitutive features of the writing of modern history itself.

In the early stages of his argument, Rancière follows a trajectory traced earlier in the work of Paul Veyne and Paul Ricoeur. Both had insisted on the inherent narrative dimension of historical writing, and had shown that despite the sociological turn in French historical thought associated with the Annales School, and the displacement of political history by analyses based on economic, geographic or demographic factors, its major works remained premised not only on remarkably literary presentation, but even on the very events and plots whose abolition they had pronounced. In *Writing History* (1971, trans. 1984), Veyne had argued in nominalist and pluralist fashion that histories are the arrangement into series of unique, nonrepeatable events, that any fact can become an event by virtue of being arranged into a historical series, and that consequently there is an indefinite number of possible histories, subject only to the time and ingenuity of historians. For Veyne there is no such thing as historical explanation, only the arrangement of facts into comprehensible series; the major contribution of the Annales School being to have enriched historical study by treating as events new kinds of facts, and therefore inventing new plots. *Writing History* is an extreme statement of a sceptical epistemology that divides the practice of the historian from any attempt to legitimate it on the grounds of its contribution to political, public or historical consciousness.

Although he accepted the tie between history and narrative, Michel de Certeau was to criticize Veyne for failing to take due account of the way in which the choices of historians were themselves circumscribed by their own desires, and by their institutional, historical and political situation (1972: 1323; 1988: 60); and had also stressed the connection between history and the suppression of the past. In turn, Paul Ricoeur had shown in much greater detail the way in which the writing of the Annales School (in particular, that of Fernand Braudel) relied on what he called 'quasi-events' (cf. 1984: 206–25). Ricoeur further suggests that the attempted displacement of the history of events by those of structures and conjunctures must remain incomplete because an event (of whatever scale and duration) is always a function of emplotment. For the historian to make historical change visible requires the construction of narratives in which the long sequences of historical time are treated as if they were events. Whereas for Veyne this results from the subjective action of the historian in his composition of a historical plot, for Ricoeur this instead reflects characteristics of time itself. Ricoeur argues that history is a distinctive form of knowledge because of its relationship to narrative on the one side and to scientific objectivity on the other: 'a discipline that, in virtue of its scientific ambition, tends to forget this line of derivation which continues nevertheless tacitly to preserve its specificity as a historical science'. (1984: 91) Compare Rancière: 'the power of articulation of names and events that is tied to the ontological indeterminacy of the narrative, but that nevertheless is alone suited to preserving the specificity of a *historical* science in general' (1994: 7).

In his later work, *Memory, History, Forgetting*, Ricoeur notes Rancière's original extension of his own analysis of Braudel's work, through which both demonstrate the recurrence of a plot based around events in the heart of the new history (2004: 341). Rancière argues that Braudel inherits Michelet's refusal to maintain a clear distinction between the present tense of the historian's narration, and the past tense in which the events he is retelling occur. The events speak; the historian situates himself and his implied addressee among them, in an ongoing process. In effect Rancière provides an analytic demonstration of de Certeau's suggestion that the function of history is as much to impose the present on the past as it is to let us perceive the past in its absence. It introduces a rift between past and present as much as it joins them in a continuity (de Certeau 1988: 85).

For Rancière, the discourse of the historian is 'the neutralization of the *appearance of the past* [which] takes on what is said of nontruth: uncertainty, death, inessentiality' (1994: 49).

The audacity of the historian in the Annales line is a figure of his subtlety: this is most clear in the ambivalent role played by Michelet in Rancière's argument. On the one hand, 'Michelet is the initiator of this revolution in the system of tenses which characterizes the writing of the new history' (1994: 48). This is to take seriously the claims of Lucien Febvre, one of the founders of the Annales School, who calls Michelet 'the very embodiment of history' (1973: 28), and in doing so to seek to understand more clearly the political implications of their historical poetics. As the epitome of the democratic Republican historian, Michelet exemplifies the way in which the people are silenced by their historians; and the institution of 'republican-romantic' history echoes – but displaces and shuts down – the founding of the Republic itself. Indeed, Rancière's chapter heading puns on the '*récit fondateur*', although the complex term *récit* is flattened in English translation as 'narrative': we might take this to refer to the story that Michelet tells about the revolution which founds the history of the people, and his own historical project; the founding role of his own story in relation to the new history; but also as the organizing role to be played by the example of Michelet in Rancière's staging of his own explication.

But for the thinker attuned to equality, the replacement of one regime of historicity by another is the substitution of one form of inegalitarian story for another. So, while revolutionary in both politics and methodology, Michelet is also the first to put into operation the new historiographical displacement of politics. The historian fabricates the nation out of the voices of the poor, but its visibility depends on precisely this substitution of the historian's account for the hubbub of the mass. Through the invention of a new narrative technique, the historian's reading of the documents of the past allows us to understand the structural conditions of events, but allots to the historian the privileged focal point from which the new history is given visibility. Unity comes out of plurality through the intervention of a single organizing intelligence. Here again Rancière is close to Michel de Certeau, who also cites Michelet in *The Writing of History* to illustrate the proposition that the historian's production of the people depends on their silence:

Another, graver mourning is added to the first. The People are also separated. 'I was born of the people. I had the people in my heart [. . .] But I found their language inaccessible. I was unable to make it speak.' It is also silent, in order to become the object of this poem that speaks of it. (de Certeau 1988: 2)

The historian becomes the privileged interpreter of the people's past, dependent on the literary production of a scientific warrant that undermines the people's ability to understand their own history without the mediation of the historian.

For de Certeau, as for Rancière, the work of the historian becomes a privileged form of a more generalized conception of social praxis as productive. Yet the subsequent accommodation to the place of narrative in history among leading figures in French historiography is not necessarily a progressive transformation but rather a repetition of some of its leading features. When Roger Chartier cites Rancière alongside de Certeau and Ricoeur in recognition of this settlement, he neglects the specific difference of Rancière's account: the political question of equality (1997: 16). Since it is already internal to the constitution of the discipline, a new self-consciousness about the implication of narrative in history need not mean a political transformation. In this sense, Rancière may be closer to Veyne's scepticism, closely allied to that of Foucault, about the efficacy of history, than to de Certeau. Moreover the thrust of his argument about the subsumption of politics in any statement of identity should lead us to question any temptation to organize an account around assertions about cultural identity or ethos.

Rancière's procedures are more descriptive than directly critical. It is not a question of attacking the methodology of the new history, or of claiming that it is insufficiently grounded in theory. This is appropriate to the claim being made: a story is not something that can be disproved, although it may always be retold from another point of view. This kind of approach to intellectual history is familiar from the techniques laid out by Foucault in *The Archaeology of Knowledge*. Foucault suggested that in the analysis of a particular discourse what one seeks is 'a group of rules that are immanent in a practice, and define it in its specificity' (2002: 51). His work directs us away from the analysis of different forms of knowledge as the expression of an underlying cultural unity to an analysis of heterogeneous discursive practices, each following its own developmental trajectory. Moreover, as de Certeau notes, *The Archaeology of Knowledge* also marks the intrusion into Foucault's problematic of the social conflicts in which historiography, as a discursive practice itself, must be involved (1988: 60).

Rancière's definition of his aim in *The Names of History* is similar: 'It is a question of the conditions in which the writing of the knowledgeable historical narrative takes place in the democratic age, of the conditions of articulation of the threefold – scientific, narrative, and political – contract' (1994: 21). In fact one could see Rancière as radicalizing a proposition of de Certeau who notes: 'Stable societies allow history to favor continuities and tend to confer the value of a human essence upon a solidly established order. In periods of movement or revolution, ruptures of individual or collective action become the principle of historical intelligibility' (1988: 48). Insofar as for Rancière the point is to intervene in the present by affirming the possibility of discontinuity, all forms of stability become forms of ordering, or what he calls, in *Disagreement*, policing. Policing implies a homogeneous time of planning and control which is in fact heterogeneous to our experience of time:

There is an event, history happens (in the sense that things happen) insofar as the human being is a being who is non-contemporaneous with itself. Events happen because there are different times which are jumbled together, events happen because there is futurity, the future in the present, because there is also a present which repeats the past, because there are different temporalities within the 'same' time, etc. (1994b: 93, my translation)

I quote from an interview given following the publication of *The Names of History* in order to remark the fact that this question of the constitutive temporal disorder of human existence is given no place in the book.

Having shown that the invention of history for the democratic age is constituted around the substitution of the nation, or the people as bound to a specific territory, for the voices of the people, Rancière contrasts this with the actual nature of democratic politics. Democratic politics is not the emancipation of a specific defined group, but the assertion of the equality of anyone with anyone. It is limitless, and must call into question all forms of bounded politics:

The class that declares itself in the pure invocation of its limitlessness of number is rather identified with the act of a speech without place and of an uncountable collectivity, one impossible to identify. It is the advent [avènement], in the field of politics, of a subject that is such only in its recrossing and disjunction of the modes of legitimacy that established the affinity between discourses and bodies. (1994: 92)

The movement of democratic politics specifically calls into question political settlement based on territory or on belonging, whether portrayed in biological, spiritual or civic terms. Rancière contrasts the disorderly and anachronistic way in which politics makes use of names and precedents to the historians' desire for the ordering of events. In a later essay he phrases this more unequivocally: history 'functions as an ethical principal of adherence, defining what can be felt and thought by the occupants of a space and time' (2006: 8). The emergence of the democratic political subject is not the birth of the Republic, but the violent eruption of the democratic *avènement*.

We might take Rancière's term *avènement* to signal something more than an event [*evènement*]. Bernard Flynn's gloss of the use of the term by Merleau-Ponty and Lefort is helpful here: 'The advent, unlike the event, is not absolutely singular and, unlike the essence, is not subject to identical repetition; although historical, the advent has a signification which overflows its possibility. It continues to preside over a certain space and time; it opens possibilities, even ones it does not itself realize' (2005: 44). The advent of the modern age of democratic politics is a scandal that exceeds the orderly recounting of history. A subject without limit cannot be the object of a history, which as Rancière notes, 'is a series of events that happen to subjects who are generally designated by proper names' (1994: 1). We can tell the story of a political event, but the temporality of a political advent is predicated on the impropriety of the subject constituted and the possible anachronism of the name invoked.

If one of the objects of a poetics of knowledge is to allow for the improper time of political advent, it must in some sense outflank the ordering of historical time. Moreover, it sharpens the political question as to the efficacy of historical understanding or knowledge. In fact this was implicit in Rancière's rejection of the possibility of social history: he suggested in 1981 that 'perhaps we overestimate history as a form of memory leading to self-possession and self-recognition' (1981: 268). Democratic man is not chained to the narrative of his own proper people, class or nation, nor does the researcher trawling the archives to establish a faithful record of times past best represent him: 'the democratic man is a being who speaks, which is also to say a poetic being, a being capable of embracing a distance between words and things which is not deception, not trickery, but humanity' (1995: 51). Questioning the political efficacy and presuppositions of history and memory is to challenge both progressive and conservative accounts of the political value of historical consciousness yet to affirm that the democratic condition of politics is latent in every social formation because innate in man's intelligence.

Although Rancière argues that politics exceeds history, this does not mean that he makes the modern subject of politics unspeakable. Clearly one aim of the poetics of knowledge is precisely to try to make democracy apparent through tracing the pressure that the excess of the political advent exerts on the discourse of history. A similar project is at work in *Disagreement* where Rancière traces the parallel deformation of political philosophy by its attempt to reckon with democracy. But beyond what could be mistaken for something akin to psychoanalysis, a way to make the absence of politics from history and philosophy felt as an absence, the poetics of knowledge also puts into operation a powerful affirmative impulse, stemming from the term 'poetics' itself. The poetics of knowledge is an ambiguous term in *The Names of History* because it describes both the work of the historian and Rancière's own project. In refusing the authority of history Rancière not only asserts the equality between his project and theirs, but an underlying kinship, a point reiterated in his recent essay on method:

> He thinks it is possible to construct in that way interesting and useful poems (you must remember that this term has no pejorative overtone for him), interesting paths allowing us to move from one point to another on the territory of the war of discourses, on condition that they opt out of the pretension to give us the 'foundations' of knowledge and action. (2009: 119)

This privileged place of poetics in Rancière's writing brings into the foreground the extent to which his procedures flow from the challenge of equality.

Poetics in its most general sense refers to production or making. Traditionally, *poiesis* is distinguished from *praxis* or action, on the grounds that *poiesis* aims at, and is subsequently judged in terms of its success at, the production of a work, whereas an action produces an event. The end of *poiesis* is in the work, but *praxis* is consumed in the action (cf. Volpi 1999: 13–14). Because of the relationship between *poiesis* and mimesis, or imitation, this distinction has often been moralized in favour of praxis. In *The Human Condition*, for example, Arendt distinguishes *praxis* as the virtue specific to politics from *poiesis*, and diagnoses both the failure of political philosophy and the ills of the modern age in 'the substitution of making for acting and the concomitant degradation of politics into a means to obtain an allegedly "higher" end' (1998: 229). Reversing the formula, Rancière tends to make action an example of a more widespread imitative making. An example would be the way in which democratic politics seizes on names and examples from elsewhere in historical time and space in order to underscore the universal dimension of the principle of equality being invoked.

Rancière reverses the traditional philosophical disdain for *poiesis*. There are two grounds for this defence. The first is that *poiesis* is in some sense already demystified: it knows itself to be more than and less than the truth.

Poetic language that knows itself as such doesn't contradict reason. On the contrary, it reminds each speaking subject not to take the narrative of his mind's adventures for the voice of truth. Every speaking subject is the poet of himself and of things. Perversion is produced when the poem is given as something other than a poem, when it wants to be imposed as truth, when it wants to force action. Rhetoric is perverted poetry. (1991: 84)

The second is more strategic, and stems from the role given to poetry and language within the text of Rancière's own production. By treating poetics as prior to rhetoric, Rancière suggests that even debased speech testifies to a fundamental equality. Eloquence, whatever its aims or effects, attests to the human capacity to make things in language. Rancière draws the political consequence. Man is neither a political nor a speaking animal, but first and foremost a *poetic* animal. This returns us to the point made in *On the Shores of Politics*:

The democratic man is a being who speaks, which is also to say a poetic being, a being capable of embracing a distance between words and things which is not deception, not trickery, but humanity; a being capable of embracing the unreality of representation. A poetic virtue then, and a virtue grounded in trust. (1995: 51)

Rancière rehabilitates *mimesis* as a fundamental constituent of human intelligence. In *The Names of History*, for example, he hints at the value of a more rhetorical form of history writing, in which the historian (the example is Tacitus) creates speeches, and in doing so 'creates a model of subversive eloquence for the orators and simple soldiers of the future' (1994: 29). To emphasize poetics rather than fiction is to emphasize the making of a work rather than the accomplishment of an action. To treat the production of life as the production of works is to emphasize human experience as something that might be repeated, or imitated, without identifiable beginning or implied end.

By contrast, modern historical procedures, distinguishing rigorously between the voice of the subjects and the voice of the historian, and by turning from those who speak on behalf of the people to the mute forces whose representatives are the people, re-routes the power of mimesis.

> Historical science doesn't win against the temptations of *narrative* and literature; it wins by the involvement of *mimesis* in narrative. It doesn't win in spite of the excesses of romanticism; it wins in the very heart of the movement called romanticism, which first of all signifies the end of the mimetic reign and the transformation of the rules of belles lettres into the unconditioned of literature. (1994: 51)

The tie between literature and history here sets the co-ordinates for the future development of Rancière's work. His later work on literature exploits the tie between what he calls literariness, meaning not the formal quality of the text as an artwork, but rather the lack of a specific addressee of any piece of writing, which implies therefore the potential equality of any reader with any other reader, and the historical characteristics of the age of democracy. But it also describes a repression of literariness inherent in the modern idea of literature, parallel to the suppression of the people's voices in the historical poem in which the historian gives voice to the earth or the nation on their behalf. I note in passing that two further questions arise here: one as to the nature of the tie between the age of democracy and the 'romantic' revolution in forms of knowledge; the second as to the privilege accorded this knot which makes possible not only the modern regime of history, but also those of literature and art, in Rancière's larger project.

If reading Rancière has proved perplexing, as the troubled responses from those who demand something more than the peripatetic pursuit of equality indicate, that may be because of the centrality to his work of this scene of endless reading, translation and making. To practise the poetics of knowledge is to attempt a form of writing that recognizes itself as poetry. But as Rancière demonstrates in *The Names of History*, for the writer or reader to know this is no more and no less than to affirm their equality with the historian, the philosopher or with whomever else they are conversing. So it costs Rancière little to admit that at the heart of history is the same poetics that his own book displays and exemplifies. The passage to the shores of history and back is not a debunking or a critical demystification, but an experiment in making visible the democratic condition as a facet of human experience.

Works Cited

Arendt, Hannah (1998), *The Human Condition*, Chicago: University of Chicago Press.

Badiou, Alain (2006), *Metapolitics*, trans. Jason Barker, London: Verso.
Certeau, Michel de (1972), 'Une épistémologie de transition: Paul Veyne', *Annales E.S.C.* 27: 1317–27.
— (1988), *The Writing of History*, trans. Tom Conley, New York: University of Columbia Press.
Chartier, Roger (1997), *On the Edge of the Cliff: History, Language and Practices*, trans. Lydia G. Cochrane, Baltimore: Johns Hopkins University Press.
Farge, Arlette (1997a), 'L'histoire comme avènement', *Critique* 53 (601–602): 461–6.
— (1997b), *Des lieux pour l'histoire*, Paris: Éditions du. Seuil.
Febvre, Lucien (1973), *A New Kind of History*, trans. K. Folca, ed. Peter Burke, New York: Harper and Row.
Flynn, Bernard (2005), *The Philosophy of Claude Lefort: Interpreting the Political*, Evanston: Northwestern University Press.
Foucault, Michel (2002), *The Archaeology of Knowledge*, trans. A. M. Sheridan Smith, London: Routledge.
Nancy, Jean-Luc (2009), 'Rancière and Metaphysics', in *Jacques Rancière: History, Politics, Aesthetics*, eds Gabriel Rockhill and Philip Watts. Durham: Duke University Press: 83–92.
Rancière, Jacques (1981), '"Le Social": The Lost Tradition in French Labour History', in *People's History and Socialist Theory*, ed. Raphael Samuel, London: Routledge & Kegan Paul: 267–72.
— (1986), 'The Myth of the Artisan: Critical Reflections on a Category of Social History', trans. David H Lake, in *Work in France: Representations, Meanings, Organization and Practice*, ed. Steven Laurence Kaplan and Cynthia J. Koepp, Ithaca: Cornell University Press: 317–34.
— (1991), *The Ignorant Schoolmaster: Five Lessons in Intellectual Emancipation*, trans. Kristin Ross, Stanford: Stanford University Press.
— (1992), *Les noms de l'histoire*, Paris: Éditions du Seuil.
— (1994), *The Names of History: On the Poetics of Knowledge*, trans. Hassan Melehy, Minneapolis: University of Minnesota Press.
— (1994b), 'Histoire des mots, mots de l'histoire', entretien avec Martyne Perrot et Martin de la Soudière, *Communications*, no. 58: 87–101.
— (1995), *On the Shores of Politics*, trans. Liz Heron, London: Verso.
— (1997), 'Democracy Means Equality: Jacques Rancière Interviewed by Passages', *Radical Philosophy*, 82: 29–36.
— (2000), 'Dissenting Words: A Conversation with Jacques Rancière', interview with Davide Panagia, *Diacritics*, 30 (2): 113–26.
— (2004), *The Philosopher and His Poor*, trans. John Drury, Corinne Oster and Andrew Parker, Durham: Duke University Press.
— (2006), *Hatred of Democracy*, trans. Steve Corcoran, London: Verso.
— (2006b), 'Thinking between Disciplines: An Aesthetics of Knowledge', trans. Jon Roffe, *Parrhesia*, 1 (1): 1–12.

— (2009), 'A Few Remarks on the Method of Jacques Rancière', *Parallax*, 15 (3): 114–23.

Ricoeur, Paul (1984), *Time and Narrative vol. 1*, trans. Kathleen McLaughlin and David Pellauer, Chicago: University of Chicago Press.

— (2004), *Memory, History, Forgetting*, trans. Kathleen Blamey and David Pellauer, Chicago: University of Chicago Press.

Ross, Kristin (2002), *May '68 and Its Afterlives*, Chicago: University of Chicago Press.

— (2009), 'Historicizing Untimeliness', in *Jacques Rancière: History, Politics, Aesthetics*, eds. Gabriel Rockhill and Philip Watts. Durham: Duke University Press: 15–29.

Veyne, Paul, (1984), *The Writing of History: Essay on Epistemology*, trans. Mina Moore-Rinvolucri, Manchester: Manchester University Press.

Volpi, Franco (1999), 'The Rehabilitation of Practical Philosophy', trans. Eric Buzzetti, in *Action and Contemplation: Studies in the Moral and Political Thought of Aristotle*, eds. Robert C. Bartlett and Susan D. Collins, Albany: SUNY Press: 3–25.

Anti-Sociology and Its Limits

Alberto Toscano

I.

Reflecting on the current fortunes of emancipatory political thought, it is difficult to shake off the nagging impression that, in a time still marked by accumulated defeats and resilient obstacles to the emergence of effective oppositional politics, the burdens of historical necessity are often turned into theoretical virtues. This is particularly evident in the pervasive preoccupation with identifying an elusive and *sui generis* form of action and subjectivity, *politics*, beneath the deceptive spectacle of social complexity.

In the context of a normalization of political life and a concomitant desublimation of the aspirations and energies that had coursed through the 'red decade' after 1968 – in other words, in the midst the neoliberal glaciation that some have referred to as the long 1980s or the Restoration – abstract and formalistic attempts to define anti-systemic practice could be understood as a way of retaining those very energies while withstanding the pressures of pragmatism and renegacy.[1] Though it is perhaps facile to say that the activity of defining politics is inversely related to the strength of political movements, it is undeniable that the draw of contemporary invocations of politics in a radical vein is intimately linked to a widespread perception of political disorientation and social powerlessness.

In this respect, some features of a current preoccupation with the politics of emancipation, whose roots lie principally in a philosophical response to May '68 and its afterlives, are of interest. The first, and perhaps more debilitating one, is the implicit equation between the politics of emancipation (or communism, or equality, or radical democracy . . .) and politics *tout court*. There is a certain comfort in this move, which is of an exquisitely philosophical character, even if it is often accompanied by criticisms of philosophy's pretension to oversee political practice. Rather than defeat at the hands of rival political projects, emancipation suffers because of the very disappearance or retreat of politics itself. This definitional move is philosophical to the extent that it judges the only *real* politics to be the one that is somehow identical, as a kind of singular universal, with the category of politics itself. The declaration that something is 'just not politics' then acquires the same dubious, self-satisfied ring that accompanies the judgment that something is 'not philosophy'.

While providing a sense of purity and nobility in defeat, withdrawing the politics of emancipation (itself hardly a unified entity) from a strategic and agonistic field, in which it would be enmeshed with the politics of conservation, interest, inequality, conformity or management, makes a reckoning with the dynamics of historical failure and the possibilities of recomposition well-nigh impossible. Questions of tendency, opportunity, alliance, strategy, preparation, and so on – that is, questions having to do with the 'dirty' dialectic of building-up an alternative together with the means of implementing it – become unintelligible if what an emancipatory political perspective faces is not a multifarious, even if largely hostile, political field, but simply *not-politics*.

This radical alterity, of politics to its others (power, capital, knowledge, the police, the economy, etc.), translates into a second dimension common to a number of contemporary philosophical invocations of politics, the claim that politics (i.e. emancipation, equality, communism) is rare. What might be perceived as a massive, global setback for the cause(s) of equality is in this way given a kind of transcendental status. From such a vantage point, it is not that moments of genuine political transformation have *become* rare, but that they always were so. This may succeed in short-circuiting those liberal and conservative critics who gloated at the collapse of movements who thought they had history, and to a certain extent necessity, on their side; but it also stifles a sustained reflection on the organizational, ideological and strategic reasons behind the triumphs of reaction and normalization.

The rarity-of-politics thesis has the salutary effect of quelling the despondency of those who've come to realize that history, far from being one's ally, is, in Fredric Jameson's words, 'what hurts'. We should not mourn living in seemingly apolitical times, since in a sense all times are apolitical. But the price of this move, together with that of a dualism between true politics (of radical equality and emancipation) and politics in its everyday usage, is to turn the recent history of painful setbacks for the radical Left, *the very reason for the attractiveness and resonance of such a thesis*, into an unintelligible phenomenon, due to some combination of insufficient will, sheer contingency, or indeed the quasi-transcendental fact that true politics – being entirely other than what generally goes by this name – is not a power that can (or should) consolidate itself into institutions and orders. Accordingly, the very idea of political transformation is sundered between its subjective or 'aesthetic' side (the affirmation and/or experience of equality) and its objective or 'material' side (social change, the establishing of a new order, a lasting mutation in everyday life) – which is regarded at best as an effect of true politics on not-politics (the economy, society, knowledge, etc.) or, at worst, a reification of emancipation into an order which, though it may be deemed better or worse than others, is different in kind, *qua* order, from politics itself.

Such a distillation and definition of politics can serve, as it arguably has, a tonic role in countering both the effective ideology of our systems of government and the theoretical common sense in the social sciences and humanities. Much like the slogan 'another world is possible', though not as openly drawing upon utopian discourse, the radical alterity claimed for a politics of emancipation forcefully asserts that, however hegemonic they may be, parliamentary capitalist democracies of a neoliberal stamp by no means exhaust the possibilities of human collective action. This alterity translates, at a high level of abstraction, the widespread, exasperated judgement that this is just not politics, that this can't be all there is. It also breaks with the inevitable anti-politics that is but the other side of this apparent closure of possibilities: a hatred of politics based on the experience that politics can only be but the management of collective life for the sake of the privileged, at a far remove from human needs and aspirations. But it also bucks the tendency, present in much contemporary social theory, to entangle questions of emancipation in the endless 'negotiation' of differences and complexities – a move which, in its understandable wish to go beyond the sterile verities of classical sociology and political theory, ends up submerging moments of rupture and equality in a micropolitics where the micro ultimately prevails over the politics (see Toscano 2009).

Having said that, welcoming antidotes to the ideological monotonies of neoliberalism and complexity, and their foreclosure of the question of radical change and emancipation, should not blind us to some of the limitations of this turn to the affirmative definition of politics. One of its most striking aspects is a hostility towards 'sociology', often identified (not necessarily as a discipline, sometimes just as a generic intellectual attitude) as the key obstacle to grasping the specificity of politics. In Rancière's work in particular, we could speak of the elaboration of a veritable anti-sociology. Exploring this dimension of Rancière's political thought can help us to weigh up its important contribution to the revival of egalitarian thought, as well as to confront the way in which it instantiates some of the deeper limitations of the broader turn to radical redefinitions of politics. In the final analysis, the wish to rescue political action from the clutches of social conformity and economic determinism risks jettisoning some of the resources of emancipation, among them ones that can be developed under the rubric of sociology.

II.

Rancière's condemnation of sociology, like the repudiation of Althusserian 'science' with which it is basically continuous (Rancière 1974), stems from his steadfast opposition to any conception of political subjectivation that would posit a relation between a social structure of places and roles, on the one hand, and the experience of emancipation, on the other. In what is perhaps his most drastic repudiation of the very idea of a critical social science, Rancière argues that to approach political change beginning from social structure, that is, beginning from *inequality*, can only ever result in the reproduction of inequality. Thus theories of the obstacles to emancipation that base themselves on an investigation of differential access to culture, taste and speech, and especially of a differential access to political consciousness – *in primis* Pierre Bourdieu's theory of dispossession – simply *redouble* oppression by giving it their academic and analytical imprimatur.[2]

Rancière's opposition to sociology, broadly construed to include Marxian critiques of political economy,[3] brings together questions of modality, knowledge and competence. Rather than siding with that Spinozist strand within Marxism, which sees the knowledge of necessity as the key to freedom, Rancière takes to its ultimate conclusions the view according to which ideology is that which passes off the contingency of domination as necessity. But this seemingly classical proposition is understood by him to mean that any order of domination is *purely* contingent, and that the very attempt to discern any kind of logic or regularity in the forms of dispossession is an act of unnecessary complicity with domination itself. Hence, on the basis of a key tenet of the theory of ideology – namely, that ideology eternalizes or naturalizes a contingent social structure – Rancière can end up suggesting that any theory of ideology is ultimately ... ideological.

Such a position is in part rendered possible by a systematic evacuation of any nuance in thinking the question of modality in the social and political domains: for Rancière it seems that *either* a social order is necessary *or* it is purely contingent: intermediate notions such as tendency, probability, likelihood – arguably the only ones with which to think political change as neither miraculous nor mechanical – vanish. Marxism itself is rather cavalierly reduced to a science of social necessity, and, in a move Rancière is not alone in making, its explanations of supposedly ineluctable economic dynamics are presented as precursors to neoliberal market fundamentalism.[4] In a society whose 'governing intelligence today is nothing but the knowledge of the automatism of the great global stomach of wealth' (Rancière 2005: 13), any concession to the idea of economic necessity is suspect.

Likewise, far from being an eminently equivocal term, a marker of cynical conformism as well as militant tenacity, for Rancière 'realism' becomes simply synonymous with the hypostasis and reduplication of reality as destiny:

Realism claims to be that sane attitude of mind that sticks to observable realities. It is in fact something quite different: it is the police logic of order, which asserts, in all circumstances, that it is doing the only thing possible to do. The consensus system has absorbed the historical and objective necessity of former times, reduced to the congruous portion of the 'only thing possible' that the circumstances authorize. The possible is thereby the conceptual exchanger of 'reality' and 'necessity'. (1999: 132)[5]

Ideology, kicked out of the door, comes back through the window, as realism comes to be defined as the 'system of belief peculiar to the consensus system' (1999: 132).

Rancière does not set out to *demonstrate* the feebleness of arguments about necessity, to propose alternative modes of explanation that could undermine the belief in necessity – a task to which others in the Althusserian orbit, as well as Althusser himself, set themselves with considerable industriousness. Claims about social causality and necessity are in the end for Rancière 'tautologies', just like his own affirmation of axiomatic equality. In spite of all their epistemic trappings, tautologies of inequality – for instance those that seek sociologically to explain why those 'left behind' by modernization may have a proclivity for racism – simply declare that 'the backwards are backwards' (2005: 28). When it comes to society, it seems that knowledge can only ever take the form of the reproduction and reassertion of inequality; the social sciences are ultimately sciences of ignorance, of the gap between the intelligence of the master and that of the incompetent, who will never be able to make the famed transition to intelligence itself.[6]

In starting from inequality, the social sciences subordinate the possibility of emancipation and equality to the reality (which for Rancière is easily recoded as necessity) of hierarchy and disempowerment; in so doing, whether wittingly or otherwise, they pose themselves as the competent overseers and mediators of this passage from necessary 'minority' to possible maturity, ignorance to necessity – in a pedagogical scenario whose inegalitarian aporia Rancière has powerfully explored in numerous texts. The sociologist or critical theorist (or indeed the Marxist scientist-politician, who serves as their precursor and the ultimate object of Rancière's animus) thus positions himself as the master of the gap between structure and agency, ignorance and knowledge, minority and maturity, thereby foreclosing the very possibility for real emancipation, which is always a contingent and immediate affirmation of the equality of intelligences, a taking of knowledge and rights, but above all a taking of speech (a *prise de parole*), which abhors any political oversight or scientific guarantee.

Rancière also refuses the view according to which, in lieu of the guidance provided by scientists or intellectuals, impersonal social processes themselves could mediate between passivity and activity, submission and emancipation. His research into the intellectuality of nineteenth-century workers led him to the conclusion that it is *not* the passage to industrialization, and the harsh experience of hierarchy and exploitation, which functions as a kind of material pedagogue for the working class; instead, 'the real movement of workers' emancipation takes place against great industry' – in idleness, the affirmation of craft, evasion, aesthetic activity, and so on (1978: 79). The momentum of capitalism does not provide a *leçon des choses*, a wrenching object-lesson that would retroactively identify radical dispossession as the precondition for full conscious reappropriation. There is no historical logic, no tendency, towards emancipation. What 1968 taught, in a lesson very different than the one which thoroughgoing industrialization was supposed to have imparted to the working class, is that *submission and resistance have no cause but themselves* (2007: 334).

Before we inquire further into the cogency of this refusal of any social explanation and causality for politics, it is worth delving further into Rancière's own understanding of the social. In effect, Rancière's polemic – which is sometimes rendered opaque outside of France by the combined specificity of his targets and obliqueness of his attacks[7] – is as much against sociological accounts of domination of the Bourdieusian stamp, as it is against the so-called return of political philosophy, which, from the late 1970s onwards, sought to reaffirm the values of the rule of law against anti-capitalist hostility to liberal rights, and to assert the classical virtues of political life against the disaggregating and conflictual character of the social – following here, albeit in a distinctly French-republican vein, in the footsteps of Hannah Arendt or Leo Strauss. Against sociologists and Marxists, Rancière affirms the irreducibility and self-reliance of emancipatory political action, which is not prepared but rather hindered or perverted by the attempt on the part of critical theories to master it. But against the pretensions of the political philosophers to separate off a proper space of political appearance from the social, understood as a domain of necessity, interest and mere life (a position often founded on its own pseudo-sociological accounts of increasing massification and individualism),[8] Rancière affirms that there are not two spheres, the social and the political, but rather incommensurable 'logics' that inhabit what our theoretical common sense perceives as more or less homogeneous domains. This is an operation that Rancière famously carries out in terms of the political arena, which is sundered into the inegalitarian operations of the *police* and the precarious irruptions of *politics* (here, again, synonymous with politics *of emancipation*). In what concerns the social, Rancière approaches this through the notion of homonymy.

III.

The contentions and disagreements between politics and the police are in a sense above all about homonymy – about the terms that define our collective life, like people, democracy, class, or indeed politics itself. Rancière's own disagreement with Marxism concerns especially the homonymy of the proletariat, which, like a number of his contemporaries, he is adamant to wrest away from the structural determinations and social necessities of the 'working class'.[9] '*Class*', he writes,

> is the perfect example of one of those homonyms over which the counts of the police order and those of the political demonstration are divided. In the police sense, a class is a grouping of people assigned a particular status and rank according to their origins or their activity. [. . .] In the political sense, a *class* is something else entirely: an operator of conflict, a name for counting the uncounted, a mode of subjectification superimposed on the reality of all social groups. (1999: 83)

These two classes are 'rigorously opposed', and if there is a fundamental *casus belli* to Rancière's distancing from Marxism it is what he perceives as its equivocations over this difference, which at one and the same time posit a pedagogical transitivity between police classification and political declassification, and undermine the possibility of a politics of declassification by treating politics as a mendacious surface-appearance hiding the socio-economic truth of class. Lacking an ear for the homonymy, or wilfully manipulating it for the sake of mastery, 'Marxist metapolitics introduces an ambiguity in which all the political *disagreement* about political *disagreement* is concentrated' (Rancière 1999: 84).

But Rancière does not simply wish, like Arendt or her epigones, to reclaim the rights of politics against the insidious intrusions of the social. Rather, he uses the method of the homonym to argue that both Marxist sociologism and philosophical politicism are led up blind alleys by failing to distinguish between the logic of politics and that of the police. Rancière even suggests that a mishandling of homonymy can lead to a kind of radicalism or 'fanaticism' which, instead of employing homonymy to unsettle the police order, reifies the two logics into poles between which it then oscillates violently. In the case of proletariat, this means turning it into either a sheer social fact, a complete passivity which is in a way indistinguishable from the police order of capitalist classification, or into a purely active revolutionary leadership, a 'nonclass': 'These two extreme poles strictly define two extremisms: an infrapolitical [i.e. sociological] extremism of class, that is, of the social embodiment of political classes, and an ultrapolitical extremism of nonclass – opposing extremisms whose homonyms, class and nonclass, allow them to come together in the single figure of the terrorist' (Rancière 1999: 85).[10]

Against this misuse of homonymy, Rancière appears to suggest that we affirm the internal division between two logics that are different in kind, while nevertheless not reifying or ontologizing these into entities or spheres (as is done, for instance, by those political philosophers who wish to put 'the social' at a distance from 'the political'). Importantly for Rancière's sustained polemic against sociology, it is the social that according to him has been 'the decisive homonym', the foremost field of contention between, on the one hand, those attempts to connect the unconnected, 'the forms of visibility of the egalitarian logos with the places where it is invisible', and, on the other, 'metapolitical' attempts to freeze the relationship between the political and the social – making the social either into the obstacle to the virtues of citizenship (as in the return of political philosophy), or treating it as the real, material basis of politics' illusory appearance (as in Marxism and sociology) (1999: 91, 90). For Rancière, the social

has caused several logics and intertwinings of logics to connect and to disconnect, to oppose one another and to blur [. . .] in the modern era, the social has been precisely the place where politics has been played out, the very name it has taken on, wherever it has not simply been identified with the science of government and with the means of taking it over. This name is, it is true, similar to the name of its negation. But every politics works on homonyms and the indiscernible. Every politics also works on the verge of its radical demise, which is embodiment as the police, the realization of the political subject as social body. (1999: 91)

There are thus two socials – one of inequality, one of equality (2004: 89).[11] The social of inequality, the social of the 'police', is the one that Rancière more or less identifies with the object of sociology,[12] whether this be understood as a social-scientific discipline or as an intrinsic component of philosophy's own capture and suffocation of politics conceived as the exceptional affirmation of the equality of intelligences.[13] The latter, for Rancière, is especially evident in the archi-political and meta-political dimensions of philosophy ever since its Greek inception. It seems that, in its foreclosure of a politics premised on the unalloyed equality of intelligences, philosophy must double itself with a sociology, that is an analysis and prescription of the social which creates an order of inequalities, of proper roles and of the spaces and times that define them.

Furthermore, there is a 'socio-logy' of politics, which seeks to ground the community in a univocal distribution of the sensible, *without remainder* (2004: 250). Democracy – another intensely homonymous term – shifts from being a political practice of equality to a policing of functions and differences precisely by erasing the 'structural singularity' of subjectivities whose refusal of dominant classifications puts them at odds with the social of inequality. The ultimate consequence of this approach is a 'sociological end of politics': the transformation of democracy into the name for a social order (2004: 48, on Tocqueville). The logic of democratic politics that Rancière discerns in the interstices of ancient Greek political philosophy, in the figure of the drawing of lots, is anti-sociological precisely in the sense that it is presented as an absence of transitivity between social placement and political action, an excess ('the part with no part') over the putatively exhaustive count that makes a community coincide with itself; a 'state of exception in which no pair of opposites, no principle of the distribution of roles functions' (2004: 230).

Philosophy instead becomes anti-democratic and anti-political – which is to say, sociological – in trying to exorcize this exception. Thus Rancière sees in Plato the inventor of sociology as the necessary support for a philosophical archi-politics:

Plato invents the regime of community interiority in which the law is the harmony of the ethos, the accord between the *character* of individuals and the *moral values* of the collective. He invents the sciences that go with this internalization of the bond of community, those sciences of the individual and collective soul that modernity will call psychology and sociology. (1999: 68)

Philosophy's social, the social of an inequality that vouchsafes the superior competence of philosophy, is the utopia of a fully policed politics, which looks like an oligarchy to the oligarchs and a democracy to the demos; it is 'the utopia of a sociologized politics', the 'fanaticism' of a regime of consensus that abhors any excess, any real, unmanageable difference (1999: 74 and 111). Here, workers are *nothing but* workers (not poets or painters, and certainly not philosophers). Philosophy and sociology are therefore two different, but intimately related practices of depoliticization; that is, two ways of eliminating the difference between politics and the police, for the obvious benefit of the latter.[14]

But, as Rancière reminds us, philosophy's sociology of inequality cloaks the fundamental equality that is inequality's repressed presupposition. As he notes about the otherwise 'idiotic' tale of the war of all against all in Hobbes:

behind this feeble tale of death and salvation, something more serious makes itself felt, the declaration of the ultimate secret of any social order, the pure and simple equality of anyone and everyone: there is no natural principle of domination by one person over another. (1999: 79)

The question of modality – that is, of the *contingency* of inequality – defines Rancière's perception of the social. We could ask whether the fact that social hierarchies are stripped of a putative natural necessity really does make them simply 'contingent', and whether, for those seeking to break with the effects of a distribution of the sensible that tries to be seamless and all-encompassing, this ideology of contingency is really such a boon. I'll return to this matter in the conclusion. For now, it is worth reiterating that, unlike the French advocates of a return to political philosophy and their anglophone precursors, Rancière does not turn the social into the gelatinous repository of everything that is not politics. The thesis of homonymy, in one of Rancière's typical operations, splits the social from within, stops it from coinciding with itself – precisely by opposing a logic of coincidence to one of non-coincidence.

Rancière presents this homonymy as a distinction that cuts across social and political movements themselves. Whence the preference for the language of 'logics' rather than 'spheres' – though we might ask whether this legitimate wish not to reify distinctions does not fall, in spite of itself, into the moralistic trap of political dualism.[15] Thus, writing about the widespread movement of strikes in France in 1995, Rancière proposes a concrete case in which the tension and overlapping between these two logics becomes a political matter in itself. For Rancière, the French strike wave, like every social movement, was marked by the homonymy of the social (and one might add of 'movements' themselves). On the one hand, these movements belong to the social as the management and balancing-out of different parts of the population, the administration (which sometimes manifests itself as antagonism) of conflicts of interests and balances of forces through operations of partition and redistribution. In this sense, social movements are an integral part of the 'police' of society – an observation that is the rather formalistic echo of the long tradition of critiques of reformism and trade-unionism as integral cogs in the reproduction of a capitalist order of hierarchy and exploitation. On the other hand, according to Rancière:

The social has also meant historically the fight to bring into question this police of social relationship, to unite to a given localised and determinate demand, coming from this or that group, the repudiation of the very logic of the distribution of parts, the inclusion of the uncounted of the social order in general. [. . .] Every social movement puts into play a more or less explicit gap between what is inscribed as a negotiable demand and

what the struggle itself implies: the demonstration of this equality which ultimately
sustains the distributions of competence in the social hierarchy, because without it [...]
inequality itself cannot even be 'explained'. There is no pure social movement and
no essential distinction between defensive and corporativist struggle and universalist
and 'imaginative' social movements. (Rancière 2009: 51)

This last formulation is particularly laudable, signalling as it does an awareness on Rancière's part of the possible moralism that results from reifying logical distinctions into categorical differences. Yet Rancière's work oscillates between positing an incommensurability between the two-names-in-one (of class, proletariat, democracy, people, and so on)[16] and acknowledging, in spite of his allergy to any dialectical transition, that the 'socials' can be viewed as two logical moments in a single if discontinuous process. The more Rancière ratchets up his anti-sociology, the more his work risks producing a sterile and moralistic dualism, rather than a dialectic of homonymy in which questions of organization and social order cannot be disjoined from moments of exception. Indeed, to return to my opening remarks, it is this focus on the exceptional, shared by Rancière with many of his contemporaries, which can lead to an aestheticization of the rarity of politics, and to a rationalization and sublimation of political weakness that risks freezing into a latter-day beautiful soul posture, as well as offering a *supplement d'âme* to otherwise apolitical discourses (something present in some of the more spurious uses of Rancière in the artworld).[17]

IV.

In his intervention at the recent *On the Idea of Communism* conference in London, Rancière put his finger on this issue, when, in the context of a further iteration of his criticisms of the pedagogical model underlying Marxism, he raised the problem of the 'discipline of emancipation' in the following way:

The question is that of knowing how the collectivisation of the capacity of anyone at all [*n'importe qui*] can coincide with the organisation of a society, how the an-archic principle of emancipation can become that of a social distribution of places, tasks and powers. (2009a: 134)

How is it possible to forge some kind of relation between two incommensurable logics, that of the political equality of intelligences and that of the policed inequality of competencies? The key thinker of emancipation for Rancière, Joseph Jacotot, or 'the ignorant schoolmaster', refused any such transition: emancipation could not be social (2009: 233).[18] The thrust of Rancière's own reasoning seems generally to push his own work in this direction: though there may be a worse or a better police there can be no such thing as the overcoming of the split between the two logics. In other words, the communist dream of an association of producers (or indeed the anarchist horizon of a federation of communes) remains inexorably attached, in however attenuated a way, to the logic of the police.

In this regard, and despite his generally hostile attitude to her stance and that of her epigones, Rancière often appears to replicate Hannah Arendt's ambiguous paean to workers' councils as spaces of appearance of political freedom and equal speech betrayed by their 'sociological' corruption, that is, by the use of councils to expropriate and run factories and manage social life more generally – leading to the re-emergence of unequal functions, asymmetries of power and the dumb activity that Arendt associates with labouring.[19] Of course, Rancière, as noted above, rejects the idea of an instituted political space, which would perforce separate the competent from the incompetent, the knowledgeable from the ignorant – and yet his implicit suspicion that the goal of lasting, material emancipation will inevitably re-inscribe an inequality of intelligences makes him retread a similar path. Rancière's distrust of 'realized' emancipation derives from his insistently negative estimation of the role of science and theory in Marxism, which Rancière sees as dispossessing the political action of communist militants in the name of the interests of workers, and the intelligence of workers in the name of the leadership of communist intellectuals and apparatchiks.[20] Rancière's critique of pedagogy allows him to refresh, though not necessarily innovate upon, the long (anarchist and left-communist) tradition of critiques of elitism and substitutionism in 'authoritarian' and Leninist socialisms. And yet his answers to the conundrum of the discipline of emancipation remain unsatisfying, too cosily reliant on a rather two-dimensional perception of the history of attempts at social and material emancipation (and of Marxism more broadly), which results in a worthy if excessively rhetorical invocation of communist 'moments'.

Rancière writes commendably about collective efforts at a politics of equality, which have always shown more organizational capability than the one manifested in bureaucratic machinations, invoking an 'organization of disorder' (an unwitting echo perhaps of the transitional 'non-state state' evoked by certain Marxists). For him, in a passage that seems to run counter to the temptation to separate off emancipation from the mess of social production and reproduction, communism is only worth reviving as a tradition

> created by those moments, whether celebrated or obscure, in which simple workers, ordinary men and women, have shown their capacity to struggle for their rights and for the rights of all, to run factories, companies, administrations, schools or armies by collectivising the power of equality of anyone with anyone. (2009: 240)

But aren't these moments defined precisely by the attempt to generate new orders? Orders which, while recognizing the dangers of hierarchy and dispossession, actually confront the need to collectively control the institutions of power, hierarchy and authority that accrue to the running of political systems and to the division of labour, without allowing them to overwhelm the principles of egalitarianism? The fact that the problem of the discipline of emancipation has received some incomplete, feeble, or at times repugnant responses, doesn't mean it does not remain the chief problem for egalitarian politics, nor that we can simply dispatch it with the argument about the homonymy of the social. A 'non-police police', so to speak, remains a real organizational and strategic question.

V.

Though Rancière's explorations of emancipation can help us to pose these questions and to remain vigilant against elitist temptations, I think his anti-sociologism is in the final analysis an obstacle to tackling the question of how the equality of intelligences can be combined with radical social transformation. Rancière's now rather outdated fixation on a dogmatic Marxism that would read off political action from social analysis (hardly a hegemonic position today!), leads him to an anti-explanatory ideology of contingency that would be seriously debilitating if it were actually imported into the practice of social and political movements. Unsurprisingly, collective drives to emancipation have generally been accompanied by attempts to analyse the mechanisms of domination. Politics may indeed always be 'a leap that no knowledge can justify and no knowledge can exempt us from' (2005: 186), but that does not mean that knowledge (of bureaucratic structure, class fractions, forms of exploitation, military forces, financial systems, commodity chains, and so on) is something that politics can do without.

The 'situational representation' or 'cognitive mapping' of one's position vis-à-vis the often invisible forces and agencies that impinge on the affirmation and flourishing of one's capacities is a vital dimension of political action (see Jameson 1988; 1991). Indeed, the formation of counter-knowledges and counter-cartographies can be regarded both as a creative opposition to the policing of what can be seen and said, but also as a strategic tool in organizing against the 'social of inequality'. The kind of knowledge produced by the Detroit Geographical Expedition, for example, which brought together radical geographer William Bunge, community activists and ordinary residents of Detroit's dispossessed black neighbourhoods, was not merely an affirmation of the contingency of domination, but an inquiry into *how* and *where* and *for whom* that domination operated. The production of knowledge and of explanations became an emancipatory activity, as it cut through representations of urban space, to remap Detroit's street-plan in terms not of the normal tropisms of traffic and commerce but of 'Where Commuters Run Over Black Children' or the regional map in terms of the net flows of wealth from the inner city 'slums' *out* to the rich suburbs (Wood 2010: 114–15, 166–71).[21] Within the workers' movement itself, it could be argued that the 'workers' inquiry', from Marx's 1880 questionnaire for the *Revue Socialiste* to the Italian workerist debate on the socialist uses of sociology[22] and more recent attempts at inquiring into call-centres, migrant labour or sex work, has precisely been the emblem of a form of knowledge that does not involve the ideological superiority of communist intellectuals over ignorant workers, but which is also capable, *for the sake of equality*, to draw on different capacities, in fraught but potentially emancipatory processes of collective learning and explanation – in which knowledge becomes itself a force for displacement, disappropriation and declassification.[23]

In such practices, we can glimpse that sociology too can be turned into a 'homonym'; though it may 'begin' from inequality (and how could it not ...) it can also function as a sociology of equality, for instance in combining a meticulous, 'scientific' knowledge of cycles of production with the strategic capacity to interfere with them, and with the political will to make radically egalitarian wage demands.[24] By continuing to struggle doggedly against the chimerical figure of a knowledge substituting itself for politics and dispossessing the incompetent, rather than investigating the forms of emancipatory knowledge that may be produced from below – and across different competencies – for the sake of equality, Rancière risks sacrificing the (counter-)epistemological dimension of politics to its aesthetic one, missing the potentially fruitful links between the two.

Recognizing the non-naturalness of domination is all the more reason to inquire into the specificities of its functioning. To think that explanation, strategy and knowledge, and indeed sociology itself, are not intrinsic components of politics is not only debilitating, it dispossesses – potentially in a more severe way than Bourdieu's sociology – those forced into positions of 'minority' of the very tools of emancipation. If it is not simply to turn into a spectacle for the melancholy enjoyment of the theorist or the historian, emancipation is a process that cannot simply be reduced to the affirmation of equality but of necessity drives one towards investigating the conditions for the institution and durability of equality.

Finally, breaking with the ideology of pure contingency that underlies Rancière's anti-sociology can allow us to be true to his inspiring studies of emancipation while not succumbing to what we could call a meta-sociology. By the latter, I want to refer to the paradoxical result of Rancière's position which, eschewing explanation, nevertheless seems to eternalize an invariant and transcendental structure of domination and incapacitation (the 'police') which, for all of its unnaturalness and contingency, seems to congeal into a figure of destiny. Among other things, sociology, along with other social and historical sciences, can also provide us with a knowledge of contingency capable of fuelling the imagination of other forms of social order, including ones in which a redistribution of economic, political and aesthetic resources would not be incompatible with the maximization of equality; where systematic and durable social transformation would not need to be viewed as incommensurable with the affirmation of an equal capacity for politics.

If moments of communism are to be rather more lasting and expansive than they have been, and to attain a greater momentum, some advance between the threadbare dichotomies of social knowledge and political truth, necessity and contingency, will have to be made. This will also mean, learning from Rancière, spying out the homonymy within academic disciplines themselves and fostering forms of knowledge that cannot be so easily dismissed as elitist and disempowering. It will also entail not dispossessing, as anti-sociology risks doing, those struggling against domination of their rightful claims not just to the experience of equality but to forms of power and of knowledge that can permit the affirmation of equality to have lasting consequences.

Notes

1. For Rancière's own defence of the politics of form, see *Disagreement* (Rancière 1999: 87).
2. In a judicious and intelligent account of the Rancière/Bourdieu differend, Charlotte Nordmann has criticized Rancière for treating intellectual dispossession as a cause rather than, as she argues it remains in Bourdieu, an *effect* of domination, and for discounting the fact that the capacities of individuals are *really* determined and delimited by the process of dispossession (Nordmann 2006: 143). For a critical if sympathetic investigation of Rancière's critique of pedagogy and its contemporary political relevance, see Power (2009). Rancière's principal attacks on Bourdieu can be found in the chapter devoted to the latter in *The Philosopher and His Poor* (2004a), as well as in 'L'éthique de la sociologie', in *Les scènes du peuple* (2003), which collects articles from *Les Révoltes logiques*, the journal Rancière co-edited between 1975 and 1985, and which also published the collective volume *L'empire du sociologue* (1984). For a more recent and ironic take on sociology, see Rancière's *Chroniques des temps consensuels* (Rancière 2005: 51–2), on Lévi-Strauss's encounter with the Bororo people of the Amazon, who are even more 'sociological' than Comte or Durkheim, and on classical sociology's 'idea of a society which transforms its science into common rituals and beliefs'.
3. In effect, 'Marxist metapolitics' is identified by Rancière as the source for the 'rules of the game' which define sociology's own elision of politics, understood in terms of 'the shift between the real social body hidden beneath political appearances and endless assertion of the scientific truth of political falseness' (Rancière 1999: 92).
4. *Chroniques des temps consensuels*, p. 46; more specifically on the question of the supposed affinities between Marxist determinism and neoliberal necessitarianism in their shared dismissal of democratic politics, see *Disagreement*, pp. 96–7. Bruno Latour is another author who views neoliberalism as a kind of 'second Marxism'. See 'Never Too Late To Read Tarde', *Domus*, October 2004, available at: *http://www.bruno-latour.fr/presse/presse_art/GB-DOMUS %2010–04.html*. Here Latour speaks of 'Marxists from the Left' and 'Marxists from the Right'.
5. Note once again the thesis of a continuity between Marxist determinism and the neoliberal creed that 'there is no alternative'.
6. See the very perspicuous comments on Rancière's anti-scientism and its political limitations in Hallward (2006). According to Hallward, the 'political price to be paid for this downplaying of knowledge is prohibitively high' (2006: 127).

7. This is especially the case in what concerns *The Hatred of Democracy*, a book whose polemical objects don't have such obvious analogues in a British or American context.
8. See Arendt's *The Human Condition* (1958), much of whose argument hinges on a particularly bleak and US-centric vision of the depoliticizing effect of 'consumer society', itself reliant on 1950s American sociology.
9. 'This multiple without a name which in Latin is called *proles* and *proletarius* and which the modern age has picked up on in the homonymy of the "proletariat", which makes of it less the name of a social category than that of a singular multiple, an analyzer of being-together, an operator of distance for productive and reproductive bodies from themselves' (2004: 187). See also Blechman et al. (2005: 285–301), where 'class struggle' is redefined as that power of declassification that moves the proletariat from a social identity to an egalitarian experience of disidentification, as in Rancière's repeated reference to Blanqui's courtroom claim to be a proletarian – a claim evidently devoid of sociological truth. For a particularly stark statement of the foreignness of the proletariat to the working class, see Agamben (2005: 31).
10. Similarly, the Marxist abuse of the homonym is responsible, in Rancière's eyes, for brutally reincorporating the politics of declassification into the social, triggering 'the most radical figure of the archipolice order' (90) – clearly an allusion to the kind of 'politics' which begins with the interpellation: 'What is your class background?'
11. It is worth noting that, for Rancière, the social of equality is primarily connected to a legal-political inscription – exemplarily, the Declaration of the Rights of Man and Citizen.
12. Whereas politics is a matter of subjectification, sociology is for Rancière caught up in the problem of identity (1999: 118).
13. The 'police' itself has a quasi-transcendental relationship to the constitution of a social of inequality: 'Police is not a social function but a symbolic constitution of the social' (2004: 240). In the 'aesthetic' sense, it is above all a way of shaping what can be seen and what can be said.
14. Nonetheless, philosophy retains an emancipatory potential not accorded to sociology. It seems that Rancière is much more sanguine about the possibilities of a plebeian philosophy than he would be about a plebeian sociology.
15. 'Dualism is, I believe, the strong form of ideology as such, which may of course disguise its dual structure under any number of complicated substitutions. This is so, I want to assert, because it is the ultimate form of the ethical binary, which is thus always secretly at work within ideology' (Jameson 2009: 198).
16. These would moments of what, in the wake of Badiou's work, Bruno Bosteels has elaborated as 'speculative leftism'. On the presence of such a speculative leftism in Rancière's *Disagreement*, see Bosteels (2009).

17. Détourning Kierkegaard, as taken up by Schmitt and then Agamben, we could say that *endless talk about the exceptional becomes boring, there are universals; if the general cannot be explained, then the exception can't either.*
18. The two emblematic thinkers of emancipation for Rancière, Jacotot and Schiller, both develop their intuitions in the wake of the excesses, defeats and misfortunes of revolutionary politics aimed at taking power and creating a new order. Though Rancière is conscious of the problems inhering in purely aesthetic or (anti-)pedagogical models of emancipation, in the final analysis he seems to be closer to the likes of Jacotot and Schiller than to proponents of a social revolution that could build the institutions of freedom and bring about a non-policed order.
19. 'The fatal mistake of the councils has always been that they themselves did not distinguish clearly between participation in public affairs and administration or management of things in the public interest. In the form of workers' councils, they have again and again tried to take over the management of the factories, and all these attempts have ended in dismal failure' (Arendt 1990: 273–4). It could of course be noted, in the light of numerous historical examples, from the Russian Revolution to the occupation and self-management of the Lip factory in Besançon in the 1970s, to the recent case of factory occupations in Argentina, that there is no necessity inhering in such 'failures', and that their causes are often extrinsic and political. The incompatibility of political freedom with collective control over social and economic life is a liberal dogma impervious to counter-examples.
20. 'The competence of the proletarian cannot be *his* competence. It is the knowledge of the global process – and of the reasons for his ignorance – a knowledge accessible only to those who are not caught up in the machine, to communists inasmuch as they are nothing but communists' (Rancière 2009: 237).
21. The practice of counter-mapping, as Wood shows, has long been an important political tool in the production of strategic, anti-systemic knowledge, and has attained remarkable prominence in recent art and activism.
22. See the whole 1965 issue of the *operaista* journal *Quaderni Rossi*, featuring the key article by Raniero Panzieri, 'Uso socialista dell'inchiesta operaia' [Socialist Use of the Workers' Inquiry]. The problem of the consciousness of equality – posed in terms which would doubtless be castigated by Rancière – is at the core of the inquiry itself: 'It is a matter of verifying to what extent workers are conscious of demanding, in the face of an unequal society, an equal one, and how conscious they are that this can take on a general value for society, as a value of equality in the face of capitalist inequality' (74–5). For an important study of workerism through a radical sociological prism, which also explores the contemporary challenges of co-research (*conricerca*), see Borio et al. (2004).

23. To offset the monolithic view of Marxist and communist politics as a politics of pedagogical mastery so dear to Rancière, it would be worth contrasting his thinking to that of Gramsci, who combined, in both theory and practice, a commitment to the equality of intelligences with a staunch interest in questions of linguistic and political pedagogy that could not do without some degree of transmission and explanation. For a fascinating account of Gramsci's 'art of listening', his practical egalitarianism and his work to promote workers' writing in the journal *Ordine Nuovo*, see Bermani (1980/81: 11–20). (Bermani's text is followed by a few specimens of this proletarian literature, making it an interesting counterpoint to Rancière's own *Nights of Labour*). In order to promote a literature by rather than about workers, Gramsci, exemplifying some of the ambiguities of pedagogy that the model of the ignorant schoolmaster seems to evade rather than resolve, spent hours and hours polishing and proofreading their texts, so that their equal intelligences, which he wished to affirm, did not end up being overshadowed by their unsurprisingly unequal linguistic resources.
24. On this dynamic, see the excellent chronicles of workers' militancy in the petrochemical complex of Porto Marghera in Sacchetto and Sbrogiò (2009), which provides a detailed record of the articulation between egalitarianism, knowledge of the production cycle and the capacity for these struggles to break through the confines of factory demands.

Works Cited

Agamben, Giorgio (2005), *The Time That Remains*, Stanford: Stanford University Press.
Arendt, Hannah (1958), *The Human Condition*, University of Chicago Press.
Arendt, Hannah (1990), *On Revolution*, London: Penguin.
Bermani, Cesare (1980/81), 'Gramsci operaista e la letteratura proletaria', *Primo Maggio*, 14: 11–20.
Blechman, Max, Chari, Anita and Hassan, Rafeq (2005), 'Democracy, Dissensus and the Aesthetics of Class Struggle: An Exchange with Jacques Rancière', *Historical Materialism*, 13 (4): 285–301.
Borio, Guido, Pozzi, Francesca and Roggero, Gigi (2004), *Futuro anteriore. Dai "Quaderni rossi" ai movimenti globali: ricchezze e limiti dell'operaismo italiano*, Rome: DeriveApprodi.
Bosteels, Bruno (2009), 'Rancière's Leftism, or, Politics and Its Discontents', *Jacques Rancière: History, Politics, Aesthetics*, ed. Gabriel Rockhill and Philip Watts, Durham: Duke University Press: 158–75.
Hallward, Peter (2006), 'Staging Equality: Rancière's theatrocracy', *New Left Review*, 37, January/February: 109–29.

Jameson, Fredric (1988), 'Cognitive Mapping', *Marxism and the Interpretation of Culture*, ed. Cary Nelson and Lawrence Grossberg, Evanston: University of Illinois Press.
— (1991), *Postmodernism, Or, The Cultural Logic of Late Capitalism*, Durham: Duke University Press.
— (2009), 'Deleuze and Dualism', in *Valences of the Dialectic*, London: Verso: 181–200.
Latour, Bruno (2004), 'Never too late to read Tarde', *Domus*, October, available at: *http://www.bruno-latour.fr/presse/presse_art/GB-DOMUS%2010–04.html.*
Nordmann, Charlotte (2006), *Bourdieu/Rancière. La politique entre sociologie et philosophie*, Paris: Amsterdam.
Power, Nina (2009), 'Axiomatic equality: Rancière and the politics of contemporary education', *Polygraph* 21. Also available at: *http://www.eurozine.com/articles/2010–07-01-power-en.html.*
Rancière, Jacques (1974), *La Leçon d'Althusser*, Paris: Gallimard.
— (1978), 'Utopistes, bourgeois et prolétaires', in *Le discours utopique*, ed. M. De Gandillac and C. Piron, Paris: UGE.
— (ed.) (1984), *L'empire du sociologue*, Paris: La Découverte.
— (1999), *Disagreement: Politics and Philosophy*, trans. Julie Rose, Minneapolis: University of Minnesota Press.
— (2003), 'L'éthique de la sociologie', *Les scènes du peuple*, Paris: Horlieu.
— (2004), *Aux bords du politique*, 2nd ed., Paris: Gallimard.
— (2004a), *The Philosopher and His Poor*, trans. John Drury, Corinne Oster and Andrew Parker. Durham: Duke University Press.
— (2005), *Chroniques des temps consensuels*, Paris: Seuil.
— (2007), Postface to Alain Faure and Jacques Rancière (Eds), *La parole ouvrière*, Paris: La Fabrique.
— (2009), 'Les raisins sont trop verts', *Moments politiques. Interventions 1977–2009*, Paris/Montréal: La Fabrique/Lux.
— (2009a),'Communistes sans communisme?', in *L'idée du communisme*, ed. Alain Badiou and Slavoj Žižek, Paris: Lignes.
Sacchetto, Devi, and Gianno Sbrogiò (eds) (2009), *Quando il potere è operaio*, Roma: manifestolibri.
Toscano, Alberto (2009), 'Partisan thought', *Historical Materialism*, 17 (3): 175–91.
Wood, Denis (2010), *Rethinking the Power of Maps*, New York: The Guilford Press.

Against an Ebbing Tide: An Interview with Jacques Rancière

Jacques Rancière

Translated by Richard Stamp

Some recent scholarship has argued that your political position is best described as 'anarchist'. How do you respond to this?

At a fundamental philosophical level my position can be called anarchist *stricto sensu* since I hold that politics exists insofar as the exercise of power does not rest upon any *arkhê*. In Greek, the *arkhê* is the identity of commencement and commandment: the fact that the exercise of power is the exercise of an already active superiority that precedes it, and which in return it confirms. This is what happens when the exercise of power is identified with the power of science, of birth, of wealth or any other entitlement to govern founded upon an unequal distribution of positions. Conversely, a government is political when it claims the people as its subject, that is to say the collection of those who have no more reason to govern than to be governed. It is in this sense that democracy – the power of those who have no particular entitlement to wield it – is the very principle of politics and not a particular form of government. Working on this principle involves putting two ideas at the base of politics at the same time: the idea of a final illegitimacy of every employment of power and that of a competency that belongs to anyone. It's clear that this approach is a long way from all those for which politics is first of all the conquest of the State, the exercise of power or avant-garde science. What is precisely proper to the State in general is to seal the democratic breach that lies at the basis of every exercise of power, to make this final illegitimacy that defines power as political, disappear. It is in this way a permanent work of depoliticization, which also means a permanent work to transform the power of the people into the impotence of the people. My 'anarchism' doesn't signify a disinterest in what States do. Quite the contrary, I have always sought to redirect attention upon the State practices, while those who reproach me for my anarchism generally practice a convenient short circuit between the general tendencies of Capital and those phenomena labelled as society. I've insisted upon the properly state forms of a 'cold racism' whereas many analyses, faced with the question of racism, content themselves with hackneyed analyses that turn it into the distressed expression of declining social categories.[1] I've insisted on the contemporary forms of State reinforcement while, from all sides, we're told about its effacement in the age of the global market; and I've indicated all the anti-democratic practices of our governments while others mollify us with the fable of triumphant 'liberalism' and the great democracy of consumers inundated by freedoms of all kinds. I've done it precisely on the basis of tightening the knot between three terms that are ordinarily disjointed: politics, democracy and anarchism. That said, this idea of anarchism has not been strongly shared by historically active anarchisms. All sorts of theories and practices have declared themselves anarchist in the modern epoch: some have placed greatest importance on the idea of the collective capacity of the anonymous. But others have shared with Marxism the cult of science, or have repeated the 'liberal' opposition of the enlightened individual to the stupid mass. Still today we find that both doctrines of direct action based on a Nietzschean denouncement of democratic gregariousness, and thoughts that aim at replacing politics with ecology (just as some anarchisms, in the nineteenth-century, wished to substitute it with the economy) are declared anarchist.

Often, the same sorts of themes and concerns recur within your works, even as the conceptual language and approach shifts – for example, the conceptual chain of 'theatrocracy' – 'police' – 'distribution of the sensible'. This variation and continuity gives the impression that you have an underlying 'project'. You have certainly made it very clear from time to time that you want to intervene into various debates – theoretical, political, national. So, do you have a project? Either way, how then do you see the nature of your interventions?

There are two questions here: one bears upon the preoccupations that guide my research, the other upon the forms of my intervention. Let's begin from the point of departure represented by my choice, in the 1970s, to turn away at once from the academic philosophical scene, from intra-Marxist debates and from the mediatized intellectual scene in order to shut myself away in archives and libraries researching the forms of thought of yesterday's workers. From the beginning there was a refusal and an idea, both very simple: the refusal to follow an ebbing tide [*la vague du reflux*], a refusal to decree that all these ideas of emancipation and revolution were an error or a crime, and thus a resolute opposition to notions of the end – the end of illusions, of utopias, of politics, of history. The idea was that these ways of rejecting an entire revolutionary tradition in the name of denouncing Marxism's crimes extended the life of precisely those intellectual schemas that had been transmitted by the Marxist tradition. A common thread throughout my work is this attention to the ways in which arguments circulate between reasons of order and the reasons of those who claim to attack it: this critical attention was already at the heart of *La Leçon d'Althusser*, and it's still at the core of *Hatred of Democracy* or *The Emancipated Spectator*. Resisting this refluent thought first of all meant going back prior to Marxist and anti-Marxist certainties, trying to find out what and whom was being spoken about in the use of words like 'workers movement' or 'proletariat', ideology or 'class consciousness'. Who were these people, what did they do, think, want, say? It was a task of recovering the texture of a perceptual experience [*une expérience sensible*]: what singular experiences make a condition become intolerable? For what kinds of gaze did this intolerability become visible? By what use of words might it be expressible? This is where we can see the origin of the idea of a 'distribution of the sensible': in the idea that to consent and to refuse are first of all a matter of sensible perception because domination itself operates across an organization of the visible, the sayable, the thinkable and the possible. Whence comes my way of posing problems from scenes that are scenes of interpretation – and eventually of quarrels over interpretation – of a perceptible datum: what permits a poet (Wordsworth) to read the reality of a Revolution in the contrasts of a landscape; or permits a novelist (Balzac) to symbolize the criminal subversion of a social order through the dreamy narrative that a scrap-metal merchant's daughter casts upon an island? How to decide whether the noise made by plebeian mouths is really argumentative speech? What is at stake in the glance that a carpenter casts through a window, or at stake in the way that workers dissect the minutiae of their masters' and judges' discourses? What interests me, as a researcher and as a writer, is to follow these fluctuations of perception and speech and to try to let their power and their stakes be felt. It's clear that this attention follows its own temporality which is not that of public events, and more importantly that it obliges us to break up the borderlines between the genres of discourse that define accepted 'competencies' in public speech.

This means that my public interventions are not the natural continuation of my research. Instead, they are born of occasions when the 'simple ideas' that underpin my research take on a topicality in contexts that aren't dependent upon me, but lie at the junction between external instigations and my own personal intolerances. As, for example, when some artists asked me to elaborate a reflection on the spectator starting out from Jacotot and this request brought me to put the implications of the thought of inequality into the form of a polemical relation with the reigning post-Situationist mood. Or else such a context places me in the situation of being the voice sounding a discordant note in the chorus of opinion: for example, the surge of a new anti-democratic discourse in the left-wing intelligentsia was an opportunity for me to put to the test of the present everything that I'd been able to learn about the complicities between the discourses of domination and those who claim to criticize them. But also it is often circumstances out of my control that can transform a text into an 'intervention'. *The Politics of Aesthetics* [*Le Partage du sensible*] was at the outset an interview given to a limited circulation journal.[2] As chance would have it some people in the art world read it and told others about it, who saw in it weapons to get out of the routine pseudo-critique that prevailed in their world – and so this confidential text became a reference text in the contemporary art world.

There appears to be a tension between your proposition that, on the one hand, in any given context there will be a 'distribution/partition of the perceptible' demarcating, structuring and reigning over thought and action, and on the other hand, your proposition that, at any time at all, any individual at all might simply shake off the stultifying effects of all of this and emancipate themselves. Is it the case that these distributions and partitions are little more than discursive inventions and institutional implementations (inscribed within and structuring scholarship, institutions, legislations, policies, practices, and so on); and that these discursive inventions are produced in ignorance or blindness or denial of the infinite complexity of individuals' emancipatory agency?

There are two questions here as well: one about the possibility of escaping from a given distribution of the sensible; and one about the relations between the collective distribution of positions and individual forms of emancipation. On the first point, I must insist on the fact that the distribution of the sensible is not an ideological machine or the disciplinary rule, fixing individuals in their places by a mechanism of necessary illusion or a control of the body. It is the play of relations between the visible, the sayable, the thinkable and the doable at the heart of which gazes operate, things are named, discourses produced, actions undertaken. From one perspective, the forms of distribution of the sensible are like a datum, more or less accepted, more or less conscious – which forms and limits the capacities of perceiving and thinking. But on the one hand this datum defines a plurality of different articulations between its elements, a multiplicity of possibilities that combine together in different ways; on the other, it is constantly modified, for individuals and collectivities, either by singular sub-systems, or by events that, breaking the ordinary temporal logic, deploy other forms of possible experience, other possible ways of giving sense to these experiences. Insurrectional experiences have taught us how unimaginable things can very quickly enter into the field of possibilities. The judgement and sentencing to death of the king of France by an assembly of representatives of the people was something unimaginable in 1789. The institution of worker power in French factories was something perfectly imaginable at the end of May 1968, etc. In the experiences of workers' emancipation that I have studied, one sees how the very forms that structure the community and assign individuals their places – work, family, national belonging, religious belonging, forms of cultural (or other) identity – are in each case susceptible to being deviated and of provoking a reorganization of the whole: national belonging becomes an affirmation of republican equality that entails a certain idea of the worker's independence, which is itself combined with the fraternity of new religions and appropriates the indecisive identities of romantic literature. Emancipation, for individuals and for the collectives in which they gather, is the work that undoes the order of positions and identities that define what is possible. This work of subjectivation operates by taking on diverse forms of experience that define subject-forms, ways of being an individual and those of being a small or large collectivity. Being subject is something that draws on forms of juridical inscription or forms of labour relation, on religious narratives, on models taken from school books, on ways of being alone or of meeting others that are put into circulation by literature, on definitions of bodily health and corruption circulated by life sciences, on ways of seeing and hearing formed by metropolitan cultures with their modes of strolling and display, etc. The religious phrase that should subjugate, the spectacle that should fascinate, the juridical inscription that should set things in order – they constantly lend themselves to the construction of unforeseen trajectories of looking and speaking, to the formation of deviant lines of subjectivation. The complexity of which we speak doesn't isolate individual forms of emancipation in relation to great collective signifiers. It is much rather identified with the voyage between these different registers of subjectivation. Deviant lines of subjectivation at once produce individualities, inter-individual relations and new modes of collective subjectivation. This is why that canonical opposition between individual and collective is so pointless. It is much rather a question of seeing how singularities get defined – whether as ways of being one or of being together – at odds with constituted identities.

From The Ignorant Schoolmaster *to* The Emancipated Spectator, *your perspective on emancipation has been focused on the individual. It seems to us that this is because you see a problem in the 'macro' perspectives of socio-political work, perspectives which 'flatten' specificity by leading people to speak reductively of 'the masses', 'the poor', and so on. The scholarly, ethical and political virtues of pointing out the skewing effects and reductiveness of these macro-political and sociological perspectives seem eminently valid and important to us. But does this make your position* individualist?

First of all, we have to leave behind the false obviousness – as much Marxist as liberal – that opposes the individual and the collective. Indeed, one way of taking part in a community goes hand in hand with a way of being an individual. Moreover, this has been the historical problem of emancipation. Communities composed of communists have generally collapsed: they were composed of men of the people who hardly attained the possibility of being individuals or of living family lives freed from very old communitarian rules. They weren't 'individualists' for all that, they were sincerely communist, but this new communism did not recognize itself in the rules of communitarian discipline to which, in contrast, groups founded on a religious rule or a charismatic authority adapted very well. The sociological or macro-political models that you mention have generally focused upon an imaginary vision of the collective according to which the latter collectively puts to work common interests and values rooted in a communal experience. At the beginning of my research, I too believed things worked like that. I looked for *the* workers' authentic thought that expressed the life experience and the struggle of a class forged in the workplace. Research forced me to find out that this was not the case, and that there were always, on the basis of an experience, several antagonistic ways of constructing common interests or common values. There is always a plurality of ways of constituting the common of a community, just as there is in defining the singularity of an individual. This is what 'subjectivation' means, either for an individual or for a collective: you construct a way of being 'one' in opposition to the identity you've been assigned; you also construct it by combining ways of life that were supposed to belong to separate identities. This construction is the work of individuals and random groupings of individuals who have formed as such through singular paths between the ways of being subject that collective structures and signifiers allow to be built. But these ways of being-subject are always at the same time ways of world-making, ways of being counted as members of a certain collectivity. And the collectivity built in this way is not the sum of individuals who belong to such and such a group of the population, or share such and such a situation. To mark the gap between subjectivation and identification doesn't characterize an individualism.

In The Ignorant Schoolmaster, *you argue for the suspension of mastery in the name of emancipation, and claim that the mastery of the teacher has nothing to do with the content of his knowledge, and everything to do with the pedagogical power he holds over the gap between ignorance and knowledge. How do you answer the complaint that your insistence on this formal power of the 'master' blunts from the outset any possibility of communicating better the knowledge and expertise involved in intervention? In other words: is there not a pedagogical value in mastery and expertise worth preserving?*

Several questions appear to be mixed together here. First of all, I have not opposed mastery and emancipation in general and I have always hated forms of guilting that prove to the master that he is guilty in advance due to his institutional position. The 'ignorant master' is an emancipating master. From a Jacotist perspective, a master is an emancipator if he dissociates his mastery – that is, the effect his will can have upon the actions of his pupil – from his own knowledge. It's a principled dissociation [*une dissociation de principe*]. Here the principle is not the opposite of reality, it is a way of distinguishing between two sides of the same 'reality'. It's a fact that the effects one produces through mastery are distinct from those produced by one's expert capacity. It's another fact that these effects are often produced by the same acts and within the same institutional apparatuses [*dispositifs*], and thus constantly mixed together. On that basis, the logic of domination is to make indistinguishable in order to identify in general the exercise of a power with that of a form of knowledge. The function of the distinctions I make is to enable judging and acting in confusing situations. The distinction is like a Kantian formula that helps to distinguish what is, in such and such a situation, the maxim to adopt, the reasons one has to adopt it, the type of effect one want to favour. What we generally call 'transmitting' is allowing the other to produce performances equivalent to those produced specifically for him. That can be very effective for enabling people to pass an exam that will enable them to get a better job – and I've got absolutely nothing against the fact that we enable people to pass exams. I find that preferable to pseudo-radical attitudes that refuse students the benefits of the master's knowledge. It is necessary to know simply that the beneficial effect of 'transmission' is limited, that this benefit doesn't produce any emancipation and very likely comes at the price of losing one's own intellectual capacity. The experience of each day and of a lifetime teaches us to distinguish between the results of knowledge and those of mastery, the effects sought by one kind of intelligence and those produced by another, as it teaches us to distinguish the different indeed contradictory effects of an apprenticeship. We can certainly use our status as legitimate 'transmitters' to put our knowledge at others' disposal. I'm constantly doing it. But what is 'stultifying' from a Jacotist perspective is the will to anticipate the way in which they will grasp what we put at their disposal. From this point of view, Jacotist radicalism strikes me as much closer to experience and good sense than those discourses that first liken the exercise of mastery to the transmission of a body of knowledge and then class this transmission of knowledge as the awakening of a soul, as the acquisition of critical thought or sense of citizenship [*sens citoyen*], or some other warmed-over fairytale served up for us on a daily basis by good progressive souls.

Many readers are struck by the affinities in your work with the works of Michel Foucault and Jacques Derrida. It might be argued that your argumentative moves are very often deconstructive, while your focus on the messy realms of individuals operating in particular situations seems concerned with distinctly Foucauldian 'visibilities'. However, while you often criticize deconstruction, Foucault rarely surfaces explicitly in your work. Is this because you feel a greater sense of proximity to Foucault's project(s) and approach?

I've been influenced very little by Derrida's thought and I've never thought of myself as practising deconstruction. Doubtless there is in me, as there is in both Derrida and Foucault, a calling into question of dominant categories that are used to describe forms of experience. But beyond this work of putting categories into aporia, it seems to me that deconstruction is caught between the Heideggerian form of awaiting the complete reversal of a civilization's development and the Kierkegaardian privilege of the decision in a situation of radical uncertainty. Basically, it's a matter of making a logical aporia lead on to an ethical confrontation with the impossible. That is to say, it's a matter of getting philosophy to recognize an outside – an unknowable and an unmasterable – that is of a religious nature. As far as I'm concerned, my approach has never been to deconstruct in order to come back to the undecidable via the mediation of the aporia, but to bring to light, through the checking of contradictions, a heterogeneity of logics that is, in the final instance, a conflict of worlds. It wasn't the double aspect of the pharmakon that interested me in the Platonic critique of writing but the articulation between a theory of speech and a social stratification. In other words, the outside that interests me is not the ethico-religious outside, but the one of forms of domination that come to be internalized in the thoughts and practices of speech and of discourse. It is the latter that draws me closer to Foucault's thought, the only contemporary thought, in fact, to have strongly influenced me. What that also means is that it's the only one I've been able to incorporate in my own way, without therefore needing to comment on it, or take it as an external reference point. That said, the aspect of Foucault's thinking that I've been able to turn into my own is that which first asks itself *how* such a thought is thinkable and *who* can think it. It is a thought that takes philosophy out of its privileged domain, forcing it to encounter all those discourses and practices in society that mark out the discursive lines and material barriers separating the possible from the impossible, the permitted from the forbidden, the thinkable from the unimaginable. The force of Foucault's thought is located at the point where it allows one to wonder: what thought is at work in a regulation or in a building? But also: what happens, what worlds confront each other in the insignificant words of some individual or other? That for me was an organon, allowing one to think the way in which words manifest the tension of lives caught between two possible universes (*Nights of Labour*) or the way in which literature deploys this tension as the tension of fictional logics (*Politique de la littérature*), or the way cinema deploys it as a conflict of temporalities (*Film Fables*), etc. It seems to me that this tension of lives gripped by relations of possibility and impossibility has been nullified by the dominant discourse about Foucault today, the biopolitical discourse. Whatever radical political references it may be given, the discourse of biopolitics repatriates Foucault's thought onto traditional philosophical terrain, that of a metaphysics of life, and rids it of the subversive potential it got precisely from its capacity to problematize the conflict *of lives*.

Several of your works make use of what might be read as a rhetoric of utopian failure – one thinks, for example, of the final pages in The Ignorant Schoolmaster, *where it is stated that universal teaching wouldn't 'take' but doesn't die, and the essays in* Film Fables *that treat of the 'thwarted' fables animating cinema. Some of your critics read this recurrent oscillation between failure and hope in your work as a refusal of political engagement; but what, for you, is the political import of the experience of 'failure' and of being 'thwarted'?*

The 'thwarting' ['*contrariété*'] that *Film Fables* speaks about is the tension between two logics: a logic of linkage and a logic of suspension. I show that for cinema as for literature this tension is a productive force and not an obstacle. The most beautiful films like the most beautiful novels are the result of this tension. It's not a matter of failure, except for those specialists in literary theory or film semiotics who will endeavour, until the end of the world, to maintain the illusion that literature or cinema are arts solely the concern of their own concept, employing their own language, etc. And the fact that universal teaching doesn't 'take' marks not the failure of intellectual emancipation, but of those who want to transform into a social institution a thought and a practice that cuts across the logic of social institutions. In fact, there are a vast number of things that 'don't take', but which are no less those that have changed our lives and those worth living for. Men live and die for words that never entirely keep their promise. This excess of words is itself the object of pleasure [*jouissance*] and is the energy source for the creation of individual works like collective uprisings or forms of community. This is what I meant by saying that man is a political animal because he is a literary animal. It is this capacity to be disappointed, to bear the disappointment and if needs be enjoy it that I tried to show in the thought and the practice of these men and women of the people that the learned always wanted to confine within a positive story of gains and losses, and it is precisely this that allows them to create works and forms of community. I have constantly tried to challenge the simplistic way in which success and failure, faith and disillusion are conceived. I've attempted to show that a movement of emancipation is never simply an instrument for ends that might be objectively judged according to whether or not they've been reached, but already a way of transforming the forms of what is thinkable and possible in the present. Many have enjoyed the communist fraternity far more than they were saddened not to have founded a dictatorship of the proletariat. The great hopes of workers' emancipation have often met with failures, sometimes ending in social reforms by which the learned claim that capitalism has only been adjusted. But for many militants the failures, on the one hand, and the limits of success, on the other, have contributed towards maintaining the very meaning of the struggle between two worlds that their movement brought to life. Dominant thought, including its 'progressive' and 'radical' variants, always operates according to a caricatural logic of ends to come and means to attain, of expectations and balance sheets. This logic spends its time blocking any experimentation with life, in art or knowledge, in the name of an entirely imaginary knowledge that it grants itself over what is possible and what is impossible, as well as over the means to realize the possible. In the past it functioned as a means of submitting every emancipatory aspiration to pseudo-scientific strategies. Today it functions as a way of crushing them beneath the endless and acrimonious stocktaking of dead illusions. I've always insisted on the contrary upon the ambiguity of these expectations that one opposes to results, and upon the precise difficulty of knowing what is success and what is failure.

You use the word 'police' to illuminate your argument about the rarity of politics. However, because of the rhetorical and semiotic baggage of the word 'police', it is very easy to read in your usage as signifying the negative in a binary of 'police' versus 'politics'. But is your use of the word 'police' always negatively charged? Is there a good and bad police? Is there a good and bad politics?

We must pay attention to the fact that a concept rarely designates a unique and univocal thing. A concept often says several things at once because it tries to bring together several lines of reflection. So the concept of 'police' in my work tries to respond to two problems. I first proposed the term in response to a question that was put to me: 'what is the political?' It seemed necessary to me at that time to unravel the confusion that identifies political activity with the various practices of government. I therefore proposed the term 'police' in order to designate the set of practices associated with the operation of institutions, with the management of populations and the administration of things. It's in this sense that one can say that there is a good and a bad police. I have said that there is politics when this set of practices happens to come up against another set of practices that put into operation the verification of equality. I have subsequently been led to clarify — that is, to displace — the politics/police relation, by rethinking it in terms of the distribution of the sensible. At the time I insisted on another signification of the 'police', namely the type of community that it constructed: a saturated community, defined as the entirety of places, functions and identities, ruling out any supplement. And I defined politics as the activity that breaks this closure through the intervention of subjects in excess of any social identity. From this point of view the two terms are necessarily opposed, and this opposition can't be reduced to the opposition between spontaneity and institution. It doesn't mean that politics is good, as opposed to police being bad. They are two forms of the distribution of the sensible that are at once opposed in their principles and yet constantly intermixed in their functioning. The State is an institution whose operation tends to transform the political scene into purely a matter of police management. But that's exactly why it needs political legitimization. And its managerial operations, therefore, constantly lead to the opening of scenes of political debate and action. The State presents such reforms of social insurance or retirement schemes as a purely technical matter of redistributing resources and expenditures, and of future projections. But technical optimization has to be considered a matter of common good, thus such projection asks the question: who is capable of thinking the future? Whence opens the quarrel about the stakes of equality and inequality set out by these 'technical' reforms. That also means that the common space opened by the political difference lends itself to all sorts of perversion. I've often insisted on the fact that one of the reasons for the success of certain far-right groupings, like the National Front in France, came from their capability of restaging an idea of popular power abandoned by the purely managerial discourse and practice of the right- and left-wing parties. The empty concept of 'populism' is a handy way of concealing this reality of the extreme-right's seizure of political signifiers abandoned by the 'left'. Instead of talking about a bad politics, it's better to say that political division also produces bad things.

Does your emphasis on the disarticulation of equality place too much emphasis on the individual (qua 'subjectivization') at the expense of addressing the problem of contemporary political organization? In other words, isn't the organizational logic of police rejected too quickly for the interruptive moment of politics? And might it not call for a closer examination of what might be called the 'politics of police' in the formation of collectivities? Or, reciprocally: Is it possible for an individual to make politics happen?

Once again, the question of subjectivation isn't that of the relation between individual and collectivity. A political subjectivation is the constitution of a collective capable of speaking in the first person and of identifying its affirmation with a reconfiguration of the universe of possibilities. To contrast the moment of interruption with organizational continuity is a handy way of masking the basis of the problem: to what extent is a collective capable of giving this reconfiguration of the universe of possibilities an autonomous temporality? All those who deafen us with their old refrain about the critique of spontaneity and the necessity of organization forget precisely that an organization is only political if it is 'spontaneous' in the strict sense of the word, that is to say if it functions as a continuous origin of an autonomous perception, thought or action. The question is not how long an organization lasts, but what it does with this time, that is to say how it transforms this time into something political. To put it another way, it's a question of which forms of the present are in themselves future-bearing. That's precisely the question at the heart of the thinking of emancipation: how the break with the time of domination is at work in the present. Both organizations and individuals live in several times simultaneously. The same goes for both the organizational and the pedagogical successes we spoke about earlier. The question is what they consist of, what organizations do. There is no denying that those who tell us what to do first of all set about reinforcing their collective identity and that, as regards an autonomous temporality, they extend their continuity in the relation between two temporalities: that of expiry dates imposed by the dominant power – whether that be elections or capitalist outsourcing – and that of a revolutionary process now forever comfortably installed.

Notes

1. *Translator's note*: see Rancière, 'Cold Racism, *July 1996*', in *Chronicles of Consensual Times*, trans. Steven Corcoran, London & New York: Continuum (2010), pp. 12–15.
2. *Translator's note*: 'Le partage du sensible' originally appeared in *Alice* (issue 2, Summer 1999) and is archived online at *multitudes-web* – http://multitudes.samizdat.net/Le-partage-du-sensible.

Select Bibliography

Althusser, Louis (1971), 'Ideology and Ideological State Apparatuses (Note towards an Investigation)', in *Lenin and Philosophy and Other Essays*, trans. Ben Brewster, London: New Left Books: 127–86.

Arditi, Benjamin, and Valentine, Jeremy (1999), *Polemicization: The Contingency of the Commonplace*, Edinburgh: Edinburgh University Press.

Badiou, Alain (1985), *Peut-on penser la politique?* Paris: Seuil.

— (2003), *Saint Paul: The Foundation of Universalism*, trans. Ray Brassier, Stanford: Stanford University Press.

— (2005), *Metapolitics*, trans. Jason Barker, London: Verso.

Blechman, Max, Chari, Anita and Hassan, Rafeq (2005), 'Democracy, Dissensus and the Aesthetics of Class Struggle: An Exchange with Jacques Rancière', *Historical Materialism*, 13, 4.

Bosteels, Bruno (2009), 'Rancière's Leftism, or, Politics and Its Discontents', *Jacques Rancière: History, Politics, Aesthetics*, ed. Gabriel Rockhill and Philip Watts, Durham: Duke University Press: 158–75.

Bourdieu, Pierre (1992), *Distinction: A Social Critique of the Judgement of Taste*, trans. Richard Nice, London: Routledge.

Bourriaud, Nicolas (2002), *Relational Aesthetics*, trans. Simon Pleasance and Fronza Woods with the participation of Mathieu Copeland, Dijon: les presses du reel.

Bowman, Paul and Stamp, Richard (2009), eds, *Jacques Rancière: In Disagreement*, *Parallax* 52, 15 (3), (July–September).

Certeau, Michel de (1988), *The Writing of History*, trans. Tom Conley, New York: University of Columbia Press.

Chambers, Samuel A. (2003), *Untimely Politics*, Edinburgh: Edinburgh University Press.

— (2005), 'The Politics of Literarity', *Theory & Event*, 8 (3). (Original version presented at *Fidelity to the Disagreement: Jacques Rancière and the Political*, Goldsmith's College, University of London, September 16–17.)
De Man, Paul (1996), 'Kant and Schiller', in *Aesthetic Ideology*, ed. Andrzej Warminski, Minneapolis: University of Minnesota Press.
Deranty, Jean-Philippe (2003a), 'Jacques Rancière's Contribution to the Ethics of Recognition', *Political Theory*, 31 (1),136–56.
— (2003b), 'Rancière and Contemporary Political Ontology', *Theory & Event*, 6 (4).
Derrida, Jacques (1994), *Spectres of Marx: The State of the Debt, the Work of Mourning, and the New International*, trans. Peggy Kamuf, London & New York: Routledge.
Dillon, Michael (2003), '(De)void of Politics? A Response to Jacques Rancière's Ten Theses on Politics', *Theory & Event*, 6 (4).
— (2005), 'A Passion for the (Im)possible: Jacques Rancière, Equality, Pedagogy and the Messianic', *European Journal of Political Theory*, 4: 429–52.
Foucault, Michel (1970), *The Order of Things: An Archaeology of the Human Sciences*, trans. Alan Sheridan, London: Tavistock.
— (1975), *Discipline and Punish: The Birth of the Prison*, Vintage, London.
— (1978), *The History of Sexuality: An Introduction*, trans. Robert Hurley. New York: Vintage.
— (2002), *The Archaeology of Knowledge*, trans. A. M. Sheridan Smith, London: Routledge.
Hallward, Peter (2006), 'Staging Equality: Rancière's Theatrocracy', *New Left Review*, 37, January/February: 109–29.
Hardt, Michael and Negri, Toni (1999), *Empire*, London and Cambridge: Harvard University Press.
Highmore, Ben (2002), *Everyday Life and Cultural Theory*, London: Routledge.
Labelle, G. (2001), 'Two Refoundation Projects of Democracy in Contemporary French Philosophy: Cornelius Castoriadis and Jacques Rancière', *Philosophy and Social Criticism*, 27: 75–103.
Laclau, Ernesto (2005), *On Populist Reason*, London: Verso.
Lacoue-Labarthe and Philippe, Jean-Luc Nancy (1997), *Retreating the Political*, ed. Simon Sparks, London and New York: Routledge.
Lacoue-Labarthe, Philippe, Nancy, Jean-Luc et al. (1983), *Le retrait du politique*, Paris: Galilée.
Lefort, Claude (1988), *Democracy and Political Theory*, Minneapolis: University of Minnesota Press.
Marchart, Oliver (2007), *Post-foundational Political Thought. Political Difference in Nancy, Lefort, Badiou and Laclau*, Edinburgh: Edinburgh University Press.

May, Todd (1994), *The Political Philosophy of Poststructuralist Anarchism*, University Park: Pennsylvania State University Press.
— (2008), *The Political Thought of Jacques Rancière: Creating Equality*, Edinburgh: Edinburgh University Press.
Nancy, Jean-Luc (2009), 'Rancière and Metaphysics', in *Jacques Rancière: History, Politics, Aesthetics*, ed. Gabriel Rockhill and Philip Watts, Durham: Duke University Press: 83–92.
Nordmann, Charlotte (2006), *Bourdieu/Rancière. La politique entre sociologie et philosophie*, Paris: Amsterdam.
Panagia, Davide (2001), '*Ceci n'est pas un argument*: An Introduction to the Ten Theses', *Theory & Event*, 5 (3).
— (2006), *The Poetics of Political Thinking*, Durham: Duke University Press.
Power, Nina (2009), 'Axiomatic Equality: Rancière and the Politics of Contemporary Education', *Polygraph*, 21. Also available at: http://www.eurozine.com/articles/2010-07-01-power-en.html.
Rancière, J. and Panagia, D. (2000), 'Dissenting Words: A Conversation with Jacques Rancière', *Diacritics*, Summer.
Rancière, Jacques (1974), *La Leçon d'Althusser*, Paris: Gallimard.
— (1981), '"Le social": the lost tradition in French labour history', in *People's History and Socialist Theory*, ed. Raphael Samuel. London: Routledge & Kegan Paul, 267–72.
— (1986), 'The Myth of the Artisan: Critical Reflections on a Category of Social History', trans. David H. Lake, in *Work in France: Representations, Meanings, Organization and Practice*, ed. Steven Laurence Kaplan and Cynthia J. Koepp, Ithaca: Cornell University Press, 317–34.
— (1989), *The Nights of Labor: The Workers' Dream in Nineteenth-Century France*, trans. Donald Reid, Philadelphia: Temple University Press.
— (1991), *The Ignorant Schoolmaster: Five Lessons in Intellectual Emancipation*, trans. with an intro. Kristin Ross, Stanford: Stanford University Press.
— (1992), 'Politics, Identification, and Subjectivization', October 61, 'The Identity in Question' (Summer 1992): 58–64.
— (1992), *On the Shores of Politics*, trans. Liz Heron, London: Verso.
— (1994), *The Names of History: On the Poetics of Knowledge*, trans. Hassan Melehy, foreword Hayden White, Minneapolis and London: University of Minnesota Press.
— (1994), 'Histoire des mots, mots de l'histoire', entretien avec Martyne Perrot et Martin de la Soudière, *Communications*, 58: 87–101.
— (1995), 'Politics, Identification, Subjectivization', in *The Identity in Question*, ed. John Rajchman. New York: Routledge, 63–72.
— (1995), *On the Shores of Politics*, trans. Liz Heron, London and New York: Verso.

Select Bibliography

— (1997), 'Democracy Means Equality: Jacques Rancière Interviewed by Passages', *Radical Philosophy*, 82: 29–36.
— (1999), *Disagreement: Politics and Philosophy*, trans. J. Rose, Minneapolis: University of Minnesota Press.
— (2000), 'Dissenting Words: A Conversation with Jacques Rancière', interview with Davide Panagia, *Diacritics*, 30 (2), 113–26.
— (2001), 'Ten Theses on Politics', trans. Rachel Bowlby and Davide Panagia, *Theory & Event*, 5 (3).
— (2003), 'L'éthique de la sociologie', *Les scènes du people*, Paris: Horlieu.
— (2003), 'Politics and Aesthetics: An Interview', trans. Forbes Morlock, intro. Peter Hallward, *Angelaki: Journal of the Theoretical Humanities*, 8.2 (August 2003): 191–211.
— (2003), *Short Voyages to the Land of the People*, trans. James B. Swenson, Stanford: Stanford University Press.
— (2003), 'Comment and Responses', *Theory & Event*, 6 (4).
— (2004), *Aux bords du politique*, 2nd ed., Paris: Gallimard.
— (2004), *The Philosopher and His Poor*, trans. John Drury, Corinne Oster and Andrew Parker, Durham: Duke University Press.
— (2004), *The Politics of Aesthetics: The Distribution of the Sensible*, trans. and intro. Gabriel Rockhill, London and New York: Continuum.
— (2004), *Malaise dans l'esthétique*, Paris: Galilée.
— (2004), *The Flesh of Words: The Politics of Writing*, trans. Charlotte Mandell, Stanford: Stanford University Press.
— (2004), 'Who Is the Subject of the Rights of Man?' *South Atlantic Quarterly*, 103 (2–3) (Spring/Summer): 297–310.
— (2004), 'The Sublime from Lyotard to Schiller: Two Readings of Kant and Their Political Significance', *Radical Philosophy*, 126: 8–15.
— (2005), 'From Politics to Aesthetics?' *Paragraph*, 28 (1): 13–25.
— (2005), *Chroniques des temps consensuels*, Paris: Seuil.
— (2006), *Film Fables*, trans. Emiliano Battista, Oxford and New York: Berg.
— (2006), 'Problems and Transformations in Critical Art/2004', trans. Claire Bishop, assisted by Pablo Lafuente, in *Participation* (Documents of Contemporary Art Series), ed. Claire Bishop, London: Whitechapel; Cambridge, MA: MIT Press, 83–93.
— (2006), *Hatred of Democracy*, trans. Steve Corcoran, London and New York: Verso.
— (2006), 'Thinking between Disciplines: An Aesthetics of Knowledge', trans. Jon Roffe, *Parrhesia*, 1 (1): 1–12.
— (2007), 'What Does it Mean to be Un?' *Continuum: Journal of Media and Cultural Studies*, 21 (4), (December), 559–69.

— (2007), Postface to Alain Faure and Jacques Rancière (eds), *La parole ouvrière*, Paris: La Fabrique.
— (2007), *The Future of the Image*, trans. Gregory Elliott, London and New York: Verso.
— (2008), 'Why Emma Bovary Had to be Killed', *Critical Inquiry*, 34 (Winter): 233–48.
— (2008), 'Aesthetics against Incarnation: An Interview by Anne Marie Oliver', *Critical Inquiry*, 35 (Autumn).
— (2008), 'Democracy, Anarchism and Radical Politics Today: An Interview with Jacques Rancière', *Anarchist Studies*, 16 (2), 173–85.
— (2009), *Moments politiques. Interventions 1977–2009*, Paris/Montréal: La Fabrique/Lux.
— (2009), *Aesthetics and Its Discontents*, trans. Steven Corcoran, Cambridge and Malden: Polity Press.
— (2009), 'A Few Remarks on the Method of Jacques Rancière', *Parallax* 52, 15 (3), (July–September): 114–23.
— (2009),'Communistes sans communisme?', in *L'idée du communisme*, ed. Alain Badiou and Slavoj Žižek, Paris: Lignes.
— (2009), *The Emancipated Spectator*, trans. Gregory Elliot, London: Verso.
— (2009), 'Contemporary Art and the Politics of Aesthetics', in *Communities of Sense: Rethinking Aesthetics and Politics*, ed. Beth Hinderliter, William Kaizen, Vered Maimon, Jaleh Mansoor, and Seth McCormick, Durham: Duke University Press: 31–50.
— (2010), *Dissensus: On Politics and Aesthetics*, ed. and trans. Steven Corcoran, London and New York: Continuum.
— (2010), *Chronicles of Consensual Times*, trans. Steven Corcoran, London and New York: Continuum.
— (ed.) (1984), *L'empire du sociologue*, Paris: La Découverte, 1984.
Ricoeur, Paul (2004), *Memory, History, Forgetting*, trans. Kathleen Blamey and David Pellauer, Chicago: University of Chicago Press.
Robson, Mark (2009), '"A literary animal": Rancière, Derrida and the literature of democracy', *Parallax*, 52, 88–100.
Rockhill, Gabriel (2004), 'The Silent Revolution', *SubStance*, 103, 33 (1), 54–76.
— (2009), 'The Politics of Aesthetics: Political History and the Hermeneutics of Art', in *Jacques Rancière. History, Politics, Aesthetics*, ed. Gabriel Rockhill and Philipp Watts, Durham and London: Duke University Press, 195–215.
Ross, Kristin (1991), 'Rancière and the Practice of Equality', *Social Text*, 29: 57–71.
— (2002), *May '68 and its Afterlives*, Chicago: University of Chicago Press.
— (2009), 'Historicizing Untimeliness', in *Jacques Rancière: History, Politics, Aesthetics*, ed. Gabriel Rockhill and Philip Watts. Durham: Duke University Press: 15–29.

Valentine, Jeremy (2005), 'Rancière and Contemporary Political Problems', *Paragraph*, 28 (1), 46–60.
Žižek, Slavoj (1999), *The Ticklish Subject*, London: Verso.
— (2005), 'The Lesson of Rancière', in *The Politics of Aesthetics*, ed. Gabriel Rockhill, New York: Continuum, 69–79.

Index

Abraham, J. 158
absoluticization 9–11, 16
Adorno, T. W. 9, 11, 108
aesthetic community (*sensus communis*) 180, 182
aesthetics 7, 167–8
aesthetics-art 113, 116, 119, 122, 125–6
Agamben, G. xiv, 11, 79
Althusser, L. xi, 20, 23, 45, 61, 63–4, 95, 163, 200, 222
anarchism 19–20, 27, 239
  May's defence of 27–35
Aranda, J. 111
archipolitics 29
Arendt, H. 3, 11, 20, 22, 26, 212, 223, 229
  The Human Condition 26, 212
Aristotle 1–2, 26, 203
arkhê 15, 18, 87, 136
art 7, 167–8
  boundaries in relation to 44–7
  critical art xvi, 112–14, 117–18, 127
  artwork as trap 54–61
Ashington Art Group 101–2
Au hasard, Balthazar (film by Bresson) 193
avant-garde 102–3

Badiou, A. xii–xiv, 5, 15, 130–1, 135, 164, 204
Balibar, E. 130, 163
Barry, A. 150–2, 158–9

Barthes, R. 165, 176
Bataille, G. 116
Baudelaire, C. 171
Bazin, A. 188–91
Benjamin, W. 45, 108
Bentham, J. 55
Bernard, J.-J. 194
Blanchot, M. 9
Blanqui, A. 106
Bourdieu, P. xi, 95, 202, 220, 232
Bowman, P. xiv, 163, 183
Brecht, B. 117–18
Bresson, R. 198
Brown, W. 75
Bunge, W. 231
Bürger, C. 107
Bürger, P. 107
Bush, G. W. 4, 75

captation 57
Carpenter, D. 158
Centre for Philosophical Research on the Political 129
Chambers, S. xv, 35
Chow, R. xv–xvi
Citizen Kane (film by Welles) 188
Clark, T. J. 103
class war 1–2
Clifford, J. 51
  The Predicament of Culture 51

Clinton, B. 78
Coldstream, W. 102
Connolly, W. 73
Cousins, M. (film critic) 196

Daemmrich, A. 154
Danto, A. 53
Davidson, D. 90
Dean, J. xv, 18, 153
Debord, G. 9
De Certeau, M. 207–9
　The Writing of History 208
deconstruction 1, 171, 202, 246
de-democratization 75, 77
Deleuze, G. xi, 116, 163, 189
De Man, P. 164, 169–74, 179–82
Demeritt, D. 155–6
democracy 33, 76, 81, 84, 138–43
　and politics 36–7
democratic apriorism 138
Demos 138
de-politicization 75–6, 78–9, 85, 152
Deranty, J.-P. 32
Derrida, J. xi, xiv, 1, 12–14, 44, 56, 80, 130, 163, 166
　Specters of Marx 13
de Tocqueville, A. 160
Dewey, J. 107
Dillon, M. 21, 150
dissensus xiv–xv, 1–2, 4–5, 9, 12, 15, 35, 105, 127, 130, 179–80, 182–3
　politics as 32
Dos Passos, J. 188
Duchamp, M. 45, 56

economism 3
Eliot, T. S. 48
emancipatory apriorism 133–5, 138
Empire (Hardt and Negri) 12
Epstein, S. 154–5
equality of intelligence 14
Establet, R. 163
ethnic identitarianism 4
Europa '51 (film by Rossellini) xvi, 186–7, 191, 198

Farge, A. 204
Faulkner, W. 188

Febvre, L. 208
Ferraris, M. 166
Ferry, L. 130
Fischer, M. M. J. 51
Flaubert, G. 47–50, 53, 58, 65, 190, 192–3
　Madame Bovary xvi, 47–8, 50, 57, 61, 165, 190–1
　as the scene of a disagreement 47–51
Foster, H. 111, 114
Foucault, M. xi, 22, 44, 51, 55, 163, 209
　The Archaeology of Knowledge 46, 209
　Folie et déraison 44
French Revolution 8, 173
Freud, S. 10

Gell, A. 51–4, 56
　Art and Agency 51
Gell, E. xvi
Germany Year Zero (film by Rossellini) xvi, 186–8, 191, 193
Gillick, L. 114, 123, 125–6
Gilroy, P. 194–5
Godard, J.-L. 165
　Histoires du Cinéma 165
Gowing, L. 102
Graham, D. 148
Gramsci, A. 141
Greene, J. 154, 158

Haacke, H. 113
Habermas, J. 32, 73, 76, 89–90, 135
Hallward, P. xi
Haneke, M. xvi, 187–8, 193–5, 197–8
Hardt, M. 12, 15, 79, 87
Harris, G. 156–8
Harrisson, T. 102
hauntology 14
Heartfield, J. 113
Hegel, G. W. F. 9, 52, 166–7, 174
Heidegger, M. 12, 167
Hemingway, E. 189
Hepworth, B. 103
Herodotus 174
heterology 58–9
Hidden (*Caché*) (film by Haneke) xvi, 188, 194, 196–7
Highmore, B. xvi
Hirschhorn, T. 116–19, 122

Hobbes, T. 1, 11, 29
Hölderlin, F. 8–9
Hundley, K. 156

intolerance 4

Jackson, E. 158
Jacotot, J. xii–xiii, 14, 175–9
Jameson, F. 231
Johann-Liang, R. 157

kallipolis 26
Kant, I. 10, 105, 170, 176, 180, 182
Kittler, F. A. 51
Kleist, H. von 180
  Über das Marionettentheater 180
Kropotkin, P. 31

Labelle 152
Lacan, J. xi, 10, 81, 86, 90, 93, 135
Laclau, E. 4, 73, 131, 140
Lacoue-Labarthe, P. 129–31
Lakoff, G. 75
la police 36
Lefort, C. 130–1, 133, 140–1, 143, 211
  La question de la démocratie 130
Lenzer, J. 159
Lessing, G. E. 49
Lind, M. 123–4
The Lives of Others (*Das Leben der Anderen*) (film by von Donnersmarck) 61, 64
  the plot of 61–2
Lyon, R. 102
Lyotard, J.-F. xi, xiv, 1, 9–10, 130, 165
  The Differend 9
  Heidegger and "the jews" 10

Macherey, P. 163
Malik, S. xvi
Marchart, O. xv
Marks, H. M. 158
Marx, K. 9, 29
Mass-Observation 102
May, T. xv, 19, 24–5, 27–36
  The Political Thought of Jacques Rancière xv, 27
McCaffery, S. 55

McGoey, L. xv, 158, 160
McQuillan, M. xvii, 166
Meckseper, J. 114, 122–3
Merleau-Ponty, M. 142, 211
Mosholder, A. 157
Mouffe, C. 73, 131, 140
Murphy, M. 151–2

Nabokov, V. 55
  Lolita 55
Nancy, J.-L. xi, 129–31, 204
Negri, A. xiv, 12, 15, 79, 87
neoliberalism 20, 25, 27
Nicholson, B. 103
Nietzsche, F. 170–1

Obama, B. 75
On the Idea of Communism conference 228
ontology 14
organizational life, the anti-politics of 148–60
  FDA, anti-politics at the 157–60
  the Ketek case 148, 156–7
Osama bin Laden 4

Panagia, D. 18, 21, 152
Parreno, P. 123–4
people 5
  demos 5
  ethnos 5
Pettman, D. 55
Phillips, A. xvi
Pickpocket (film by Bresson) 193
Plato 7–8, 15, 20, 26, 28–9, 115, 139, 165, 176, 202–4
  Phaedrus 15
  Republic 7–8, 15
Pliny 174
poiesis and *aisthesis* 114–16, 120
police order 23, 127
politics 2, 4, 6, 8, 18, 26, 32–3, 35, 74, 88–9, 98, 126–7, 149, 154
  aestheticization of 7
  May's misreading of 35
  and police 18–19, 20–7, 32, 35, 131, 149
populism 4, 250
Porter, T. 151

postdemocracy 25–6
   Rancière's definition of 25
   practices of negation 103 *see also* avant-garde

Rancière, J. xii–xiv, 5, 9, 11, 23, 27, 30, 35–7, 47–8, 51, 58, 75, 82, 86–7, 89, 111–15, 119, 121, 131, 138, 140, 149–50, 152–3, 155, 160, 165, 167–8, 175–7, 179–81, 183, 186–7, 190, 200, 206, 220–1, 224, 228
   as an art critic 99–108
   the distribution of the sensible (*le partage du sensible*) 96–101, 143, 167
   interview with 238–51
      on affinities with Foucault and Derrida 246–7
      on anarchism 38–9
      on the concept of 'police' 248–50
      on individualism 243–4
      on mastery and emancipation 244–5
      on subjectivation 250–1
      themes and concerns 239–41
   the political 129–33
   as a post-political thinker xv
   the syllogism of equality 133–8
Rancière's works
   Disagreement xiv, 18–19, 21, 23, 26–8, 31, 76, 82–5, 87, 89, 106, 112, 121, 210, 212
   The Emancipated Spectator xvii, 114, 175, 178–9, 182
   Film Fables 189
   Hatred of Democracy 26–7, 139, 201
   The Ignorant Schoolmaster xii, 107, 175, 200–1
   La Leçon d'Althusser 45
   Les Révoltes Logiques xii, 200, 203
   The Names of History 14, 205–6, 210, 212–14
   The Nights of Labor (*La Nuit des prolétaires*) 97–8
   On the Shores of Politics 26–7, 76, 84, 87, 133, 201, 213
   The Philosopher and His Poor (*Le philosophe et ses pauvres*) 130, 201

The Politics of Aesthetics 189, 191
   'Ten Theses on Politics' 23, 28
Rawls, J. 32
religious fanaticism 4
Ricoeur, P. 206–7
   Memory, History, Forgetting 207
Robson, M. xvi
Rockhill, G. xii, 132
Rogozinski, J. 130
Rohrhuber, J. xv–xvi
Rome, Open City (film by Rossellini) 191
Rose, N. 151, 157
Rosler, M. 113–14
Ross, D. 148, 153, 156–9
Ross, K. 203–4
   May '68 and Its Afterlives 203
Rossellini, R. xvi, 186–92, 198
Rousseau, J.-J. 82

Schelling, F. W. J. 9
Schiller, F. 8–9, 49, 112, 170, 176, 178–81
   On the Aesthetic Education of Man 112
Serres, M. 44, 45
The Seventh Continent (film by Haneke) 187, 194, 198
Sheppard, J. 158
sociocracy 201
Soreth, J. 156
Soulez, A. 130
Spinoza, B. 116
spontaneism 3
Stamp, R. xiv, 163, 183
state apparatus 23
Stendhal 99–100
Strauss, L. 3, 223
subjectification xvi, 86, 119–22, 126, 140, 224

Taussig, M. 51
   Mimesis and Alterity 51
Thatcher, M. 73
Thomson, A. xiii, 6, 27, 36
Thoreau, H. D. 55
Thrift, N. 152
Thucydides 174
Toscano, A. xv, 219
trap as artwork 51–4
Trevelyan, J. 102–3, 106

unprofessional painting (exhibition) 101–6
   Ashington Art Group 101
   Ashington Miners 103–4
   pitmen painters 102
   Sunday painters 101

Veyne, P. 206, 209
   Writing History 206
Vicinato (Parreno) 123
Volpi, F. 212
Von Eschenbach, A. 157

Wallis, A. 103
Ward, C. 34
Watts, P. xii
Wodizcko, K. 113
Wood, D. 231
Workers Education Authority (WEA) 102

Žižek, S. xiv, 6, 74, 78, 80–1, 83–4, 87–91, 140
   The Ticklish Subject 87
Zola, E. 189–90

www.ingramcontent.com/pod-product-compliance
Lightning Source LLC
Chambersburg PA
CBHW052217300426
44115CB00011B/1720